Pleasures of the Table

Florence Fabricant's

Pleasures of the Table

Innovative menus for entertaining,

easily prepared recipes, and the

wines to serve with them

Introduction by Sam Aaron

with photographs by Matthew Klein

Galahad Books • New York

To Richard, Patty, and Robert.
My severest critics, my greatest fans.

Project Director: Darlene Geis
Editor: Ruth A. Peltason
Designer: Darilyn Lowe
Photo Editor: Eric Himmel

Frontispiece (page 24): *Paupiettes of Sole with Shrimp*

Portions of this book have appeared previously in a different form in
Signature magazine.

First Galahad Books edition published in 1989.

Galahad Books
A division of Budget Book Service, Inc.
386 Park Avenue South
New York, NY 10016

Galahad Books is a registered trademark of Budget Book Service, Inc.

Published by arrangement with Harry N. Abrams, Inc., a division of
the Times Mirror Company.

Library of Congress Catalog Card Number: 85-28791

ISBN: 0-88365-748-1

Printed in China.

Acknowledgments

Most immediately my thanks go to Horace Sutton, who encouraged me to write the *Signature* magazine column, "Pleasures of the Table," from which this book evolved. I am grateful to Paul Gottlieb, Darlene Geis, Sam Antupit, Ruth Peltason, Darilyn Lowe, and Eric Himmel of Harry N. Abrams Publishers, all of whom contributed considerable talent and care to the project. Matthew Klein's photographic skills and good taste were indispensable. Barbara Coats and Susan Shipman of *Signature* also helped make this book possible.

Looking back, I owe an infinite debt of gratitude to the late Everett Rattray of the East Hampton *Star*, and to his wife, Helen, now the publisher; also to Alden Whitman, as well as to Craig Claiborne, Michael Leahy, and Stewart Kampel of the *New York Times* for their past and continued confidence. And to Niki Singer for her friendship.

Contents

5 Acknowledgments

8 Introduction by Sam Aaron

9 About This Book

12 Planning a Menu

13 Selecting and Serving Wines

16 **Dinners: Intimate, Informal, and Grand**

18 **INTIMATE DINNERS**

19 Dinner for Two
Beaujolais or Beaujolais Nouveau

23 Seafood and Chablis
French Chablis

27 Breaking the Rules
Red Bordeaux

31 A Luxurious Italian Menu
Tuscan White Wine, Brunello di
Montalcino

36 Cool Food for a Warm Evening
California Chardonnay

40 Northern Italian Specialties
Soave, Amarone

44 A 700-Calorie Dinner
White or Red Wine Spritzers

48 **INFORMAL DINNERS**

49 Dinner in Under an Hour
Red Côtes du Rhône

52 Summer Menu on the Grill
California Fumé Blanc

56 East Coast Informality
White Table Wine or Beer

60 West Coast Informality
Dry Chenin Blanc

63 Après Outdoors—Before an Open Fire
American Pinot Noir

68 A Bouillabaisse Supper
Châteauneuf-du-Pape Blanc

72 A South-of-the-Border Spread
South American Sauvignon Blanc and
Cabernet Sauvignon

75 An Alsatian Feast
Alsatian Gewürztraminer

79 A Hearty Belgian Menu
Belgian Beers

82 **GRAND DINNERS**

83 An Evening in Spring
Pouilly-Fumé or Pouilly-Fuissé

87 A Zesty Summer Dinner
Dry and Sweet Orvietos

90 Grilling with Style
California Gewürztraminer, California
Cabernet Sauvignon

93 A Dinner for a Chilly Evening
California Sauvignon Blanc or
Chardonnay, California Merlot

97 An Autumn Holiday Celebration
California White and Red Zinfandels

101 An Eclectic Menu for Six
German, Alsatian, or American Rieslings

106 A Grand Dinner Party for a
Special Occasion
White and Red Burgundies

112 **Lunches, Brunches, Picnics,
and Parties**

114 **WARM WEATHER LUNCHES**

115 A Spring Luncheon
Muscadet

118 Cool Italian Classics
Pinot Grigio

122 A Casual Summer Lunch or Supper
Red Table Wine

125 Lunch Alfresco
New York State White Wine

128 **COOL WEATHER LUNCHES**

129 An Autumn Lunch
Chianti Classico

133 A Pasta Menu for Lunch or Supper
Barbaresco

136 Lunch, Brunch, or Supper for Twelve
Riojas, Beer

140 Brunch with a Portuguese Touch
Vinho Verde

144 **A TRIO OF PICNICS**

Picnic Quaffs—Rosé Wines,
Sangria, Beer

146 Mexican Picnic

148 Greek Picnic

151 Indian Picnic

154 **A HOLIDAY BUFFET**

Champagne or Sparkling Wine,
Tropical Citrus Punch

162 About Cheese

163 Just Dessert . . . and Dessert Wines

164 Coffee and Tea

165 A Listing of Menus

168 Index

176 Credits

Introduction by Sam Aaron

When future observers survey the history of gastronomy in America, I believe they will view the four decades following World War II as the dawn of a golden age. These years have seen a revolution in the appreciation of food and wine at the American table.

Among the pioneers of this creative era who introduced the culinary arts of Europe, Asia, and South America to our kitchens were James Beard, Craig Claiborne, and Julia Child. A number of sociological and cultural phenomena made Americans attentive to the message of these innovators. Air travel enabled millions of us to experience the delights of foreign foods and wines. A shorter workweek provided increased leisure time for cooking as an avocation and for experimentation in the kitchen. Widespread affluence made a larger range of ingredients and wines affordable for a greater number of people. Food and wine societies flourished, and food and wine became ever more popular subjects for books, newspaper articles, magazines, radio, and television.

While the interest in creative cooking has greatly expanded, the role of wine in cookbooks, restaurants, and menu planning has lagged behind. This courageous tome you hold in your hand is a brilliant expression of a new and growing awareness in this area. Florence Fabricant is among the first to create a book that reveals the myriad ways in which wine, when properly coordinated with food, can turn a mundane meal into an eventful dinner, and an eventful dinner into an outstanding gastronomic experience.

As you turn the pages of *Florence Fabricant's Pleasures of the Table*, you will see that the wines accompanying the menus have been skillfully chosen to marry magnificently with the foods. One has the sense that the recipes have been inspired by the wines, making each meal a symphonic whole.

Florence Fabricant's text moves gracefully from simple intimate and informal dinners to grander feasts, then on to a festive assortment of lunches, brunches, picnics, and parties. She makes each of the thirty-five menus a highly individual celebration of the compatibility of food and wine.

Her encyclopedic knowledge of both wine and food, as well as her exquisite taste, keen selectivity, and finely tuned sense of the harmony between the various elements of a meal, has produced the imaginative groupings of wines and recipes that follow. Often surprising yet always felicitous combinations of foods are beautifully integrated with a wide range of potables, each chosen to heighten the enjoyment of the meal and make it an even more special occasion. Simply browsing through the menus one can perceive Florence Fabricant's enjoyment in creating meals as interesting as they are delicious. Cooks and wine lovers of all persuasions will be inspired by her inventiveness.

Equally impressive is her insightful understanding of the characteristics of the wines of the world; her descriptive notes succinctly capture the essence of a variety of wines from France, Italy, California, Germany, Spain, Portugal, and South America. She offers not only clear, up-to-date background on each type of wine, but also a balanced view of the wine in relation to the food it complements.

Achieving equilibrium in writing about food and wine is not easy. Cookbook writers rarely give proper attention to the role of wine; wine writers rarely tackle the subject of food in depth. Florence Fabricant transcends the partisan approach of each world, and combines the best of both.

About This Book

I began writing about food in East Hampton, a community near the tip of Long Island that combines seashore and farmland. In my first column for the East Hampton *Star* nearly fifteen years ago, I deplored the quality of tomatoes in the supermarkets and pointed out that commendable hothouse tomatoes, raised in nearby Riverhead, could be purchased in a certain few markets as a stopgap (it was then May) until late July when vine-ripened field tomatoes would become available.

It cheers me that now the situation has changed. Hothouse tomatoes are becoming an off-season staple, and decent field tomatoes can be found in urban markets as well as at country farm stands from July through September. The food scene has evolved considerably. My *Star* column, "In Season," dealt with the strawberries, peaches, apples, cucumbers, zucchini, corn, eggplant, herbs, mussels, bluefish, fresh tuna, scallops, and even the free-range chickens and thick-shelled fresh eggs that have made this region such a joy for the lover of good food. Many of these treasures now reach a wider market as chefs and consumers insist on them.

The new ingredients that have generated so much excitement in recent years—the fragrant extra-virgin olive oils, rich balsamic vinegars, cultivated exotic mushrooms, and game—are everywhere. Gone are the days when buying a piece of fresh ginger meant making a trip to Chinatown or that a decent goat cheese was hard to find; now ginger has become a staple of the supermarket produce department and fine goat cheese is made here. As for wine, the choice offered the consumer is dazzling. Nowhere in the world are the wine shops as well stocked as they are in the United States. Keeping up with all the new wines is downright daunting.

I much prefer to cook in East Hampton, where in a big open kitchen, I am never more than a few steps from my guests, where herbs and peppers flourish in my garden, and where, over the years, the quality of ingredients has not diminished while the variety has increased by geometric progression. The majority of the recipes in this book were conceived, attempted, tested, and savored in that country kitchen. I taste everything and I trust my taste buds—I always have.

My introduction to the kitchen came at home from my mother, a wonderful cook who liked to experiment, frequently entertained, and derived great pleasure from setting an elegant table. Like my mother, I am willing to experiment, and like the typical American, I have trouble pledging allegiance to any one cuisine.

Travel, dining out, collecting cookbooks—beginning with James Beard, Craig Claiborne, and Julia Child—cooking on my own, and in the course of my career as a food writer for numerous publications including the *New York Times*, interviewing chefs, good home cooks, cooking teachers, and other experts in the field have all contributed to my skills and understanding. It is to so many of my colleagues (literally hundreds of them) that I owe my thanks.

Five years ago I began writing a monthly feature for *Signature* magazine called "Pleasures of the Table" in which a menu with appropriate wines was presented with both wine and food discussed in detail. This book is based upon that column and it reflects my personal approach to entertaining.

The pleasure of entertaining is threefold: we delight in the food, the wine, and the company. Like the word companion, "company" has its roots in the sharing of bread. The guests who share it are as crucial to the success of a meal as are the food and wine.

When I entertain I expect to enjoy my party totally, to derive as much pleasure from being with my guests as in serving them a delicious, homemade meal. The com-

pany and the occasion determine the nature of the menu, which is affected by the season, the budget, my equipment, and the time at my disposal—I rarely spend days in the kitchen preparing for a dinner party anymore. Mine is also a pragmatic, efficient nature. I want to avoid expeditions scouting out offbeat ingredients when I'm under pressure, or toiling at length in the kitchen away from my guests. If I plan to serve three wines, I make sure I have enough glassware without having to wash any between courses.

The menus in this book are complete, and many of them reproduce my favorite recipes and dinners. Some are more elaborate than others, some throw any notion of calorie counting to the wind, and some qualify for serving barefoot at the beach. I have planned dinners for guests who are dieting without drawing attention to their particular needs, and I have created menus keyed exclusively to white wines (for example, we have a friend who is allergic to reds). But they all share a sense of relaxed unself-conscious good spirits so that dining on good food and sipping pleasant wine become the focus of an occasion peppered with interesting conversation.

The menus and recipes in *Pleasures of the Table* reflect the evolution of cooking and eating in present-day America, with our country's cross-cultural mix of flavors, its astonishing range of choices from the world's larder and wineries, and its newly awakened interest in unprocessed, fresh food. Simplicity affects us all: you will not find any pretentious roasts wrapped in pastry here; however, an old-fashioned, hearty stew is a welcome entry.

A few of the menus can be prepared literally in minutes, others are almost totally fat-free. Don't hesitate to substitute if you must, whether because an ingredient is unavailable (celery plus a sprinkling of fennel seeds can stand in for fresh fennel, for example), or time is short (fresh berries with sweetened puréed berries spooned over as a sauce can replace a tart).

The choice of wines is not rigid either. Unlike Tuscans who mainly drink their native Chianti, Americans can opt for almost any wine in the world. The style is an important factor—a wine for brunch would not likely be the same as one (or several) for a formal dinner and the rules, such as they are, can be artfully broken to surprise and satisfy.

Above all, serve the wines you enjoy with food you like to prepare to people whose company delights you. That is the true pleasure of the table.

Florence Fabricant
East Hampton, New York

Almond-Apricot Torte (recipe, page 164)

Planning a Menu

Ease of entertaining is directly proportionate to the amount of time spent planning and organizing. Make lists. Write out an approximate timetable for serving. A well-planned dinner, brunch, or party saves you from that last minute trip to the store for some forgotten item, when time may be at a premium.

Whatever the occasion's starting point—it might be a certain guest, a particular event, a great bottle of wine to share, or a dish you just feel inspired to prepare and serve—all these elements must be taken into account and coordinated. It is rather like ordering in a Chinese restaurant; balance is essential, whether you are considering two courses or ten.

Many years ago I was a student living in France. My host family had a housekeeper whose responsibility it was to plan the midday meal on Thursdays, when the lady of the house went to a concert. Invariably she served us a monochromatic meal: cauliflower soup followed by fish in cream sauce with mashed potatoes and a molded rice dessert. I never forgot those unintentionally funny midday dinners that also came in green, yellow, red, orange, brown, or even purple.

Without some compelling reason, a menu should not be designed as if by Johnny-one-note. There are occasions when an all-fish menu or an all-salad buffet would be appropriate, but even then contrast and variety of texture, flavor, and form, as well as color, should be the goal. Quiche and fruit tart do not belong in the same menu, nor do mushroom soup and mushroom stuffing, or mayonnaise and hollandaise sauces.

A well-planned menu would not call for two dishes requiring different cooking temperatures baking simultaneously in the kitchen's only oven. Nor would it call for two dishes to be stir-fried at the same time by one cook.

Finally and most importantly, the menu should be governed by the seasons. Winter appetites do not crave cool summer soups, nor does a light springtime lunch satisfy as the leaves fall. Despite the year-round availability of so many ingredients, there still may be seasonal differences that affect flavor and quality. The lusciousness of locally grown, vine-ripened tomatoes in summer is never matched by the Florida crop in the winter. (On the other hand, superb hothouse tomatoes from Israel and the Netherlands will satisfy a craving for a recipe out of season—at a price.)

The seasons notwithstanding, when it comes to perishable foodstuffs—produce, seafood, poultry, meat, cheese, coffee—it does not pay to compromise on quality. Food is too expensive and cooking requires too much time and effort for that. It is better to substitute: if the weather has been too hot for the markets to stock unwilted arugula or watercress, try spinach or romaine lettuce in a salad instead.

As for nonperishable grocery items, I have certain preferences. For general cooking purposes the olive oil I prefer is imported virgin olive oil from Italy or France, reserving the fragrant green extra-virgin olive oil for flavoring purposes, to be added at the end. Quality extra-virgin olive oil is cold-pressed and unrefined so it burns more easily at high temperatures. Oriental sesame oil, toasty and brown, is also a condiment heated briefly at best.

For most cooking and seasoning, I use a very light soy sauce rather than one labeled dark soy or that is unspecified. Try to find an imported brand of soy rather than one that is made under license in this country.

Parmesan and Gorgonzola cheeses are best imported from Italy (some imported Parmesan comes from Argentina, but is inferior to the Italian), and Parmesan should always be freshly grated as needed. Unbleached all-purpose flour, pure chili powder without added salt, kosher salt which tends to be sweeter than regular table salt, unsulfured dried fruits, and stone-ground cornmeal are some of my other preferences.

Dried herbs and spices are sold in containers that are far too large, so I discard them long before the contents have been used up. Faded herbs and tasteless spices will not properly season a dish.

I keep shelled, chopped, and ground nuts in the freezer, while specialty oils like hazelnut, which I do not use frequently, are kept in the refrigerator to prolong their freshness.

Having a freezer is an enormous convenience, but its capabilities should not be overestimated. I tend to use the freezer when keeping food in a "holding pattern" for shorter term storage than is customary. Food can deteriorate in the freezer, becoming unpalatable even though it might not be dangerous. Wrap food airtight and in a couple of layers, label the package with the storage date, and use it within a few months (breadstuffs and cakes should be used even sooner).

By keeping in mind balance—the occasion, the season, and your guests—you can begin planning your menu at any point (maybe with fresh strawberry tartlets for dessert when beautiful berries are on the market) and go on from there. A sense of good menu design becomes second nature after a while, so that even an everyday lunch or dinner is well planned, efficient to serve, and enjoyable to both eye and palate. That is the basis of pleasurable entertaining.

The menus that follow have been designed, each with a particular number of guests in mind. In some instances, notably desserts such as pies, there might be leftovers . . . on second thought, there might not!

Selecting and Serving Wines

I select the wines for a menu with the same care as I take in planning the courses and marketing for the ingredients. Wine selections should be balanced so that color, style, and quality are appropriate to the food and the occasion. A simple white jug wine that might suit picnic fare does not belong with a relatively extravagant poached salmon, for example.

It would simplify matters considerably to drink and serve only American wines. Limiting one's choices to the regional quaff is traditional in wine-producing countries: few Frenchmen drink Riojas, and it is a rare Roman who would open a bottle of Sancerre rather than a Frascati. But winemaking on a large scale is relatively recent in the United States, and despite the sophistication of Thomas Jefferson's cellar or the example set at George Washington's headquarters, no established wine-drinking tradition has existed in this country. Only lately has wine been accepted as an integral part of a meal.

Which wine remains the question. In a country that has become, in effect, a market for all the wines of the world, making the decision can be an agonizing, complicated process for some. It is important to realize that, as in most matters of taste, there are no rules, only some sensible guidelines, and with a little experience you can begin to trust your judgment.

Generally speaking, wine and food work well together when they represent a marriage of comparable intensities. Light wines are more suited to light flavors; the more forthright, robust, and complex selections should accompany assertive tastes and rich textures. If a wine is used in a sauce, it is likely to be a good choice for the glass as well. When more than one wine is served with a meal, the progression should be from light to full-bodied.

The cuisine—the nationality of the food—can provide a sensible clue. For many of the menus in this book I have followed the regional route in choosing a wine, because for me such combinations have an interesting and satisfying logic.

In selecting wines to accompany a full dinner, calculate about a half-bottle per person as an average. With an appreciative assembly, there is no reason why the service of a given wine course should be limited to one wine, either. Open three different zinfandels or St. Émilions, or several bottles of the same wine in different vintages for eight or ten people, and compare them.

Serve wines in stemware, the simpler the better, and larger rather than smaller in capacity. A ten-ounce glass (filled no more than halfway) is a good all-purpose size. I always open and sample the wine I plan to serve before the guests arrive. The unexpected bad bottle can crop up, even from the most reputable wine shop, or you might find that the wine you have been waiting to drink has been in the cellar a trifle too long—it might be acceptable for a family dinner, but perhaps not for guests.

The general rule that white wines be served chilled and reds at room temperature requires some explanation. It is accurate up to a point. For example, chilling will mask defects in a wine, so a mediocre white jug wine, or even a marginal red, will benefit from chilling or being served on the rocks. A well-made white wine, however, should be served cool, never ice cold, allowing the fullness of the fruit, the balance in its structure, and the richness of its bouquet to be appreciated. The younger the wine, regardless of whether it is white or red, the cooler it can stand to be.

"Room temperature" for a red wine customarily referred to rooms in houses that were not centrally heated to 75 degrees. By our standards they were downright chilly. Fine red wines brought from a cellar where they were maintained at 55 degrees were allowed to "warm" to about 68 degrees in the dining room. Ideally, that is the temperature at which most red wines should be served. Beaujolais and other young, fruity reds are best enjoyed a trifle cooler than that, at about 60 degrees.

Finally, a point should be made about the practice of allowing a wine to "breathe." Merely opening the bottle of a red wine whose tannins are harsh and need exposure to oxygen to soften will not accomplish much. If, upon tasting your wine, you feel this might be the case, pour it directly into the glasses where, in thirty minutes or so, it will indeed soften. Decanting the wine may also help.

A very old, fragile wine is likely to be best when decanted or poured and served immediately, before contact with the air causes its evanescent character to dissipate. Older red wines that show sediment (usually evident if you hold the bottle up to the light) should be allowed to stand upright for a few days to permit the sediment to settle to the bottom of the bottle. Such wines may also be carefully decanted, but that is not absolutely necessary.

Equip yourself with a good corkscrew, one with a long, spiral worm, remove the metal or plastic capsule from the top of the bottle, and wipe the top before pouring the wine. Much as wine holders and baskets are attractive accessories, I find them to be unnecessary. A coaster on the table is useful to have.

Discussions of vintages and equipment aside, enjoying wine is not a complicated matter. Whether the menu is simple or sumptuous, there will be many wines to suit it. Guidelines exist, but the final arbiter should be your own taste.

Dinners: Intimate,

Butterflied Lamb with Rainbow Peppers
(recipe, page 91)

Informal, and Grand

INTIMATE DINNERS

The closeness with just a few dear friends, family members, or even the right business associates permits a level of social warmth and relaxation that evenings on a larger scale do not allow. These occasions can be memorable on many levels, not the least of which might be the quality of the food and wine. With fewer to entertain, the menu can be designed with more luxurious ingredients, accompanied by finer wines than you might serve to a crowd. Consider pouring a noble Bordeaux or red Burgundy, an elegant California chardonnay, or a well-aged Italian brunello.

Furthermore, there are any number of dishes that are wonderful to prepare and serve, but which are simply unsuited for quantity cooking. Sushi is too time-consuming, calves' liver is too specialized, casserole-roasted Cornish hens or poached fish are too bulky. A restaurant chef can sauté six portions of swordfish at one time, but in a home kitchen that becomes nearly impossible, so in practical terms the wonderful swordfish in green peppercorn sauce is best on a menu for two or four people.

The menus are all gracious and designed to enhance convivial intimacy. They consist of multiple courses (and where cheese has not been included, feel free to add it) in order for dining to be the evening's entertainment.

Dinner for Two

Beaujolais or Beaujolais Nouveau

Cranberry Borscht
Casserole-Roasted Cornish Hens
Baked Barley
Bibb and Watercress Salad
Cheese

Sabayon with Nectarines

Whole Cornish hens, roasted in a casserole, require a good deal of space which is why this kind of dinner is best for two. A simple sauce which accompanies the game hens is enriched with onions and mushrooms and tastes earthy and mellow. Barley, an underutilized nutty grain, bakes in the oven with the birds. The first course is a ruby-colored borscht sharpened with cranberries. Follow the main course with a salad, then serve a cheese with some bite, such as Reblochon or a chèvre, with good bread.

The sabayon can be whipped up in advance, and served chilled if last minute preparation is inconvenient.

Beaujolais or Beaujolais Nouveau

Conventional attitudes toward red wines do not apply to Beaujolais. It should be served lightly chilled, when it is still young and fresh, to accompany almost anything you happen to be eating, including fish. It may even be argued that for enjoyable quaffing you never need any other kind of wine.

This is easy, undemanding wine to drink and at its best provides enough structure to balance its exuberant, youthful fruitiness. No wonder it remains France's most popular wine, the wine of the bistro. Ideally, the production of a given vintage of Beaujolais and Beaujolais-Villages should be consumed before the next year's wine is ready to be sold, as much of Beaujolais is not for keeping.

In Beaujolais, the large district at the southern extreme of the Burgundy region, the grape is gamay. The rolling countryside between Villefranche-sur-Saône and Lyon is where most of the wine labeled Beaujolais is produced. Better yet are the nine *crus* or selected Beaujolais growths, Moulin-à-Vent, Morgon, Chénas, Fleurie, Saint-Amour, Chiroubles, Juliénas, Brouilly, and Côtes de Brouilly; all of these can improve with some bottle aging, and have a higher alcoholic content than regular Beaujolais or Beaujolais-Villages, as well as more bouquet, complexity, and finesse. North of Villefranche, nestled into more hilly terrain, is the collection of thirty-six villages linked by narrow, winding roads that produce wines entitled to the appellation Beaujolais-Villages.

Beaujolais comes on the market in April and May following the harvest. Beaujolais nouveau, a wine country tradition that has now become an international fad, can be released on the third Thursday in November. This is a frivolous wine, light, full of fruit, and meant to be consumed within a few months of production. Whole bunches of grapes are not pressed but are fermented in tanks of carbon dioxide to preserve the fruit and impart less tannin, a method called carbonic maceration. But without tannins the red wine has a brief life span.

Cranberry Borscht

A traditional beet borscht looks no different with the addition of cranberries but has a fruitier, richer flavor. Keep cranberries in the freezer to have them on hand for any season.

   ½ pound beets
   1 cup cranberries
   1½ cups water
   4 to 5 teaspoons sugar
   Pinch of salt
   ½ tablespoon lemon juice
   ⅓ cup sour cream
   1 teaspoon minced fresh dill for garnish

Peel and grate the beets. You may want to wear rubber gloves or slip plastic sandwich bags over your hands to protect them from staining.

Place beets in a saucepan with the cranberries and water, and simmer for 20 minutes until the cranberries and beets are very tender. Strain them, reserving the liquid. Purée the beets and cranberries in a food processor, combine with the reserved cooking liquid, and return to the saucepan. Add sugar, salt, and lemon juice, and bring to a simmer.

Stir the sour cream so it is smooth, then stir into the gently simmering soup. Reheat but do not allow to boil. Alternatively, the sour cream may be used as a garnish, with a dollop floated on each serving and decorated with cranberries. Borscht can also be chilled and served cold. Garnish with dill before serving.

2 servings

Casserole-Roasted Cornish Hens

   2 Cornish hens, about 1 pound each
   Salt and freshly ground black pepper
   2 tablespoons sweet butter
   2 tablespoons minced shallots
   1 teaspoon minced garlic
   6 ounces small white onions, peeled
   6 ounces small fresh mushrooms
   ½ cup dry white wine
   ¼ cup well-flavored chicken stock
   ½ teaspoon dried thyme or 1 teaspoon fresh, if
      available
   1 tablespoon minced fresh parsley

Rinse and dry the hens inside and out; season the cavities with salt and pepper. Tuck the wing tips in back and using clean white cord, tie the legs together.

Melt 1 tablespoon of butter in a heavy casserole that will comfortably hold the hens. On top of the stove, brown the hens in the butter on all sides. Remove the hens from the casserole. Preheat oven to 400 degrees.

In the butter remaining in the casserole, sauté the shallots over low heat until soft. Add the garlic and sauté a moment longer. Remove casserole from heat. Return hens to the casserole, along with any juices that may have collected around them.

In a separate pan, melt the remaining tablespoon of butter and toss the onions in it over medium-high heat until they are lightly browned. Transfer the onions to the casserole. Add the mushrooms to the pan in which the onions were browned and toss them over medium-high heat until they begin to brown. Add them to the casserole, scattering them around the hens.

Add wine, stock, and thyme to the casserole. Bring to a simmer, taste for seasoning, and season with salt and pepper. Cover the casserole and place in the oven to cook for 25 minutes.

Remove hens to a serving platter, draining them

well. Remove trussing string. Cook sauce in casserole over high heat for about 2 minutes until it has reduced and thickened somewhat. (If you like a thicker sauce, you may stir in 1 teaspoon of cornstarch which has been dissolved in 1 tablespoon of cold water.) Taste and season with salt and pepper, if necessary. Pour sauce over hens, dust with minced parsley, and serve.

2 servings

Note: This recipe may be doubled to serve 4, but you will need quite a large casserole to hold the hens.

Baked Barley

    1½ tablespoons sweet butter
    ¼ cup finely chopped onions
    ⅔ cup medium barley
    ½ teaspoon salt
    ¼ teaspoon thyme
    1⅓ cups hot chicken stock, preferably homemade
        (see following recipe)

Preheat oven to 400 degrees. Melt butter in a small ovenproof casserole or saucepan. Add the onions and sauté until tender. Add barley, salt, thyme, and ⅔ cup of the stock. Bring to a simmer, cover, and place in the oven to bake for 20 minutes.

Stir barley once, add another ⅓ cup of the stock, and return casserole to the oven for 20 minutes. Stir once more, add remaining ⅓ cup of stock, and continue baking for 15 to 20 minutes, until the liquid is absorbed and the barley is tender.

2 servings

Chicken Stock

Use either a whole chicken or chicken parts for making stock. Do not use the livers as they will make the stock bitter. Adding unpeeled onions to the stock, a trick that Craig Claiborne once wrote about, gives the stock a rich color.

  3½ to 4 pounds chicken, whole or parts
  4 quarts cold water (approximately)
  2 large onions, trimmed but unpeeled
  1 large leek, white part only, well rinsed
  3 celery stalks, including the tops
  2 large carrots, scraped
  1 clove garlic (optional)
  2 small sprigs parsley
  2 small sprigs dill
  Kosher salt

Place chicken in a large kettle, cover with water, and bring to a boil. Allow to boil for about 10 minutes. During this time skim the surface of the liquid to remove any foam or other particles that accumulate.

Once the surface is relatively clean, add remaining ingredients, including salt to taste. Lower heat to a gentle simmer. Simmer uncovered for about 2 hours, skimming the surface occasionally. Check seasoning.

Strain the stock. A fine strainer will only do an adequate job. It is better to strain the stock through a strainer or colander lined with a clean linen napkin, several thicknesses of cheesecloth, or coffee filter papers. To degrease the stock first chill it, then lift off the congealed fat that accumulates on top. Stock can be frozen for many months.

About 3 quarts

Bibb and Watercress Salad

  2 small heads Bibb lettuce
  1 bunch watercress
  1 tablespoon red wine vinegar
  ½ teaspoon Dijon mustard
  3 tablespoons extra-virgin olive oil

Thoroughly rinse and dry lettuce. Tear the lettuce into bite-size pieces, and discard the cores. Trim any heavy stems from the watercress, rinse, and dry it. Combine lettuce and watercress in a bowl.

Mix the vinegar and mustard, and beat in the olive oil. Pour dressing over salad, toss, and serve.

2 servings

Sabayon with Nectarines

Nectarines are not the only fruit that a rich sabayon will enhance. Peaches, apricots, pineapple, bananas, strawberries, or blueberries can be substituted.

  2 large ripe nectarines, sliced
  1 teaspoon lemon juice
  ⅓ cup amaretto liqueur
  3 egg yolks
  2 tablespoons sugar
  Pinch of nutmeg, preferably freshly grated

Toss the nectarines in a bowl with lemon juice and one tablespoon of liqueur. Set aside. In a saucepan or a bowl that will fit over a pan of simmering water, beat egg yolks until they have thickened. Beat in the sugar.

Set the bowl with the egg yolk-sugar mixture over the simmering water and beat the mixture vigorously over very low heat. Add half the remaining amaretto and continue beating. As the eggs thicken and lighten, continue to add remaining amaretto, beating constantly. Regulate the heat so it is very low; if the egg mixture appears to coat the bottom of the bowl or pan or to coagulate, add a bit more amaretto and remove from heat. Continue beating until thick and light but still pourable.

Transfer nectarines to large wine goblets and pour the sauce over them. Sprinkle a bit of nutmeg on top and serve. This dessert may also be chilled in goblets and served cold.

2 servings

Seafood and Chablis

⟨❧⟩

French Chablis

Zucchini Fritters
Paupiettes of Sole with Shrimp
Brown Rice with Leeks and Chives

Apples Baked in Cider

I can remember my mother preparing fillets of sole wrapped around shrimp. She usually bathed them in a tomato sauce mellowed with cream. It was a dish for special occasions and that is how I still think of paupiettes of sole. It is versatile enough to have as a fine main course for a light dinner or a luncheon, or as a lovely first course for a grand event. (You might precede the quail on page 95, for example, with the sole instead of the scallop chowder.) Paupiettes of sole are quick to prepare and stylish to serve.

Both the sole and the dessert are baked in cider—one hard, the other sweet. Although a cheese course has not been included, a superb ripe Camembert would be perfect for four people, perhaps served with chilled hard cider instead of the wine.

French Chablis

Chablis should be known only as a fine white wine produced in limited quantities, about 114 miles southeast of Paris. But for several decades it has shared its name with a lesser wine made in bulk and bottled in jugs in California, an ocean and a continent away from the more

than 4,000 acres of hillside chardonnay vineyards that comprise the French Chablis district.

Authentic Chablis is a pale straw-gold color, crisp and clean tasting, with enough fruit to balance its acidity. Flinty is the term frequently applied to connote a certain well-bred austerity. In the 1950s, before the California wine industry fully realized its potential for making quality wines, it borrowed the luster of Chablis to label undistinguished white wines, often made without chardonnay grapes. The name has stuck and countless American consumers are genuinely surprised when they learn that, yes, Chablis is *also* made in France. Serious wine drinkers are never confused by this geographical swapping, and when they order Chablis they expect it to be French.

At their best the wines offer the fruit of chardonnay from vines that struggle deep in the chalky soil, which contributes to its acidity. Hard work has its rewards. Chablis is not a lush, buttery wine but has a harmonious elegance that makes it an excellent choice for a seafood menu of some delicacy. There are four classes of Chablis: the finest is *grand cru* (great growth) followed—at some distance—by *premier cru* (first growth), then Chablis, and petit Chablis.

Zucchini Fritters

These are like potato pancakes, but made with shredded zucchini. Make these fritters very small, two inches in diameter, and they can be passed as hors d'oeuvres.

1½ pounds zucchini
2 beaten eggs
½ cup flour
¼ cup freshly grated Italian Parmesan cheese
Salt and pepper
Vegetable oil
Italian parsley sprigs for garnish

Shred or grate zucchini, salt it lightly, put it in a sieve, and allow it to stand for half an hour. Press out as much liquid as possible. Combine the eggs, flour, and cheese. Mix the zucchini with this batter. Season the batter to taste with salt and pepper.

Heat vegetable oil in a large skillet to a depth of about ¼ inch. Drop tablespoons of the batter into the oil, flattening each mound with the back of a spoon to make small pancakes. Brown the fritters lightly, then turn to brown the other side. Remove fritters to paper towels and allow to drain. Continue as above until all the batter is used, adding additional oil as needed.

Serve as soon as possible, garnished with Italian parsley.

4 to 6 servings

Paupiettes of Sole with Shrimp

The apple cider used for this recipe could be replaced by a fruity white wine such as chenin blanc or riesling.

2 tablespoons sweet butter
4 tablespoons minced shallots
6 lemon or gray sole fillets, 3 to 4 ounces each
Salt and freshly ground white pepper
12 medium to large shrimp (about ½ pound), peeled and deveined
½ cup French or English cider (hard cider)
1 cup heavy cream
2 teaspoons lemon juice

Preheat oven to 425 degrees. Melt butter in a small skillet and sauté shallots until they are soft. Spread half the shallots in a lightly buttered 8-inch-square baking dish.

Season the fish fillets with salt and pepper, and spread each with about 1 teaspoon of the remaining shallots on the "skin" side of the fish, which is grayer in color. Place 2 shrimp side by side—head to tail—across each fillet. Roll the fillet around the shrimp, so that the shrimp tails poke out of the rolled fillets. Place the paupiettes, seam side down, in the baking dish.

Pour cider over the fish, cover with a sheet of buttered foil or waxed paper, and bake for 15 minutes. The fish should be nearly done, almost completely opaque. Turn off the oven. Carefully pour all the cooking liquid into a large skillet and return the fish, again covered with the paper, to the turned-off oven.

Boil the cooking liquid for about 6 minutes, until it is reduced to about 3 tablespoons and is quite syrupy. Add cream and lemon juice, and cook rapidly for about another 3 minutes, until the cream has thickened. Season to taste with salt and white pepper.

Arrange the fish on a warm serving platter or individual plates, pour the sauce over it, and serve at once.

3 to 6 servings

Brown Rice with Leeks and Chives

2 tablespoons vegetable oil
2 cups finely chopped leeks
1 cup brown rice
2 cups chicken stock, preferably homemade (page 22), or water
Salt and freshly ground black pepper
2 tablespoons minced fresh chives

Heat oil in a heavy saucepan which has at least a 2-quart capacity. Add leeks and cook very slowly, until the leeks are tender and transparent. Stir in the rice and cook, stirring, for 2 to 3 minutes.

Add stock (or water) and boil, uncovered, for 3 minutes. Lower heat, season to taste with salt and pepper, cover, and cook at a very slow simmer for 40 minutes, until the liquid is absorbed. Remove from heat and set aside, covered, for 15 minutes before serving. Sprinkle with chives.

4 to 6 servings

Apples Baked in Cider

Concentrated cider—sweet cider boiled down until it becomes syrupy—is a wonderful change-of-pace sweetener. Cider that threatens to turn before it is used can be prepared in this manner and the resulting syrup frozen in one-pint containers.

3 cups fresh apple cider (not hard cider)
¼ cup honey
4 tablespoons sweet butter
Generous pinch grated nutmeg
4 large baking apples, preferably Cortland
⅔ cup heavy cream, lightly whipped

Preheat oven to 400 degrees. Boil the cider until it is reduced by half. Stir in the honey, butter, and nutmeg, stirring until the butter melts.

Core the apples, leaving the bottom intact, and peel them two-thirds of the way down. Arrange in a small baking dish.

Spoon about 2 tablespoons of the cider mixture into the center of each apple. Pour the rest of the cider over and around the apples. Bake until the apples are tender but still hold their shape, about 40 minutes. Baste several times during baking.

Serve warm or at room temperature, with lightly whipped cream on the side.

4 servings

Breaking the Rules

❧

Red Bordeaux

Old Country Chicken Liver Pâté with Radish
Swordfish Steaks in Green Peppercorn Sauce
Garlic-Roasted Potatoes
Broccoli with Lemon Butter
Wilted Romaine and Red Onions
Cheese

Raspberry Cream Tart

If you love to throw an occasional culinary curve, as I do, this menu may intrigue and please you. Its focus is fish—swordfish steaks prepared as if they were steak au poivre, sautéed and served in a sauce finished with Cognac, red wine, heavy cream, and spicy green peppercorns. Swordfish is rich and meaty, both in texture and flavor, making it an excellent choice to pair with red wine. It is a menu that is best prepared for no more than four, otherwise it becomes difficult to manage cooking the fish.

Red Bordeaux—A Wine of Depth and Character

Say Lafite or Latour and people sit up and take notice. These, along with the other princely bottles of Bordeaux fetch staggering prices, exalt restaurant lists, and ennoble great cellars. From such wines Bordeaux derives its prestige.

But most of the wine produced in Bordeaux, the château-studded area in western France, is, as the Bordelais well knows, for the consumption of mere mortals and suitable for pouring every day. Quality ratings descend from the top, or first classified growths (established beginning in 1855) down to the unclassified estates (still

called châteaux whether or not a "castle" overlooks the vineyards), which often represent excellent value. There are also reliable wines blended in the region by major shippers, which do not state "mise en bouteille au château" (bottled at the estate) on the label.

The location of the estate, the age of the vines, and the yield per acre (a factor inversely proportionate to quality) affect the wine. That the label on a bottle of Bordeaux indicates it is a classified growth is often an accurate gauge of a wine's merits. Certainly, the vintage must also be taken into account. In the late 1970s and early 1980s there were a succession of fine vintage years resulting in good supplies and reasonable prices (helped by the favorable rate of exchange). These wines, made from cabernet sauvignon, merlot, or cabernet franc in various proportions (or, in the case of cabernet sauvignon and merlot, occasionally alone) have depth and complexity combined with rich fruit, a scent of violets and raspberries, and a flavor that lingers on the palate. In the case of the best châteaux, they are capable of long aging.

A graceful well-made red wine from Bordeaux is the perfect partner for red meat, game, veal, hearty chicken dishes, and casseroles, cheeses, and charcuterie. Under certain circumstances, it complements fish. Swordfish steak, with its "meaty" texture, is just one example.

Old Country Chicken Liver Pâté with Radish

It is arguably the homeliest and least refined of pâtés, but old-fashioned chopped liver is just delicious. One secret of its good flavor is home-rendered chicken fat, along with the resulting cracklings. In the context of an elegant dinner, the liver is served surrounded with a thatch of finely shredded white radish and slices of toasted brioche.

3 tablespoons rendered chicken fat (see following recipe)
1 cup sliced onions
½ pound chicken livers
2 hard-cooked eggs
Cracklings left from making chicken fat (optional)
Kosher salt and freshly ground black pepper
1½ cups very finely shredded or grated daikon (Oriental white radish)
Slices of toasted egg bread or brioche

Melt 2 tablespoons of the fat in a heavy skillet. Add onions and sauté over medium-low heat until they are golden. Remove onions from the pan, draining as much of the fat as possible back into the pan. Reserve the onions.

Trim the chicken livers of any connective tissue or membranes, and pat dry with paper towels. Sauté livers in the skillet over medium heat until they are lightly browned and no longer pink in the middle. Remove from heat. Combine livers, including any pan drippings, sautéed onions, 1½ hard-cooked eggs, and the cracklings, if using, in a bowl. Finely chop all the ingredients. The liver mixture can be chopped with a curved chopping blade in a wooden bowl, put through a meat grinder, or processed to a medium-coarse texture using the pulse mechanism of a food processor. You do not want this mixture to be smooth. It should have some texture. Season to taste with salt, and add remaining tablespoon chicken fat, if desired. If you refrigerate it, allow it to come to room temperature before serving.

Form mounds of the chopped liver on small plates and surround them with the grated radish. Finely chop the remaining egg yolk and some of the white and sprinkle on top. Serve with toast.

4 servings

Rendered Chicken Fat

¼ cup raw chicken fat
2 tablespoons finely chopped onion
Pinch of kosher salt

Place all ingredients in a small, heavy pan or skillet. Cook very slowly over low heat, stirring from time to time, until fat is completely liquefied and the onions and cracklings are golden brown.

Strain into a jar or crock and refrigerate. Reserve the cracklings to use for making chopped liver.

Makes ⅓ cup

Swordfish Steaks in Green Peppercorn Sauce

Be sure to cook the fish no more than medium, with a trace of pink in the center.

2 pounds swordfish, 1 inch thick, divided into four 8-ounce servings
2 tablespoons green peppercorns, drained
2 tablespoons sweet butter
1 tablespoon vegetable oil
Salt
1 tablespoon finely minced shallots
3 tablespooons Cognac or brandy
¼ cup dry red wine
⅔ cup heavy cream
1 tablespoon lemon juice
Freshly ground black pepper
1 tablespoon minced fresh parsley for garnish

It is important that the swordfish be uniformly one inch thick so it will cook evenly. Pat dry and trim away any skin. Using the back of a spoon, slightly crush the peppercorns, then spread them over both sides of the fish, pressing them into the surface. Preheat oven to warm, about 150 degrees.

In a heavy skillet (do not use one with an aluminum or iron interior surface) large enough to hold the fish in a single layer, heat the butter and oil over medium-high heat. Add the fish and sauté 4 to 5 minutes on each side, until the fish is lightly browned, but not completely cooked through. If you make a small incision, you should still see a line of pink in the middle of the fish. Season fish lightly with salt, transfer to a heatproof platter, and place in the warm oven.

Add the shallots to the skillet and sauté over low heat until they are soft and just beginning to brown. Add Cognac and cook for several minutes, stirring and scraping up any particles clinging to the pan. Add red wine and cream. Continue to cook the sauce, stirring, for a few minutes until it has reduced and thickened somewhat. Stir in the lemon juice. Keep sauce warm over low heat.

Remove the fish from the oven and drain any juices that have accumulated on the platter into the sauce. Stir the sauce, and season sauce to taste with salt and a little freshly ground pepper. Place fish in the skillet and baste with the sauce once or twice. Transfer the swordfish to a serving platter or individual plates, spoon sauce over the fish, garnish with parsley, and serve.

4 servings

Garlic-Roasted Potatoes

If you have the time and the inclination, you can "turn" potatoes French style, carving them into olive shapes. Otherwise, select small oval new potatoes and quarter them lengthwise.

> 1 large clove garlic, peeled and cut into 3 or 4 pieces
> 4 tablespoons sweet butter
> ½ cup water
> 1½ pounds small peeled and quartered or "turned" potatoes
> Salt and freshly ground black pepper

Preheat oven to 450 degrees. Place garlic, butter, and water in a small saucepan and simmer until the water evaporates and the garlic is tender.

Strain the butter through a very fine strainer, mashing the soft garlic through the strainer as well. Toss the potatoes in the garlic butter and scatter them in a baking dish large enough to hold them in a single layer without crowding.

Bake for about 25 minutes, turning them a couple of times, until they are tender and browned. Remove them from the baking dish with a slotted spoon. Season lightly with salt and pepper and serve.

4 servings

Above: Swordfish Steaks in Green Peppercorn Sauce
Below: Raspberry Cream Tart

Broccoli with Lemon Butter

1 bunch broccoli
3 tablespoons sweet butter
Juice and grated zest of 1 lemon
Lemon peel, julienned for garnish (optional)

Rinse broccoli and cut off flowerets in uniformly small pieces. Reserve stems for another use. Steam broccoli flowerets until crisp-tender, about 4 minutes.

Just before serving heat butter, lemon juice, and lemon zest in a skillet. Toss broccoli flowerets in the lemon butter and serve garnished with the lemon peel.

4 servings

Wilted Romaine and Red Onions

1 medium head romaine lettuce
½ cup sliced mushrooms
6 tablespoons olive oil
1 large red onion, in thin slices
1⅓ cups toasted croutons
2 tablespoons red wine vinegar
1 teaspoon anchovy paste
Freshly ground black pepper

Trim any unattractive outer leaves from the lettuce, remove the core, rinse the leaves, and dry them. Tear into bite-size pieces and place in a glass or ceramic salad bowl along with the mushrooms.

Heat the oil in a large skillet. Add the onions and sauté over medium-high heat until they have just wilted and lost their sharp raw taste. Add the croutons and toss a few times to coat them with oil. Remove from heat.

Beat together the vinegar and anchovy paste, combine with the ingredients in the skillet, and immediately pour over the romaine lettuce. Season with pepper, toss, and serve at once.

4 servings

Raspberry Cream Tart

This simple dessert is one of the best in my repertory.

Sweet Tart Pastry for a 9-inch one-crust tart shell
   (see following recipe)
1½ cups fresh raspberries
6 tablespoons sugar (approximately)
2 eggs
½ cup ground blanched almonds
¾ cup confectioner's sugar
1 cup heavy cream

Preheat oven to 425 degrees. Line a 9-inch straight-sided French tart or flan ring with the pastry. Prick the bottom, cover with foil, and weight with dried beans or pastry weights. Bake for 6 minutes. Remove foil, prick again, and bake another 4 or 5 minutes, until pastry is just beginning to color. Remove from oven and lower temperature to 350 degrees.

Sweeten raspberries with sugar, using more or less according to their natural sweetness. Spread raspberries in a single layer in the partly baked tart shell.

Lightly beat the eggs, almonds, confectioner's sugar, and cream. Pour over raspberries in tart shell, and bake for 30 minutes, until top is golden brown. Cool to room temperature before serving.

Makes one 9-inch tart

Sweet Tart Pastry

1¼ cups flour
Pinch of salt
2 tablespoons sugar
5 tablespoons cold sweet butter, diced
1 egg yolk
3 tablespoons ice water (approximately)

Combine flour, salt, and sugar. Cut in the butter with a pastry blender. Beat egg yolk with ice water, and moisten dry ingredients to form a dough. The dough may be mixed in a food processor: combine the dry ingredients in the work bowl, add the butter and blend it briefly, using the on-off pulse, then with the machine running, add the egg yolk and water through the feed tube until a ball of dough forms.

Pastry for an 8- or 9-inch tart

A Luxurious Italian Menu

Tuscan White Wine
Warm Artichokes with Basil Béarnaise

Brunello di Montalcino

Veal Ragout with Peas and Fresh Pasta
Arugula, Radicchio, and Endive Salad

Pear-Almond Cake with Dark Caramel Sauce

This is one of my favorite menus, one that has had enormous appeal for small dinner parties. I love the wine for its velvet-gloved strength and that it makes guests feel pampered. The food, from the artichokes through the pear cake with caramel sauce for dessert, is extremely attractive to serve.

Brunello di Montalcino

In our materialistic, label-conscious society, calling something "the most expensive" can be dangerous. It effectively obliterates those outstanding qualities that might indeed justify the price. Brunello di Montalcino, widely touted as Italy's most expensive wine, is a good example of this. In his book *Italian Wine* Victor Hazan calls it "the one Italian wine with snob appeal."

It is an outstanding wine, capable of extraordinary longevity, but its international prestige, comparable to that of Bordeaux *premiers crus*, also depends to a certain extent on people whose taste buds are in their wallets. A bottle of Biondi-Santi brunello di Montalcino can fetch hundreds of dollars, and the notion of "most expensive" has a great deal to do with the Biondi-Santi label.

The relationship between Biondi-Santi and brunello is an intimate one, since the wine originated in the late nineteenth century on the Biondi-Santi estate on the southern fringe of Tuscany. The wine is made from a clone of the sangiovese *grosso* grape (sangiovese is the dominant red grape of Tuscany) and according to Franco Biondi-Santi, present head of the family, all brunello is made from descendants of the "mother" vine first cultivated by his grandfather.

The cachet of brunello di Montalcino has increased exports to this country from many producers, some with prices that do not require taking a second mortgage on the house. From the same region also come excellent red table wines, called *rosso di Montalcino* made from younger sangiovese vines, or wines aged less than the four years required for brunello di Montalcino.

The dinner for four has been planned so that one fine bottle of brunello di Montalcino can be poured. With the veal as a main course, brunello di Montalcino, especially one with a good five or more years of age on it, is an elegant match. If an aperitif is served, select a Tuscan white wine—bianco Toscano or Galestro. The first course of whole artichokes does not require a wine and might actually countermand it since artichokes will distort the flavor of wine. Light, crisp Tuscan whites are as good a choice as any.

Warm Artichokes with Basil Béarnaise

Do not be daunted by the length of this recipe. Describing how to trim an artichoke takes longer than the task itself. I have made the artichokes extremely convenient for guests, with the fuzzy choke removed, then filled with warm sauce so the vegetable becomes its own serving dish. The béarnaise sauce holds up extremely well in the warm artichoke. If the béarnaise sauce is prepared in advance, you can store it in a thermos until you are ready to serve—a trick I learned from Manhattan cooking teacher Peter Kump.

4 large globe artichokes
1 lemon
Basil Béarnaise (see following recipe)

Select a kettle or pot large enough to hold all of the artichokes. Fill it halfway with water and set it over high heat to boil.

Rinse the artichokes, slice the stems off flush with the base so the artichokes can stand level, and pull off any tough outer leaves. Rub all cut areas with lemon. Slice off the top inch of each artichoke and rub exposed area with lemon. Using kitchen shears, snip off the top half-inch of each leaf.

Place the artichokes base side down in the boiling water, lower the heat to medium, and weight the artichokes with a dish or pot lid that fits into the pot to keep the artichokes submerged. Simmer the artichokes until the base can be pierced easily with a knife point, 30 to 40 minutes. Do not undercook. Remove the artichokes and drain upside down.

As soon as the artichokes are cool enough to handle, gently spread the leaves away from the center of each to expose the pointed inner leaves that cover the choke. Using a spoon, scoop out these leaves as well as the fuzzy choke, taking care not to remove any of the fleshy bottom beneath. When all of the fuzz has been removed, place the artichokes in a dish, cover with a clean towel wrung out in hot water, and set aside to keep warm. The artichokes should be just warm, not hot, when served.

4 servings

Basil Béarnaise

3 tablespoons dry vermouth
3 tablespoons white wine vinegar
1 tablespoon minced shallots
2 egg yolks
6 ounces sweet butter, melted
Salt and freshly ground white pepper
¼ cup very finely minced basil leaves

Combine two tablespoons of the vermouth plus the wine vinegar in a small saucepan. Add the shallots and cook about 5 minutes, until the shallots are tender and only about 1 tablespoon of the liquid remains. Stir in the remaining tablespoon of vermouth.

Meanwhile whisk the egg yolks until very thick and light. Strain the vermouth mixture into the egg yolks, whisking constantly. Discard the shallots.

Return the egg yolk mixture to the saucepan and place over very, very low heat. You might even keep the pan only partly on the burner and give it a quarter turn every 15 seconds or so; you could use a double boiler if you prefer. Still beating the egg yolks, start to add melted butter, allowing it to dribble in extremely slowly. By the time about half the butter has been added the sauce should have thickened considerably. Continue to beat in the butter and gently heat the mixture. If it shows any indication of clotting or lumping, remove it immediately from the heat and plunge the base of the pan into cold water to arrest the cooking. (If the sauce curdles you can usually repair it by beating a fresh egg yolk and gradually beating the curdled sauce into it.)

When the sauce is thickened and all the butter has been incorporated, season with salt and pepper, and stir in the basil. You can hold the sauce by putting it in a double boiler over simmering water. These proportions make about 1 cup of sauce.

When the sauce is finished, spoon about ¼ cup of the warm sauce into the center of each cooked, warm artichoke and serve.

Makes about 1 cup

A light, dry, and crisp Tuscan white wine is a fine aperitif. With its good acidity, it can complement first-course artichokes

Veal Ragout with Peas and Fresh Pasta

Try to find fresh peas for this recipe; they make all the difference. The pappardelle can be purchased or, if you are up to making your own egg pasta, homemade. Fresh fettuccine is a good substitute.

  5 tablespoons olive oil
  ½ cup finely chopped onions
  ½ cup finely chopped celery
  ½ cup finely chopped carrots
  1 large clove garlic, minced
  1½ pounds lean veal shoulder, in 1½-inch cubes
  ¾ cup dry red wine
  1 pound plum tomatoes, peeled and chopped (1½ cups well-drained canned plum tomatoes can be substituted)
  ½ teaspoon dried sage
  1 bay leaf
  Small pinch red pepper flakes
  Salt and freshly ground black pepper
  1 pound fresh peas, shelled (1 cup frozen peas can be substituted if fresh are unavailable)
  2 ounces prosciutto, cut in thin slivers
  1 teaspoon lemon juice
  ½ pound pappardelle, broad egg noodles, or fresh fettuccine (page 132)
  3 tablespoons sweet butter
  1 tablespoon minced fresh parsley

Heat 2 tablespoons of the olive oil in a heavy casserole. Add the onions, celery, and carrots, and sauté over low heat until soft but not brown. Add garlic and continue sautéing another minute or so. Remove from heat.

Dry the veal with paper towels. Heat the remaining 3 tablespoons olive oil in a heavy skillet (do not use cast iron or aluminum) and add as much of the veal as the pan can accommodate without crowding. Brown the veal over medium-high heat, placing the lightly browned pieces over the vegetables in the casserole, and adding more veal to the skillet. When all the veal has been browned and transferred to the casserole, lower heat under the skillet to medium and add the wine. Cook the wine for several minutes, scraping the skillet to dissolve any browned bits clinging to it. Pour the contents of the skillet over the meat in the casserole. Return the casserole to the stove and place over low heat.

Add the tomatoes, sage, bay leaf, red pepper, and salt and pepper to taste to the casserole. As soon as mixture starts to simmer, cover and cook for 1½ hours.

Check from time to time to make sure there is enough liquid in the casserole; meat should be nearly covered. Add a little water if too much liquid has evaporated.

At the end of 1½ hours the veal should be tender. Add the peas and cook 15 minutes longer (slightly less if they are very small). If you are using frozen peas, they will require only about 5 minutes (but don't expect the same sweet flavor as from fresh peas). Add the prosciutto and lemon juice and cook just long enough for the ham to heat through. Check seasonings.

Meanwhile boil noodles in a large pot of salted water until al dente. Fresh pasta will take 2 to 4 minutes; dried up to 7 minutes. Drain and gloss with butter. Serve noodles alongside veal ragout. Sprinkle veal with parsley before serving.

4 servings

Arugula, Radicchio, and Endive Salad

1 bunch arugula
1 head radicchio
2 endives
1½ tablespoons red wine vinegar
4 tablespoons extra-virgin Italian olive oil
Salt and freshly ground black pepper

Rinse and dry arugula, removing any heavy stems. Break any very long branches in half.

Rinse the radicchio, remove the core, and separate into leaves, breaking or tearing leaves into bite-size pieces.

Remove the cores from the endives, separate the leaves and sliver them vertically. Cut these slivers so they are no more than 2 inches long. Combine the greens in a salad bowl.

Beat the vinegar and oil together, and season with salt and pepper. Pour over the salad, toss, and serve.

4 servings

Pear-Almond Cake with Dark Caramel Sauce

This dessert can be prepared early in the day but should not be refrigerated before serving. It is an excellent recipe for entertaining, easy to prepare, and expandable. I have doubled it and baked it in an 11-inch-round pan to serve 12.

A puddle of caramel sauce spooned onto the dessert plate alongside the triangle of cake gives it extra appeal and great style.

2 pounds ripe pears
Juice of 1 lemon
10 tablespoons sweet butter, at room temperature
1 cup sugar
2 eggs
1 cup flour
½ teaspoon baking powder
½ teaspoon salt
½ teaspoon almond extract
½ cup sliced almonds
Dark Caramel Sauce (see following recipe)

Preheat oven to 350 degrees. Butter and flour a 9-inch springform pan. Peel, core, and slice pears. Toss pears with juice of ½ the lemon and set aside. Cream 8 tablespoons of the butter with ¾ cup of the sugar. Add eggs one at a time and beat well. Sift flour, baking powder, and salt together; add to batter, stirring lightly. Add remaining lemon juice and the almond extract.

Spread batter in prepared pan and cover with sliced pears. Dot with 1 tablespoon of the butter. Sprinkle with 2 tablespoons of the sugar and then sprinkle the almonds on top. Sprinkle with remaining 2 tablespoons of sugar, dot with remaining tablespoon of butter. Bake for 1 hour. Cool slightly before removing sides of pan. Serve warm or cool, with dark caramel sauce.

6 to 8 servings

Dark Caramel Sauce

Try this quick dessert sauce with the Small Steamed Chocolate Puddings (page 51), or over ice cream.

½ cup sugar
4 tablespoons water
3 tablespoons hot brewed espresso
½ cup heavy cream

Swirl sugar and water together in a heavy saucepan until the sugar dissolves. Place over medium-high heat and cook, stirring occasionally, until the mixture turns a uniform honey-brown color. Remove from heat.

Pour the hot espresso into the caramel and stir to blend. Add the cream, stirring to blend completely. If all the caramel has not dissolved, briefly reheat the sauce. Refrigerate until ready to use.

Makes 1 cup

Cool Food for a Warm Evening

California Chardonnay

Cold Cucumber and Bulgur Soup
Poached Salmon Steaks with Lemon-Mustard Sauce
New Potato Salad with Fresh Peas
Sliced Ripe Tomatoes

Double Blueberry Tart with Gingered Whipped Cream

Warm weather dining is the most relaxed there is, from the standpoint of the cook as well as the guests. Every dish is prepared in advance, then served either cold or at room temperature.

This menu, which relies upon quality ingredients, is suitable for a gracious, intimate dinner served on a terrace or in a cool, airy room indoors. Its very simplicity makes it easy to expand to serve six, even eight, but keeping the party small usually permits a splurge in the wine department.

The calorie-conscious can generously baste the cooled poached salmon with a mixture of lemon, mustard, and minced parsley instead of serving the mayonnaise sauce, and omit most of the oil for the potatoes. Replace the tart with fresh blueberries and top them with cottage cheese that has been smoothed in the blender, lightly sweetened, and seasoned with ground ginger.

California Chardonnay

The chardonnay grape has class. The white grape of Burgundy's aristocratic Montrachets, the wine that Alexandre Dumas said should be drunk on one's knees, and the backbone of Champagne, has now become the grape from which California's finest white wines are made.

Big, molten gold wine, scented of ripe peaches and apples, silken on the palate, the expansive taste lingering seductively—that's California chardonnay. But wait: sunlit, crisp, clean, elegant wines that capture a freshness are again descriptions of California chardonnay. Fickle grape? No more so than in Burgundy where it ranges in style from the leanness of Chablis in the north, the richness of the Meursaults and Montrachets of the Côte de Beaune, or the lighter style of the Mâcon area.

Climate, soil, and in the case of California, the winemaker's personal style make the difference. The problem with understanding the California interpretation of chardonnay is that the wines are not easily defined by district as they are in France. No established tradition dictates how wine from a given area should taste.

Recently there has been a trend away from the mouth-filling, oak-aged style on the theory that a lighter style better complements food. As a generalization, that is open to question. A big chardonnay is not for everyday drinking and might overwhelm a plate of oysters or a simple veal piccata, but with richer fish such as lobster (or the salmon in this menu), or with poultry or veal in a cream sauce, a lush wine should be poured. Furthermore, it would be tragic to see the California winemakers abandon the very style of chardonnay with which they have achieved their greatest distinction.

If you prefer to serve a lighter wine, the acidity of the sauce will still maintain the balance. In fact, you might consider serving a pair of chardonnays—a lighter one as an aperitif and with the soup, followed by a bigger one. With a few exceptions, look to Napa and Sonoma counties. In the fresher-tasting style, consider wider geography and more moderate price as a rule of thumb.

Cold Cucumber and Bulgur Soup

This refreshing tart cold soup suggests the cuisine of the Middle East with its combination of cucumbers, cracked wheat, and mint. Serve the frosty green soup with its contrasting herbal garnish in chilled bowls, but check seasonings since flavors are dulled by cold.

½ cup bulgur wheat
1 cup warm water
2½ cups peeled, diced cucumbers
½ cup chopped scallions
2 cups buttermilk (approximately)
Salt and freshly ground black pepper
1 tablespoon minced fresh chives
1 tablespoon minced fresh mint } for garnish
1 teaspoon minced fresh parsley

Cover bulgur with the water and set aside to soften, about 20 minutes.

Meanwhile, combine 2 cups of the cucumbers with the scallions and 1 cup of the buttermilk in a blender or food processor. Blend until finely puréed. Stir in remaining 1 cup buttermilk, season with salt and pepper, and chill at least 2 hours.

When the bulgur is soft, drain it well, pressing out as much moisture as possible. Add it to the cucumber mixture.

Just before serving, check seasonings, and stir in remaining ½ cup of the cucumbers. If the soup has become too thick, stir in a little more buttermilk. Garnish each serving with minced chives, mint, and parsley.

4 servings

Poached Salmon Steaks with Lemon-Mustard Sauce

Salmon, always delicious, is today among the best quality fish you can buy thanks to cultivation efforts in the Pacific Northwest and Scandinavia. The fish are flown to market as soon as they are "harvested," and should be of impeccable freshness when purchased from a reliable fish market. As with most fish, a touch of undercooking will keep the texture moist and succulent.

1½ cups dry white wine
1½ cups water (approximately)
1 tablespoon fresh lemon juice
6 white peppercorns, crushed
1 teaspoon salt
Parsley sprigs
1 bay leaf
1 small onion, sliced
4 salmon steaks, each about 1 inch thick (about 2 pounds salmon total; if the steaks are very large, use two steaks)
Lemon wedges and watercress for garnish
Lemon-Mustard Sauce (see following recipe)

Combine wine, water, lemon juice, peppercorns, salt, parsley, bay leaf, and onion in a deep skillet or a fish poacher large enough to hold the fish in a single layer. Do not use an aluminum or cast-iron pan—only tin-lined copper, enamel, or stainless steel should be used. A nonstick surface would also be suitable, but not necessary.

Gently lower the fish into the pan. The fish should be just covered with liquid. If not, add more water or a mixture of water and wine. Adjust heat so the liquid is just barely simmering—the surface of the water should shiver. Cook fish for 3 minutes. Remove from heat and allow fish to cool in the poaching liquid; then serve at room temperature, or refrigerate cooled fish until ready to serve, allowing it to come to room temperature first. Reserve poaching liquid for making the sauce.

Serve fish decorated with watercress and slices of lemon, with lemon-mustard sauce on the side.

4 servings

Lemon-Mustard Sauce

3 tablespoons lemon juice
3 teaspoons Dijon mustard
2 large egg yolks
1 cup light vegetable oil (French olive oil, sunflower seed oil, or light peanut oil would be best)
3 tablespoons cooled fish stock (reserved from poaching fish)
1 tablespoon grated lemon rind

Combine 1 tablespoon of the lemon juice, 1 teaspoon of the mustard, and the egg yolks in a bowl or in the container of a blender or food processor. Beat or process until well blended. Slowly drizzle in the oil, beating or processing constantly, until very thick. This is basically a mayonnaise.

By hand, fold in the remaining 2 tablespoons lemon juice, 2 teaspoons mustard, the fish stock, and lemon rind. Refrigerate sauce until ready to use, but allow to come almost to room temperature before serving.

Makes 1½ cups

New Potato Salad with Fresh Peas

1½ pounds small new potatoes, uniform in size
Salt and freshly ground black pepper
4 tablespoons tarragon vinegar
¾ pound fresh green peas, about 1 cup shelled
    peas *(see note)*
1 tablespoon sugar
2 tablespoons finely minced red onion
5 tablespoons olive oil

Boil the potatoes until they are just tender. Do not overcook. As soon as they are cool enough to handle, quarter them and place them in a bowl. Season with salt and pepper and sprinkle with 3 tablespoons of the vinegar. Set aside until cooled to room temperature.

Simmer the peas with the sugar until they turn bright green and are barely tender, about 5 minutes. Drain and set aside.

When the potatoes and peas have cooled, combine them, adding the onion and mixing very gently. Beat the remaining tablespoon of vinegar with the olive oil until well blended, and lightly fold the dressing into the salad.

4 servings

Note: If fresh green peas are not available, substitute snow peas, blanched in boiling water about 2 minutes, then finely slivered. Frozen green peas would be a very last resort.

Double Blueberry Tart with Gingered Whipped Cream

Sweet Tart Pastry (page 30)
2 pints fresh blueberries
4 tablespoons good quality blueberry preserves
1 cup heavy cream
3 tablespoons finely chopped crystallized ginger

Preheat oven to 425 degrees. Roll out pastry and line a 9-inch straight-sided French tart or flan ring with the pastry. Prick the bottom, cover with foil, and weight with dried beans or pastry weights. Bake for 6 minutes. Remove foil, prick again, and bake for about 10 minutes longer, until the pastry is golden brown. Remove from oven.

Once the pastry is prepared and is baking, mix 1 pint of the blueberries with the preserves in a heavy saucepan. Bring to a simmer and simmer for about 5 minutes, just until the berries have softened. Strain the berries, returning the cooking syrup to the saucepan. (Reserve the berries.) Simmer the cooking liquid another 5 minutes or so, until it has thickened to a heavy syrup. Recombine with the cooked blueberries and set aside to cool.

When the pastry and the berries have cooled, spread the cooked berry mixture in the pastry shell. Top with the uncooked pint of berries. (You can prepare the pastry filled with the cooked berries early in the day if you wish, but do not add the uncooked berries until within an hour of serving.)

Whip the cream and fold in the crystallized ginger. Serve alongside the blueberry tart.

6 servings

Northern Italian Specialties

❦

Soave
Mussels and Clams Aglio Olio

Amarone

Fegato alla Veneziana
(*Calves' Liver Venetian Style*)
Herbed Polenta
Bitter Greens with Sweet Vinegar

Pears in Red Wine

For ease of preparation, this is a menu for four people. And they should be individuals whose tastes are familiar to you.

The main course, *Fegato alla Veneziana*, is calves' liver, a meat that does not enjoy universal appeal. But there is no better, more delectable method of preparing it than the Venetian way in which mere liver and onions transcend the ordinary through careful cooking and seasoning.

Coordinating this menu is a trifle tricky. The dessert is prepared and set aside, well before the first course and main course are tackled. (Searing the liver is unavoidably a last minute task.) Similarly, the greens (aside from their dressing) can wait, ready to be served. If, instead of poaching the pears in wine you serve fresh pears with Gorgonzola cheese and walnuts for dessert, you have a menu that is ready in under one hour.

Soave and Amarone—Wines of the Veneto

The wines of the Veneto, the region in northeast Italy crowned by Venice, could fill a cellar with bottles suitable for any occasion. The diverse inventory begins with pale, easy Soave, the most popular white wine imported into the United States, and a fine accompaniment for mussels and clams in oil, garlic, parsley, and white wine. (Don't hesitate to splash the Soave into the pan.)

In the Veneto, the traditional grape varieties also produce light red Bardolino and Valpolicella. White varietals such as pinot grigio (see page 118) and pinot bianco introduced in the last century account for eminently drinkable still and sparkling wines. More recently the French varietals—cabernet sauvignon and merlot—have been cultivated with some good results.

But it is amarone, with its deep garnet color and extraordinary power and complexity, that stands apart from the wines of this region and is rarely matched in intensity by any other dry red wine. Grapes from the same vineyards north of Verona that produce the soft, cherry-scented Valpolicella are used to make amarone, but they are picked selectively from the tops of the bunches. These grapes, having been exposed to more sunlight, accumulate a greater concentration of sugar and are even left to dry for a month or more before being pressed, thus further concentrating the sugar. When completely fermented, they produce a blockbuster wine with at least fourteen percent alcohol. The name amarone comes from "amaro" or bitter, to distinguish it from sweet wines made in a similar fashion.

The lush wine, bottled in dark brown glass, has a heady bouquet suggesting almonds and raisins, as one might expect from a wine made with partially dried grapes. It is complex and velvety, with a subtly bitter aftertaste also characteristic of the simpler Valpolicella, and it is superb with rich meat such as liver. Amarone is capable of extensive aging but the younger amarones offer smooth fullness to balance but not overpower a simple dinner of Venetian specialties, turning it into one of splendid tastes.

Mussels and Clams Aglio Olio

Since the steaming liquid becomes the sauce, be sure the shellfish is scrubbed extremely well and that none of the mussel shells are filled with silt. Serve this with plenty of bread.

    6 tablespoons olive oil
    1 tablespoon minced garlic
    1 pound mussels, scrubbed and debearded
   18 littleneck clams, scrubbed
    ½ cup chopped fresh parsley
    ½ cup dry white wine
    A few red pepper flakes
    1 tablespoon extra-virgin olive oil

Heat the oil in a large, heavy skillet. Add garlic and sauté a few minutes, until the garlic is extremely fragrant but not beginning to brown. Add the mussels and clams and stir for several minutes. Cover the pan and cook over low heat until the mussels and clams open, about 10 minutes.

Using a slotted spoon, remove the mussels and clams from the pan, place in a bowl, and cover to keep warm. Add parsley, wine, and pepper flakes to the sauce in the pan. Taste; if the sauce is too salty, add a little water.

Divide the mussels and clams into individual bowls. Stir the extra-virgin olive oil into the sauce, pour the sauce over the mussels and clams, and serve.

4 servings

Fegato alla Veneziana
(Calves' Liver Venetian Style)

Take the time to sauté the onions slowly, then cook the liver as quickly as possible. If you have fresh sage, use a few sprigs as a garnish.

  1⅓ pounds calves' liver, in slices ¼ inch thick
    4 tablespoons olive oil
    3 cups thinly sliced onions
    Salt and freshly ground black pepper
    ½ teaspoon fresh sage leaves or ¼ teaspoon dried
    1 tablespoon dry white wine
  1½ tablespoons white wine vinegar

Trim liver very well of any sinews. Cut the slices into pieces about 2 inches long. Pat the liver dry with paper towels, then place on a platter, cover, and refrigerate until ready to use.

Heat oil in a large, heavy skillet. Add the onions, season with salt and pepper, and cook over very low heat, stirring frequently, until the onions are golden and very tender, about 20 minutes. Remove onions from the pan and place in a bowl, draining them well in order to leave as much of the oil as possible in the skillet.

Increase heat to high and add the liver, tossing it in the oil for about 3 minutes, until the liver strips are beginning to brown but are still very pink inside. Sprinkle with sage, wine, and vinegar, season with salt and pepper, and reduce heat to low. Return onions to the pan, mix to reheat, and serve liver and onions moistened with pan juices at once.

4 servings

Herbed Polenta

Polenta—the Italian name for cornmeal mush—is a trifle tricky. Try to serve it as soon as it is ready. It will hold no more than 20 minutes. But for advance preparation, the best technique is to spread the finished polenta in a buttered baking pan, dot it with butter, and bake it for 15 minutes at 350 degrees. Cut into squares for serving.

  4½ to 5 cups chicken stock, preferably
        homemade (page 22)
  1½ cups yellow cornmeal
    Salt and freshly ground black pepper
    2 tablespoons sweet butter
    1 teaspoon minced fresh sage or ½ teaspoon dried
    1 teaspoon minced fresh parsley

Bring 4½ cups stock to a simmer in a heavy saucepan. Add the cornmeal very slowly, stirring constantly. The easiest way to add the cornmeal is to allow a very thin stream of it to pour from your hand, keeping your fist closed and releasing the cornmeal very gradually. If you add the cornmeal too rapidly it will lump.

When all the cornmeal has been added and the mixture is very thick and creamy, season to taste with salt and pepper. Continue to cook, stirring, for 5 minutes or so. To serve immediately, stir in the butter, sage, and parsley, and serve.

If you are not serving the polenta immediately, add the additional half cup of stock, dot with butter, and set aside, covered. It will hold for about 20 minutes. Then when ready to serve, mix the polenta, adding a little water, if necessary, and reheat it gently, stirring. Stir in the sage and parsley, and serve.

4 servings

Mussels and clams, garlic and oil

Bitter Greens with Sweet Vinegar

Balsamic vinegar from Modena is the color of coffee and extremely mellow. It requires very little oil in a salad dressing.

½ head escarole
1 bunch watercress
½ bunch young dandelion greens or 1 bunch
    arugula
3 tablespoons extra-virgin olive oil
7 tablespoons balsamic vinegar
3 tablespoons grated Fontina cheese
Freshly ground black pepper

Rinse and dry the escarole, watercress, and dandelion or arugula. Coarsely chop the escarole and watercress. Shred the dandelion or arugula leaves. Do not add the stems. Place the greens in a bowl.

Mix the olive oil and vinegar together. Pour over salad and toss. Sprinkle cheese and pepper on each serving.

4 servings

Pears in Red Wine

4 whole, large, ripe pears with stems intact
3 tablespoons lemon juice
3 cups dry, full-bodied red wine
⅓ cup sugar
1 teaspoon vanilla extract
A cinnamon stick
2 tablespoons brandy

Peel the pears, scooping out the cores from the bottom with the point of a swivel-bladed potato peeler. Immerse the pears in water mixed with 2 tablespoons of the lemon juice. Bring the red wine to a simmer in a saucepan that will comfortably hold the pears upright. Add sugar, vanilla extract, and a cinnamon stick. Once the sugar has dissolved, add the pears and cook them gently for about 15 minutes, until they are tender but still hold their shape. Remove the pears from the pan, draining them well.

Bring the wine mixture to a boil and cook rapidly until it is reduced to about ¾ cup and has become quite syrupy. Stir in the remaining tablespoon of lemon juice and brandy, and pour the syrup over the pears. Allow the pears to cool to room temperature or chill them, basting from time to time with the syrup.

4 servings

Above: Pears in Red Wine with fresh mint garnish
Right: Fegato alla Veneziana

A 700-Calorie Dinner

❦

White or Red Wine Spritzers

Asparagus "Guacamole" with Jicama Chips
Mushroom Timbales with Red Pepper Sauce
Tilefish en Papillote
Lemon Potatoes
Steamed Broccoli with Oyster Sauce

Minted Melon and Kiwi
Chocolate Meringue Kisses

I t does seem lately that downward revisions of the number of calories, the amount of cholesterol, the percentage of dietary fat, and the grams of protein that are considered a sensible daily intake for today's adult are announced by one agency or another. And with lean bodies and happy longevity the potential reward, we submit ourselves to yet another regime.

By following certain principles calories can be trimmed, especially when the cooking is done at home where there is more control. When friends, relatives, and acquaintances share these restrictions or have similar concerns, they can enjoy a dinner party without worry. Delicious food does not have to be abandoned.

The following menu is a multicourse affair designed to keep cholesterol and calories to a minimum. Although the average "gourmet" dinner is calculated to provide an average of 2,000 calories per person, this one weighs in at closer to 700, including the drink. The caloric savings here is accomplished by removing as much fat as possible, using nonstick skillets, steaming, "sweating" onions over low heat to tenderize them without fat, and substituting cottage cheese puréed in a blender instead of cream in a quichelike mixture.

White or Red Wine Spritzers

The average glass of wine provides 100 calories. Reduced calorie or "light" wines are not worth discussing because most of them are not particularly palatable.

But through clever use of sparkling water you can create wine coolers that extend the enjoyment of wine without adding calories. I frequently prepare and serve spritzers, especially with lunch or as a cocktail. Short of plain sparkling water with lime, spritzers have fewer calories than almost any other drink, including a glass of orange juice. A spritzer made with one part wine to three of water transforms the 100 calories of wine in a typical glass into two big eight-ounce drinks. Add a judicious splash of bitters and you intensify the flavor enough to stretch it further. Serve the drink over ice (another dilutant) in handsome stemmed goblets garnished with a slice of orange.

For drinks such as these it goes without saying that the best bottles in the cellar are not pressed into service. A wine should have flavor and good acidity, and I tend to prefer red wine spritzers. I particularly like the results when made with zinfandel, barbera, or a young Chianti because they have more body. For a white wine spritzer try a forthright sauvignon blanc.

Asparagus "Guacamole" with Jicama Chips

Asparagus, puréed and seasoned to a fare-thee-well, becomes a surprisingly accurate double for traditional guacamole at about one-tenth the calories. Jicama is a crunchy tropical tuber with a flavor somewhere between coconut and apple. Slices of sweet white turnip or cucumber could be substituted for dipping.

1 pound medium-thick fresh asparagus
2 tablespoons fresh lime juice
2 tablespoons finely chopped scallions
2 tablespoons very finely minced sweet red pepper
1 canned small green chili pepper, seeded and minced (about 1 tablespoon), or minced fresh green chili to taste
1 tablespoon minced fresh coriander leaves
Pinch of salt
Cayenne pepper to taste
Slices of fresh jicama, peeled

Wash asparagus, snap off the ends, and simmer in water until very tender, about 20 minutes. Drain and allow to cool. Cut off the tips and reserve them.

Cut the spears into half-inch pieces and process to a smooth purée in a blender or food processor.

Fold in remaining ingredients. Either fold in the tips or use them to garnish the dip. Serve with slices of peeled jicama for dipping.

Makes 1½ cups

Mushroom Timbales with Red Pepper Sauce

1 pound fresh mushrooms
1½ cups finely chopped onions
1 clove garlic, minced
Salt and freshly ground black pepper
½ teaspoon paprika
½ teaspoon oregano
1 teaspoon sweet butter
1 cup lowfat cottage cheese
½ cup skim milk
2 whole eggs plus 2 egg yolks
2 large sweet red peppers, seeded and chopped
2 cups water
Pinch of cayenne pepper
6 parsley sprigs for garnish

Finely chop the mushrooms in a food processor or by hand. Place them in a strainer lined with several thicknesses of paper towels or a clean linen towel and press out as much moisture as possible. Set aside.

Place 1 cup of the onions with the garlic and a sprinkling of salt in a large skillet, preferably nonstick. Cover the skillet and allow the onions and garlic to cook until soft and translucent, about 10 minutes. Add the drained mushrooms to the skillet and continue to cook over medium-high heat until the liquid from the mushrooms has cooked out and evaporated, about 10 minutes longer. Season the mushrooms with salt, pepper, ¼ teaspoon of the paprika, and all of the oregano. Preheat oven to 375 degrees. Lightly butter six ½-cup heatproof molds, such as small soufflé dishes or custard cups.

Place the cottage cheese and skim milk in a blender jar and combine until smooth and creamy. Transfer to a bowl. Beat in the eggs and egg yolks. Stir in the mushroom mixture, which should have cooled somewhat. Carefully season the custard mixture, then divide it evenly among the prepared molds. Place the molds in a baking pan large enough to hold them comfortably, and pour boiling water into the baking pan to come halfway up the sides of the molds. Place the pan in the oven and bake for about 20 minutes, until the custards are firm and a knife inserted in the center comes out clean.

To make the pepper sauce, place the chopped peppers and the remaining ½ cup of the onions in a shallow saucepan or a skillet with 2 cups of water. Allow to simmer slowly until the peppers are tender, about 20 minutes. This can be done while the timbales are baking. Add remaining ¼ teaspoon of the paprika and cayenne pepper. When the peppers are soft, purée the mixture in a blender and season to taste.

Unmold the timbales by running a knife around the inside of each mold, and then inverting the timbale onto a plate. Spoon a little of the pepper sauce around each timbale on the plate and place a sprig of parsley on top of the timbale for garnish.

6 servings

Tilefish en Papillote

2 pounds tilefish or other meaty fillets of fish
Juice of 1 lemon
1 large onion, finely chopped
1 clove garlic, minced
Salt
2½ cups peeled, chopped tomatoes (fresh ripe or
    drained canned)
½ teaspoon crushed fennel seeds
Freshly ground black pepper
1 tablespoon vegetable oil
⅔ cup minced scallions
6 thin slices lemon

Divide the fish into 6 equal portions and place in a dish with the lemon juice to marinate briefly. Place the onion and garlic in a heavy saucepan over very low heat, sprinkle lightly with salt, cover, and cook until the onions have wilted and turned translucent, about 10 minutes. Add tomatoes and fennel, cook briefly over high heat, and season with salt and pepper.

Preheat oven to 375 degrees. Prepare six squares of heavy duty aluminum foil large enough to enclose the fish loosely but securely. Lightly brush each piece of foil with oil. Scatter half the scallions among each of the foil squares. Top each with a piece of fish, then divide the tomato mixture evenly over each. Scatter over the remaining scallions, then top with a slice of lemon.

Bake about 20 minutes. Serve by putting a package on each plate, and opening it in front of your guests.

6 servings

Lemon Potatoes

2 pounds new potatoes, as small as possible
Salt and freshly ground black pepper
Juice of 2 lemons
1 tablespoon minced fresh dill

Scrub the potatoes and peel a strip from around the middle of each. Place in a large saucepan, cover with water, bring to a boil, and simmer until the potatoes are just tender, about 15 to 20 minutes. Drain.

Return potatoes to the saucepan and add the remaining ingredients. Cook over low heat, stirring, for about 10 minutes, until the lemon juice just films the bottom of the pan. Recheck seasonings and serve.

6 servings

Steamed Broccoli with Oyster Sauce

1 bunch broccoli
2 tablespoons Chinese oyster sauce
1½ tablespoons light soy sauce

Rinse the broccoli. Cut the flowerets into small pieces. Peel and slice the stems into ½-inch thicknesses. Place the broccoli stems in a steamer basket and steam for 2 minutes. Add the flowerets and continue steaming until all the broccoli is crisp-tender, about 4 minutes longer.

Toss the broccoli with the oyster and soy sauces and serve.

6 servings

Minted Melon and Kiwi

4 kiwis, peeled and sliced horizontally
1 large cantaloupe
3 tablespoons orange juice
1 tablespoon lime juice
2 tablespoons finely chopped fresh mint

Place the kiwi slices in a bowl. Cut the cantaloupe in half, remove the seeds, and using a melon ball scoop, make melon balls using about two-thirds of the melon. Place the melon balls in the bowl with the kiwi. Dice the remaining melon. You should have about three cups of diced melon.

Purée the diced melon in a food processor or blender. Add orange juice and lime juice. Stir in mint. Pour this sauce over the melon and kiwi, and refrigerate until ready to serve.

6 servings

Chocolate Meringue Kisses

3 tablespoons cocoa
⅓ cup sugar
1 tablespoon cornstarch
3 egg whites
Dash of vinegar
Confectioner's sugar

Preheat oven to 225 degrees. Line a baking sheet with foil or parchment. Combine the cocoa with the sugar and cornstarch. Beat the egg whites with vinegar until they begin to peak, then gradually add the cocoa mixture, beating constantly. Continue beating until stiff. Pipe the meringue through a large star tube onto the baking sheet. Bake for 1 hour, then shut off the oven and leave the cookies in overnight.

The next day carefully peel the paper off the cookies and store them airtight. Dust with confectioner's sugar just before serving.

2½ dozen cookies

INFORMAL DINNERS

Informality is a mood that condones guests strolling into the kitchen (or out to the grill) to watch the cook in action, serving foods meant to be eaten with the fingers, sipping jug wines or beer, and taking off one's shoes. It means the guests help themselves. But it is never careless.

Certain details such as carefully crafted canapés, hired help, and polished silver are superfluous at an informal dinner and one rarely serves a succession of wines, but other elements must be taken into account. I find that the more informal the meal the better and larger the napkins must be. The comfort and pleasure of guests and the quality of the food you serve should remain constant.

I will never forget a boiled crab dinner served in a gracious Georgetown mansion. Rare pieces of Chinese export porcelain were lined on the Chippendale sideboard, the crystal chandelier glittered, and the large table was set for twelve—with newspaper and paper towels. Bags of highly spiced steamed hard crabs were dumped in the center of the table and everyone dug in, and drank beer. It was informality at its best.

A clambake; pizza and grilled fish; a soup and salad supper; a south-of-the-border buffet; and a chicken dinner that can be ready in less than an hour (time is often what determines the degree of formality) are some of the informal menus that follow.

Dinner in Under an Hour

Red Côtes du Rhône

Parmesan Salad with Fennel, Mushrooms, and Walnuts
Chicken with Tomatoes and Balsamic Vinegar
Potatoes with Shallots

Small Steamed Chocolate Puddings

This meal sounds far more elaborate and time-consuming to prepare than it is. Assuming you have all the ingredients on hand, total preparation time is definitely under one hour. Moreover, because the dishes can continue to cook while the first course is being served, the dinner bell can ring a mere thirty minutes from when you begin your cooking.

First light the oven and set the chocolate out to melt. Brown the chicken, then finish preparing the chocolate puddings. Continue with the preparation of the chicken; once it begins to simmer, prepare the potatoes and put them on to cook. As soon as the salad is ready, place it on the table and your guests can be seated.

To convert this menu to a low-calorie dinner, omit the walnuts from the salad and use less oil in the dressing. Cook the shallots and potatoes together in the stock without first sautéing them in butter; serve ripe melon with a wedge of lemon or lime for dessert.

Red Côtes du Rhône

The Rhône region extends from just south of Lyon nearly to the Mediterranean. Elegant, long-lived premier red wines—Hermitage, Crozes-Hermitage, Côte-Rôtie, Cornas, and St. Joseph—are produced from grapes cultivated on its northern slopes. Vineyards further south yield Gigondas and Châteauneuf-du-Pape (see page 68), as well as vast quantities of a less exalted red called simply Côtes du Rhône. Production of Côtes du Rhône (and Côtes du Rhône Villages from certain designated villages) has just about doubled since 1979.

The usual choices for blends of Côtes du Rhône are the tannic syrah grape, softened by grenache, and smoothed by cinsault. Recent vintages are fruity but have enough backbone to stand up to the flavors in this slightly Mediterranean menu of chicken enriched with tomatoes, intensified with mellow balsamic vinegar (from Italy), and served following a salad of Parmesan cheese, mushrooms, and fennel.

Look for recent vintages of Côtes du Rhône. In this region, as in Burgundy, the name of the bottler or négociant is a good indication of quality. And the three that stand out are Jaboulet, Chapoutier, and Guigal.

Parmesan Salad with Fennel, Mushrooms, and Walnuts

3 cups sliced fresh fennel bulb
¼ pound fresh mushrooms, thinly sliced
¼ pound Italian Parmesan cheese, in slivers
⅓ cup chopped walnuts
Freshly ground black pepper
2 tablespoons white wine vinegar
4 tablespoons extra-virgin olive oil

Combine fennel, mushrooms, cheese, and walnuts in a bowl and toss gently. Season with pepper.

Beat the vinegar and oil together until well blended, pour over salad, and toss to combine.

6 servings

Chicken with Tomatoes and Balsamic Vinegar

2 tablespoons olive oil
1 3½-pound chicken, cut into serving pieces and dried
½ cup chopped onions
⅓ cup chicken stock, preferably homemade (page 22)
3 tablespoons balsamic vinegar
1 cup finely chopped fresh plum tomatoes (canned tomatoes can be substituted; drain well)
Salt and freshly ground black pepper
1 teaspoon fresh chopped rosemary or ½ teaspoon dried

Heat the olive oil in a large skillet. Add chicken pieces and brown on both sides. Do not crowd the chicken in the pan; if necessary brown it in two shifts. When the chicken is browned, remove it from the skillet.

Sauté the onion in the fat in the skillet until tender. Stir in the stock and vinegar. Return the chicken to the pan, baste once or twice with the sauce, cover, and simmer slowly for about 25 minutes, until the chicken is cooked through.

Remove the chicken from the pan and set aside, covered, to keep warm. Boil the cooking liquid for several minutes until it has reduced somewhat. Add the tomatoes and cook a few minutes longer, until the sauce is slightly thickened. Season to taste with salt and pepper, and add the rosemary. Return chicken to the pan to reheat for a minute or two in the sauce, transfer to a serving dish, and serve.

4 servings

Potatoes with Shallots

  1 cup diced shallots
  3 tablespoons sweet butter
  6 cups diced large new potatoes (about 3 potatoes)
1½ cups chicken stock, preferably homemade
     (page 22)
    Salt and freshly ground black pepper
  3 tablespoons minced fresh parsley

Sauté the shallots in the butter in a heavy 3-quart saucepan until tender. Stir in the potatoes and continue cooking for several minutes, until the potatoes are well coated with the butter. Add the stock, bring to a simmer, and season to taste with salt and pepper.

Lower heat so the liquid simmers very gently, cover tightly, and cook about 20 minutes. The potatoes should be tender and have absorbed the stock. Fold in the parsley and serve.

4 servings

Small Steamed Chocolate Puddings

These puddings can also be prepared the day before, unmolded, and served at room temperature.

  2 squares unsweetened chocolate
 ⅓ cup milk
  4 tablespoons sweet butter, at room temperature
 ⅔ cup sugar
  2 eggs, separated
  1 teaspoon vanilla extract
 ⅓ cup flour
 ½ cup heavy cream, whipped

Preheat oven to 325 degrees. Butter four ½-cup ovenproof ramekins or custard cups. Line the bottoms with waxed paper.

Melt chocolate in milk over very low heat. Remove from heat and stir to blend.

Cream butter and sugar together by hand, in an electric mixer, or in a food processor. Beat in the egg yolks, one at a time. Stir in the chocolate mixture and vanilla. Stir in the flour.

Beat the egg whites until they form soft peaks and are still creamy. Fold the egg whites into the chocolate mixture and divide the pudding among the four prepared baking dishes. Place the dishes in a larger pan that will hold them comfortably, and add enough boiling water to come halfway up the sides of the dishes.

Place in the oven and bake for 35 to 40 minutes, until the tops are firm to the touch. Remove from the oven and allow to sit in the warm water bath for 20 to 30 minutes before unmolding. Run a knife around the inside edge of each baking dish and unmold the puddings onto individual plates, remove paper. Spoon whipped cream on the side and serve at once.

4 servings

Summer Menu on the Grill

▓▓▓▓▓▓▓

California Fumé Blanc

Individual Pesto Pizzas
Grilled Soy-Glazed Tuna with Eggplant and Peppers

Walnut Plum Tart

I resent aprons that make statements such as "men at work." In our house, the grilling, like the pastry-making and the vegetable peeling, is my responsibility. Luckily grilling has shed its backyard hot dog image and become synonymous with sophisticated California cuisine, food with a nice char around the edges, and a subtly smoky flavor.

This is an easygoing, unbuttoned dinner for four, California style, what with the pizza and grilling. An oven broiler is a good understudy for a grill, but your food will not be traced with the typical cross-hatchings. If you use a barbecue grill that requires charcoal, light a good quality hardwood charcoal rather than supermarket products (especially the self-lighting ones), which do not burn at as high a temperature and are saturated with chemicals.

California Fumé Blanc

It amuses me to serve a wine called fumé blanc with grilled fish as fumé means smoked. The choice of this dry, herbaceous wine is more than a play on words—it truly suits the food.

The sauvignon blanc grape was christened "fumé blanc" by Napa Valley winemaker Robert Mondavi in 1971, cleverly and successfully capitalizing on the popularity and prestige enjoyed by the French Pouilly-Fumé, perhaps the best known French wine made from the sauvignon blanc grape. Fumé blanc has since become a California classic.

Individual Pesto Pizzas

Although the recipe makes more pesto than you will need for the pizzas, leftovers can be refrigerated or frozen for future use in salads, with pasta, poultry, and seafood.

Cornmeal
Pizza Dough, divided in four (see following recipe)
¼ cup *Pesto* (see following recipe)
1 cup shredded mozzarella
½ cup freshly grated Italian Parmesan cheese
½ cup shredded Italian Fontina cheese

Preheat oven to 475 degrees. Place oven racks in the lowest possible position. Lightly oil baking pans and dust them with cornmeal. You can use 9-inch cake tins or the removable bottoms from cake or quiche pans, or large baking sheets that will each hold two small pizzas.

Roll and stretch each of the four portions of dough into an 8- to 9-inch circle, leaving a thicker border. Spread each circle with a tablespoon of the pesto and scatter the cheeses on top.

Place in the oven and bake pizzas for about 15 minutes, until the crust is lightly browned and the cheese is bubbling. For very crisp crust remove pizzas from the pans and bake directly on the oven rack for a minute or two longer.

4 individual pizzas

Pizza Dough

1 package active dry yeast
Pinch of sugar
1 cup warm water
1 teaspoon salt
2 tablespoons olive oil
½ teaspoon coarsely ground black pepper
1 cup whole wheat flour
2 cups all-purpose flour (approximately)

Dissolve yeast and sugar in the water and set aside to proof about 5 minutes. Pour yeast mixture into a bowl and add salt, olive oil, pepper, and whole wheat flour. Mix until smooth. Add remaining flour, ½ cup at a time, until the dough begins to leave the sides of the bowl. You should have some flour left.

Dust a work surface with some of the remaining flour and turn dough out. Knead until it is very smooth and elastic, kneading in additional flour as you go. Kneading should take about 8 minutes.

Place the dough in a lightly oiled bowl twice its size. Turn dough to oil the top, cover loosely, and allow to rise until doubled, about 1 hour at room temperature. Punch dough down. It is now ready to use.

Dough for 1 large or 4 small pizzas

Pesto

2 cups fresh basil leaves, packed (no stems)
2 tablespoons pine nuts
2 large cloves garlic
½ cup olive oil
½ cup grated Italian Parmesan cheese

Combine basil, pine nuts, and garlic in a food processor, and process until finely minced. With the machine running, slowly add the oil and process until smooth. Add cheese and process briefly, just to combine. Store in refrigerator for several days or freeze the unused portion.

Makes 2 cups

Grilled Soy-Glazed Tuna with Eggplant and Peppers

½ cup Oriental sesame oil
3 tablespoons rice vinegar
2 tablespoons grated fresh ginger
4 tuna, mako shark, or swordfish steaks—6 to 8 ounces each, about ¾ inch thick
1 medium eggplant, about 1¼ pounds, in ¾-inch slices
Salt
½ teaspoon sugar
2 sweet red peppers, cored, seeded, and quartered
2 tablespoons light soy sauce
Hot chili oil to taste (optional)
1 tablespoon finely minced fresh scallions
Fresh coriander for garnish

Mix the sesame oil, rice vinegar, and ginger together until smooth and thick. Arrange the fish in a shallow glass dish and spoon half the sesame oil mixture over it. Reserve unused half. Set aside to marinate for 30 minutes to 1 hour. While the fish is marinating, arrange the eggplant slices in a dish and liberally dust with salt. Cover with another dish to weight them down. Leave the eggplant to macerate for 30 minutes.

Light hardwood charcoal on a grill, or light a gas grill.

After 30 minutes, drain and rinse the eggplant slices. Dry them on paper towels. Add the sugar to the remaining marinade, and brush each eggplant slice on both sides with the marinade. Brush the peppers with the marinade. Reserve 2 tablespoons of the marinade. If you do not have that much left, mix a little more. Add the soy sauce and chili oil to the marinade and set aside.

Grill the fish and vegetables on a very hot grill, about 2 to 3 minutes on each side. As soon as you turn the fish and eggplant, brush the tops with the reserved marinade. Do not brush the marinade on the peppers. When the fish and vegetables are done, transfer them to a warm serving platter or individual plates, sprinkle with scallions, garnish with coriander, and serve.

Alternate Cooking Method—Oven Broiling: Broil fish and vegetables as close as possible to a very hot broiler, 2 to 3 minutes on each side, turning once. Be careful not to overcook the fish. As soon as the fish and vegetables are done, transfer them to a warm serving platter or individual dinner plates and brush tops with the reserved marinade. Sprinkle with scallions, garnish with coriander, and serve. Since oven broiling will not impart a smoky flavor to the food, you may wish to season more heavily with soy sauce and chili oil.

4 servings

Walnut Plum Tart

There is no substitute for the small, freestone blue plums, often called Italian prunes, in this recipe. If the plums, which are in season in late summer and early fall, are unavailable, substitute another dessert, such as the Pear-Almond Cake, page 35.

> *Basic Pastry* for a 9-inch tart shell (see following recipe)
> ½ cup ground walnuts
> ¼ cup flour
> ½ cup sugar
> 1 teaspoon baking powder
> 1 teaspoon cinnamon
> 2 eggs
> ½ cup milk
> 1 teaspoon vanilla extract
> 2 tablespoons melted sweet butter
> Italian plums, pitted and cut in eighths to make 1½ cups (about 12 plums)
> 2 tablespoons sugar mixed with ¼ teaspoon cinnamon
> 1 cup heavy cream, whipped

Preheat oven to 425 degrees. Roll out pastry and line a 9-inch straight-sided French tart or flan ring with the pastry. Prick the bottom, cover with foil, and weight with dried beans or pastry weights. Bake for 6 minutes. Remove foil, prick again, and bake 4 to 5 minutes longer, until the pastry is just beginning to color. Remove from oven. Reduce oven temperature to 400 degrees.

Mix the walnuts, flour, sugar, baking powder, and cinnamon together in a bowl. Beat the eggs and stir them into the walnut mixture along with the milk, vanilla, and butter. Pour the batter into the tart shell.

Arrange plums in a pattern on the batter (they will sink in somewhat—no matter), dust with the sugar-cinnamon mixture, and bake for about 30 minutes, or until a knife inserted in the center comes out clean.

Serve warm with whipped cream.

6 to 8 servings

Basic Pastry

> 1¼ cups flour
> ½ teaspoon salt
> 6 tablespoons cold sweet butter
> 4 tablespoons ice water (approximately)

Mix flour and salt together. Cut in butter with a pastry blender, two knives, or your fingertips, or do this in a food processor using the pulse button until the mixture resembles coarse meal. The finer the mixture the more crumbly and less flaky the pastry will be. Gradually add the water, stirring with a fork, just until a ball of dough can be formed, or add the water through the processor feed tube and process briefly. The dough is likely to require less liquid if mixed in a food processor. If possible, wrap dough in plastic and refrigerate for at least 30 minutes before rolling.

Pastry for an 8- or 9-inch one-crust pie or tart

Note: For a two-crust pastry increase flour to two cups, salt to one teaspoon, butter to 10 tablespoons, and liquid to 6 or more tablespoons.

East Coast Informality

**White Table Wine
or Beer**

**Corn and Pepper Tart
East Coast Clambake
Buttermilk Coleslaw
Whole Grain Biscuits**

**Strawberry Ice Cream
Iced Watermelon**

Modern cooking methods and contemporary tastes cannot improve on the traditional clambake. The native American recipe remains the best: build a driftwood fire in a pit on the beach, line it with rocks to hold the heat, and some six to eight hours later you can add moist seaweed to create steam for cooking clams, lobsters, and any other available seafood.

The only problem is that this system is a trifle inconvenient, especially if you live far from the beach. However, by applying the same principle, steaming, the clambake can be adapted to fit the kitchen stove and serve a party of eight.

Even though the clambake can be prepared indoors, I prefer to serve it outside, whether on a deck, by the pool, or in the garden. This is casual, summertime food—a bit messy but fun. Remember to have an ample stock of cloth napkins or even clean dishtowels to use as napkins for all this finger food, plus nutcrackers and bowls for discarded shells.

White Table Wine or Beer

Since the clambake is a thoroughly American creation, I have selected an American white wine. Something infor-

mal, perhaps available in 1.5 liter jugs, suits the occasion. Many California wineries are producing excellent table wines that are palatable, well made, and attractively priced. They are usually called white table wine or some variation thereof.

Some varietal jug wines—chardonnay or sauvignon blanc—also make for fine, dry, easy quaffing. On principle I avoid the wines called chablis—California chablis has nothing to do with the fine white Burgundy of the same name.

With a clambake, beer is a splendid alternative. Most American beer is bland and watery, with very little character. But lately a number of small, local "boutique" breweries have been started in various parts of the country, their handmade operations producing commendable beers with a depth of yeasty flavor. Select a lager (light) or a medium amber beer rather than a dark beer for this menu.

Corn and Pepper Tart

Basic Pastry for a 9-inch tart shell (page 55)
2 tablespoons sweet butter
¼ cup chopped onions
½ cup chopped green peppers
½ cup chopped sweet red peppers
1 teaspoon chopped fresh hot chili pepper
⅔ cup corn kernels, preferably fresh kernels cut
    from the cob
½ teaspoon ground coriander
1 tablespoon minced fresh coriander leaves
Salt and freshly ground black pepper
3 eggs
1 cup milk
½ cup heavy cream
2 tablespoons shredded Monterey Jack cheese

Preheat oven to 425 degrees. Roll out pastry and line a 9-inch straight-sided French tart or flan ring with the pastry. Prick the bottom, cover with foil, and weight with dried beans or pastry weights. Bake for 6 to 8 minutes until pastry looks dry but has not begun to color. Remove foil. Remove from oven.

In a skillet melt the butter and sauté the onions and peppers until soft but not brown. Stir in corn and both the ground and fresh coriander. Season mixture to taste with salt and pepper, and spread in prepared pie shell.

Whisk eggs with milk and cream. Sprinkle cheese over the vegetables in the pastry shell, then pour the egg mixture over it. Place in the oven, lower temperature to 375 degrees, and bake for about 45 minutes, until golden brown.

6 to 8 servings

East Coast Clambake

The tricky item in this recipe is the seaweed. Genuine, rubbery rockweed with little air bladders that pop when heated and release more steam is the best kind to use. Order it at least a week in advance from your fishmonger, or substitute lettuce or celery.

3 quarts fresh seaweed, if available
2 small broiler chickens, quartered
Salt and freshly ground black pepper
8 onions, peeled
8 medium, unpeeled new potatoes (optional)
4 1½-pound lobsters
4 dozen littleneck clams or mussels (or some of
    each), scrubbed
1 medium boiling potato
8 cups water, beer, or white wine
1 pound sweet butter, melted
2 tablespoons very finely minced fresh parsley
4 lemons, quartered

In a steamer pot, a large 16-quart stockpot, or in the bottom layer of a series of large Chinese steamer baskets, place about half the seaweed. Skin the chickens, season them lightly with salt and pepper, and wrap each quarter, plus an onion, in cheesecloth. Place the chickens in the pot or steamer. Place the potatoes, if you are using them, around the chicken. (If the potatoes do not fit in the Chinese basket, put them in with the lobsters.) In the steamer pot or stockpot, cover the chickens and potatoes with more seaweed; if using Chinese steamer baskets line the next one with seaweed.

Place the lobsters in next, then add the remaining seaweed (or line the third basket with it). Divide the clams and/or mussels into 8 equal portions, and wrap each in cheesecloth. Add these after the lobsters. Put the boiling potato on top.

Put 8 cups of the water, beer, or white wine in the bottom part of the steamer, or pour it into the stockpot. If you are using baskets, the liquid goes into the wok in which the Chinese baskets are set.

Put the assembled steamer on top of the stove and cook for about 1 to 1½ hours. Check it after 45 minutes to 1 hour and if the clams and mussels have opened, serve them, with some broth if you have it, in cups on the side. Usually when the potato that was put in last is tender, the clambake is done.

After the clams and mussels have been served (1 bundle to a person, with melted butter for dunking), each guest receives a plate with 1 potato, ½ a lobster (split in the kitchen before serving and drained), and half a chicken with the onion. Lightly brush the chicken and onion with melted butter and sprinkle with parsley so they will be more attractive. Lemon wedges go on the side of the plate.

8 servings

Buttermilk Coleslaw

1 small head cabbage
1 teaspoon salt, or more as needed
1 medium onion, grated
¾ cup buttermilk
¾ cup mayonnaise, preferably homemade (see
  following recipe)
2 tablespoons minced fresh chives
1 tablespoon minced fresh parsley
1 tablespoon minced fresh dill

Quarter the cabbage and remove the core and the
tough outer leaves. Finely shred the cabbage.

Place cabbage in a bowl and sprinkle with salt to
wilt it slightly. Stir in the grated onion.

Combine buttermilk and mayonnaise, mixing until
smooth. Pour over cabbage. Stir in chives and refrigerate
for several hours.

Stir coleslaw, season again if necessary, sprinkle
with parsley and dill, and serve.

8 servings

Quick Mayonnaise

*This mayonnaise, made with a whole egg instead of egg
yolks in the traditional fashion, is lighter than most.*

1 egg
1 teaspoon Dijon mustard
1 tablespoon white wine vinegar
1⅓ cups vegetable oil (approximately)
Salt and freshly ground black pepper

Place the egg, mustard, and vinegar in a food processor and process until well blended. With the machine
running, slowly add the vegetable oil in a thin stream
through the feed tube. Add only enough of the oil to
make a thick mayonnaise. Season to taste with salt and
pepper.

Makes 1½ cups

Whole Grain Biscuits

1 cup whole wheat flour
½ cup all-purpose flour
¼ cup unsweetened wheat germ
1 tablespoon baking powder
1 teaspoon salt
6 tablespoons sweet butter, chilled
⅔ cup milk (approximately)

Preheat oven to 450 degrees. Adjust oven rack to upper one-third of oven. Line a baking sheet with a double thickness of foil.

Mix whole wheat flour, all-purpose flour, wheat germ, baking powder, and salt together in a large bowl. Using 2 knives or a pastry blender, cut in the butter until the mixture resembles coarse meal. Stir in enough milk to make a soft dough. Knead for about 30 seconds on a floured board, just until smooth. Alternatively, this may be done in a food processor: using the steel blade, blend the dry ingredients together, add the butter in pieces, and blend it in by turning the machine on and off rapidly until the mixture resembles coarse meal. Add the milk with the machine running until a ball of soft dough forms. You may need somewhat less milk with the food processor-method and kneading is not necessary, but be careful not to overwork the dough.

Roll or pat the dough to a ½ inch thickness on a floured board. Using a 2½-inch round cutter, cut biscuits. Reroll scraps and cut them.

Bake biscuits on prepared baking sheet in upper third of oven until risen and lightly browned, about 15 minutes.

Makes 18 biscuits

Strawberry Ice Cream

There is a great variety of ice cream makers on the market, including simple little hand-cranked gadgets with chilled liners. While extremely inexpensive, quick, and convenient to use, these do not produce frozen desserts with as smooth a texture as a machine that churns continuously.

2 cups fresh strawberries, hulled and sliced
⅔ to ¾ cup sugar
1½ cups heavy cream

Mix the strawberries with 3 to 4 tablespoons of the sugar, depending on the sweetness of the berries. Allow to stand for about 1 hour.

Scald 1 cup of the cream and mix with remaining sugar. Allow to cool while the strawberries are macerating. Stir the remaining ½ cup of cream into the cooled cream.

Force the strawberries through a coarse sieve. You can leave a few larger pieces as well. Stir the strawberry purée into the cream and chill. Then transfer it to the container of an ice cream machine, and freeze according to manufacturer's directions.

Makes 1 quart

West Coast Informality

⁞⁞⁞⁞⁞⁞⁞

Dry Chenin Blanc

Simple Sushi
Cold Tomato, Red Wine, and Basil Soup
Chicken Baked in Walnuts and Yogurt
Bulgur Salad with Avocado

Chocolate Raisin Cake
Fresh Grapes

An easy menu? It is one that can be largely prepared in advance of the arrival of guests and does not require much attention during the dinner. That it is capable of serving eight, as in this case, so much the better.

Because the "sushi" does not have to involve raw fish or, for that matter, any specialized ingredients or equipment, it lends itself to advance preparation. Similarly, the soup, an uncooked food-processor dish, resides in the refrigerator until serving time. The chicken is meant to be served just warm so that it, too, can be readied in advance. The bulgur wheat salad is another uncooked dish. If preparing a big, moist, dark chocolate cake studded with raisins well in advance and freezing it is your idea of convenience, as it is sometimes mine, this dessert takes beautifully to the treatment.

Dry Chenin Blanc

Serious prizewinning cabernet sauvignons and chardonnays are the ultimate pride of California wineries. But for informal relaxation I prefer to tear a different page from the winemaker's book and find something lighter, softer, and less demanding to chill and quaff. Regardless of how exalted one's tastes may be or how liberal the budget, there is a time and place for simpler pleasures.

Chenin blanc, one of the two or three workhorse white grapes of California and an indispensible ingredient in many of the jug wines that constitute the backbone of its industry, invites just such enjoyment. Count on this dependable vinifera to contribute flowery aroma and fresh fruitiness, making it worth appreciating on its own merit (as it is in the Vouvrays of France). Chenin blanc can be dry or sweet, still or sparkling, but when crafted to a delightfully clean dryness, still abloom with flower and fruit, it becomes a distinguished wine. That seems to be the direction the grape is headed, led by the excellent chenin blanc of Chappellet Vineyards.

It is a wine I would select for a light menu which is fortified, California style, with avocado, sprouts, whole wheat, and fresh herbs. Although I often serve chicken with red wine, the chicken for this menu consists only of the breasts and is baked in a tangy yogurt mix, all of which easily suggests white wine with some fruitiness instead of red.

Simple Sushi

Select slender cucumbers—they will be sweeter—and use regular, not converted, rice for best results.

2 medium cucumbers
1 cup cooked white long-grain rice
2 tablespoons rice vinegar
Pinch of sugar
4 ounces thinly sliced smoked salmon or very fresh raw tuna, or some of each
Wasabi paste (Japanese green horseradish paste)

Peel cucumbers and cut off the ends. Split in half lengthwise. Using a spoon, scoop out all the seeds, leaving a thin shell of cucumber.

Mix the rice with the vinegar and sugar. Pack some of the rice mixture into the cavity of each cucumber half, slightly mounding it. To make individual pieces of sushi cut the cucumbers into 1½-inch pieces. Cut the salmon and/or tuna to fit each piece of sushi. Lightly dab each piece of fish with a very small amount of the wasabi paste and place it, wasabi side down, on the rice. Refrigerate until ready to serve.

About 20 hors d'oeuvres

Cold Tomato, Red Wine, and Basil Soup

3 pounds ripe tomatoes
Juice of 1 lemon
2 cups light-bodied dry red wine
2 tablespoons minced fresh basil
Salt and freshly ground black pepper
Fresh basil leaves for garnish

Peel tomatoes by plunging them into boiling water for about 20 seconds, then rinsing them in cold water. The skins will slip off. Remove cores and slice in half horizontally. Gently squeeze each tomato half to remove the seeds. Chop the tomatoes.

Purée the chopped tomatoes in a food processor. Stir in remaining ingredients and chill until ready to serve. Recheck seasonings and decorate each serving with fresh basil.

8 servings

Chicken Baked in Walnuts and Yogurt

4 large whole boned and skinned chicken breasts (to yield 8 halves)
1 cup plain yogurt
1 cup walnuts
2 teaspoons curry powder
2 tablespoons lemon juice
Pinch cayenne pepper
Salt
½ tablespoon vegetable oil
1½ tablespoons sweet butter
1 cup thinly sliced onions
2 teaspoons minced fresh ginger
1 lemon, cut into 8 wedges
Fresh coriander sprigs

Carefully trim chicken breasts of any excess fat. Place them in a glass or ceramic dish that will hold them snugly without crowding.

Stir yogurt. Finely grind ½ cup of the walnuts in a food processor or blender and mix with the yogurt. Add 1½ teaspoons of the curry powder, the lemon juice, cayenne pepper, and salt to taste. Spread the yogurt mixture over the chicken and turn the chicken so it is well coated on all sides. Cover and refrigerate for at least 4 hours.

One hour before serving, preheat oven to 450 degrees. Select a shallow baking pan that will hold the chicken without crowding and line it with foil. Brush the foil with vegetable oil. Arrange the chicken in the pan. It should be fairly heavily coated with the yogurt mixture. Place chicken in the oven and bake for 20 minutes. Remove chicken from the pan and arrange on a serving platter. It will need to rest at room temperature for 20 to 30 minutes so that it will be tepid when served.

While the chicken is cooking, heat the butter in a skillet. Add the onions and sauté over medium-low heat until tender and just barely beginning to brown. Chop the remaining ½ cup of walnuts and add them to the pan along with the ginger and the remaining ½ teaspoon curry powder. Continue to sauté the mixture until the onions are lightly browned.

When ready to serve the chicken, scatter the onion mixture over it and decorate the platter with lemon wedges and coriander sprigs.

8 servings

Chicken Baked in Walnuts and Yogurt

Bulgur Salad with Avocado

1½ cups bulgur wheat
6 cups boiling water
2 ripe avocados
½ cup lemon juice
1 cup chopped scallions
½ cup chopped fresh parsley
⅓ cup extra-virgin olive oil
Salt and freshly ground black pepper

Place the bulgur in a large bowl and pour the boiling water over it. Allow to soften for about 2 hours. Drain well, squeezing out as much water as possible.

Peel and dice the avocados. Immediately toss them with lemon juice. Mix bulgur, scallions, parsley, olive oil, and salt and pepper in a serving bowl. Gently fold in avocados and lemon juice.

8 servings

Chocolate Raisin Cake

Try serving fresh grapes with this dessert to play the fresh grapes against the dried ones (the raisins in the cake). A classy way to serve grapes is to pile them in a glass or china bowl half filled with ice water, which is the way grapes are always served in Greece.

1 cup all-purpose flour
½ cup whole wheat flour
¾ cup cocoa
1 teaspoon instant coffee
1 teaspoon baking soda
1 cup raisins
2 tablespoons rum or brandy
8 tablespoons sweet butter, at room temperature
1 cup sugar
2 eggs
1 cup plain yogurt, stirred until smooth
1 teaspoon vanilla extract

Preheat oven to 350 degrees. Butter and flour a 9-inch tube pan.

Mix the all-purpose flour, whole wheat flour, cocoa, instant coffee, and baking soda; set aside. In a small dish stir together the raisins and rum or brandy, and set aside.

Cream butter and sugar until fluffy. Add eggs one at a time, beating until smooth. Stir in the flour mixture alternately with the yogurt, mixing only enough to combine the ingredients. Stir in raisins and rum or brandy and vanilla.

Spread batter in prepared pan and bake for 45 minutes. Cool 20 minutes in the pan, then remove from pan and continue to cool on a rack.

8 servings

Après Outdoors Before an Open Fire

—————

American Pinot Noir

Istanbul Bean Soup
or
Split Pea and Barley Soup
Sausages Baked in Red Wine
Zucchini and Watercress Stir-Fry
Walnut Wheat Bread
Salad with Goat Cheese

Apple Charlotte with Crème Anglaise

A bowl of soup, some sausage, bread, cheese, and a mellow golden dessert are the infinitely appealing elements of a weekend or informal evening supper. This is a menu I would serve to skiers, after a hike in the woods with the crunch of fallen leaves underfoot, to celebrate the first snowfall, or the last one.

The soup is thick. I have given you a choice of one made with beans and one made with barley—both are favorites. The bean soup is called "Istanbul" based on my memory of a similar soup we enjoyed there some twenty years ago. We sought a restaurant that was not strictly for tourists and consulted the hotel concierge. After some hedging, he led us, on a dark, damp night, to a nameless basement place where the diners sat on communal benches at wooden tables and no English was spoken. The concierge put us in the hands of a waiter who invited us to order by pointing to dishes that looked appealing. A bean soup seasoned with lemon was our delicious first course. The only change I made in it over the years is the addition of the fresh coriander.

The recipes can be doubled to serve eight. In fact I would recommend making the larger quantity of the soup in any case in order to have leftovers. Depending on my mood and the particular occasion, I would even consider restructuring this menu and serving the sausages before the soup as an appetizer. In that case, I would save the zucchini recipe for another dinner.

American Pinot Noir

American winemakers have enjoyed enormous success with major French red and white vinifera grapes. But pinot noir, planted in the early years of the California wine boom with the kind of enthusiasm still lavished on cabernet sauvignon, has been the most problematic.

Too many early California pinot noirs lacked the balance and finesse of a good Burgundy, in part because the wines were too alcoholic and heavy with fruit. They won prizes but were not ideal for accompanying food. What they needed was more acid to add structure, control the fruit, and make the flavor more complex. Soil and climate have had a great deal to do with it as well. Like the recalcitrant child, the pinot noir grape has been called "difficult" and often relegated to the production of white or blush wines, with *blancs de noirs*.

Lately considerable progress has been made, not only in the Napa Valley but especially in Oregon, and wines that deserve to be called elegant in the Burgundian sense are attracting attention. Pinot noir has yet to come of age but it is showing signs of maturity. I like it with the sausages—their spiciness is nicely complemented by some pinot noirs. Because this is an informal occasion, which does not warrant two services of wine and changing glasses, I would also pour it with the hearty soup.

Istanbul Bean Soup

1 tablespoon olive oil
½ cup finely chopped onions
1 cup large, dried lima beans, presoaked if
   necessary
1 quart chicken stock, preferably homemade (page
   22)
½ teaspoon salt
Freshly ground black pepper
1 tablespoon plain yogurt
1 teaspoon lemon juice
1 lemon, cut into 4 wedges for garnish
4 sprigs fresh coriander for garnish

In a large saucepan heat the olive oil and sauté the
onions until golden. Add the lima beans and stock. Bring
to a simmer, cover, and cook for about two hours, until
the beans are tender. Remove the beans to the bowl with
a slotted spoon and roughly mash them so there are still
some pieces of lima bean.

Return the beans to the liquid in the saucepan and
stir. Add salt, pepper, yogurt, and lemon juice, and reheat, stirring, but do not allow to come to a boil. Check
seasonings. Serve garnished with lemon wedges and
coriander.

4 servings

Split Pea and Barley Soup

½ pound green split peas
2 tablespoons vegetable oil
½ cup chopped onions
¼ cup chopped celery
¼ cup chopped carrots
1 bay leaf
⅓ cup medium barley
Juice of 1 lemon
3 tablespoons minced fresh dill
Salt and freshly ground black pepper

Pick over the split peas, rinse, drain, and place
them in a saucepan. Cover with water to the depth of 1
inch, bring to a boil, and cook for 2 minutes. Remove
from heat and set aside to soften for 1 hour.

Melt oil in a large, heavy saucepan. Add the onions,
celery, and carrots and sauté over medium heat until soft

and just barely beginning to color. Drain and rinse peas
and add them to the saucepan. Add 6 cups of water and
the bay leaf.

Bring to a boil, lower heat to a simmer, and cook
for 1 hour. Add the barley and continue cooking 1 hour
longer. If the soup is too thick, add some additional
water.

Stir in the lemon juice and dill and season to taste
with salt and pepper.

4 servings

Sausages Baked in Red Wine

2 pounds Italian hot sausages or 1 pound each hot
   and sweet sausages
2 sweet red peppers, cored and cut in thin slivers
½ cup dry red wine
1 tablespoon minced scallions

Preheat oven to 400 degrees. Cut sausages into separate links and remove any strings. Slice each link at ½-
inch intervals, but cutting only about ¾ of the way
through so that the link is still in one piece.

Place links in a shallow baking pan. Bake until
crisp, 35 to 40 minutes.

Scatter the peppers in the pan, pour the wine over
them, and sprinkle with scallions. Return to the oven for
5 minutes. Serve at once.

4 servings

Zucchini and Watercress Stir-Fry

1 pound small zucchini
½ bunch watercress
½ tablespoon vegetable oil
¼ teaspoon sugar
Salt

Above: Apple Charlotte with Crème Anglaise
Below: Salad with Goat Cheese and Walnut Wheat Bread

Rinse zucchini and trim the ends. Slice into rounds ⅛ inch thick. Rinse and drain watercress. Cut off heavy lower stem ends and separate the branches.

Heat oil in a wok or skillet. Add zucchini and stir-fry over high heat 2 to 3 minutes, just until the slices look moist. Sprinkle with sugar.

Add watercress and stir-fry another 30 seconds or so, just until the watercress wilts. Salt to taste. Transfer to a serving dish. Serve hot, at room temperature, or cold.

4 servings

Walnut Wheat Bread

1 package dry yeast
2 teaspoons sugar
2½ cups warm water (about 110 degrees)
1 tablespoon salt
¼ cup finely ground walnuts
3½ cups whole wheat flour
2 to 2½ cups unbleached all-purpose white flour
1½ cups broken walnuts
Cornmeal
¼ teaspoon salt dissolved in ¼ cup cold water

Dissolve yeast and sugar in ½ cup of the warm water and set aside in a warm place for a few minutes, until it begins to froth. In a large bowl, combine remaining 2 cups water and the salt. Stir in the ground walnuts and add the yeast mixture.

Stir in 3 cups of the whole wheat flour, 1 cup at a time. Add the final ½ cup of whole wheat flour and then about 1 cup or more of the all-purpose flour, ½ cup at a time, until the dough leaves the sides of the bowl. The dough can be combined in a mixer or food processor.

Flour a work surface with all-purpose flour, turn the dough onto the floured surface and knead for about 10 minutes, kneading in another cup or so of flour until the dough is resilient and has lost most of its stickiness. The dough should not be very stiff, although it will be somewhat heavy. There should be no flour left on the work surface.

Scatter the broken walnuts on the work surface and knead them into the dough. This should take about 2 minutes.

Place dough in a well-oiled bowl and turn to coat the dough. Cover lightly and set aside to rise until dou-bled, about 1 hour. Punch dough down, knead for 1 or 2 minutes, and slice into 2 equal portions. Shape each portion into a round ball and place the balls of dough on a baking sheet that has been dusted with cornmeal. Set aside to rise again until doubled, about 45 minutes.

Using a very sharp knife or a razor blade, slash the top of each loaf to a depth of ½ inch, either in a criss-cross pattern or as a row of slashes. The blade must be extremely sharp so you can make the cuts without compressing the surface of the risen bread.

Place loaves in the middle of the oven and turn the oven to 400 degrees. Bake for 20 minutes. Brush with saltwater, lower heat to 350 degrees, and bake about 30 minutes longer, brushing the breads every 10 minutes with the saltwater.

As you will be opening the oven several times, you probably should turn the baking sheet once to ensure even baking. Bake the bread until it is nicely browned and sounds hollow when tapped. Remove from oven, carefully lift off the baking sheet, and allow to cool completely on racks before slicing. To serve the bread warm, reheat it briefly in a 300-degree oven after it has completely cooled.

Makes 2 loaves

Salad with Goat Cheese

1 head Boston or leaf lettuce
1 head radicchio
½ bunch arugula
4 ounces goat cheese
1½ tablespoons red wine vinegar
5 tablespoons extra-virgin olive oil
1 tablespoon mixed fresh herbs (parsley, thyme, tarragon)
Salt and freshly ground black pepper

Separate the lettuces into individual leaves, discard the cores, rinse, and thoroughly dry. Rinse and dry the arugula. Tear the leaves into bite-size pieces. Divide onto salad plates.

Just before serving slice or crumble some of the goat cheese onto each salad serving. Beat together the vinegar and oil, and pour over the salad. Sprinkle with herbs and season with salt and pepper.

4 servings

Apple Charlotte with Crème Anglaise

If you double this menu to serve eight, you will find this dessert can just about manage that many servings. For more generous portions, use twelve apples instead of eight, increase the sweetening, add another couple slices of bread, and bake it in an 8-cup mold. French chefs often prefer our Golden Delicious apples for baking because they are naturally sweet and have a dry texture.

12 tablespoons sweet butter
8 Golden Delicious or Granny Smith apples, peeled, cored, and coarsely chopped
½ cup sugar (approximately)
1½ teaspoons vanilla extract
3 tablespoons apricot preserves
5 tablespoons Calvados
12 slices firm-textured white bread, thinly sliced
4 egg yolks
1¼ cups milk

Lightly butter a 5- or 6-cup charlotte mold, soufflé dish, or deep baking dish.

Melt 2 tablespoons of the butter in a large, heavy skillet. Add the apples and ¼ cup of the sugar and cook over medium-high heat, stirring frequently, for about 10 minutes, until the apples have softened and most of the liquid has evaporated. When the apples begin to cohere in a soft purée, add 1 teaspoon of the vanilla, the apricot preserves, and 4 tablespoons of the Calvados. Lower heat and continue cooking for another 10 minutes to make a thick purée. Sweeten with additional sugar if the apples taste too tart, as this is how they will taste in the finished dessert. Remove from heat.

Preheat oven to 425 degrees. Melt remaining 10 tablespoons butter in a saucepan and clarify it by skimming off as much of the white, milky residue as possible. Trim away the bread crusts, and cut 8 of the slices in half to form rectangles and 4 to make triangles. Heat some of the clarified butter in a clean skillet and over medium heat sauté the rectangles until they are golden brown on one side; do not turn. Remove from skillet and set aside. Sauté triangles on one side, adding more butter if needed.

Fit the triangular pieces tightly into the bottom of the baking dish, sautéed side down. Do not overlap them. Trim off any excess pieces and reserve. Arrange the rectangles standing up around the sides of the dish, sautéed side out, overlapping them slightly. Fill the cen-ter with the apple purée and, if necessary, trim the tops of the rectangles so that they are flush with the purée. Scatter any extra bread trimmings on top.

Cover the dish with foil and bake for 30 minutes. Remove from the oven and allow to cool at room temperature for at least 1 hour before unmolding.

Meanwhile, prepare the crème anglaise. Beat the egg yolks with remaining ¼ cup sugar in the top of a double boiler. Scald the milk, then add it to the eggs and sugar, pouring it very slowly in a thin stream while stirring the egg yolks with a whisk. Cook the mixture over simmering water, stirring, until the custard thickens enough to coat a spoon. Do not allow it to come to a boil.

Add remaining ½ teaspoon vanilla and remaining 1 tablespoon Calvados and chill until ready to serve.

Unmold the charlotte on a platter and pass the sauce alongside, or first nap the serving platter with some of the sauce if desired.

6 servings

A Bouillabaisse Supper

Châteauneuf-du-Pape Blanc

Assorted Olives
Quick Bouillabaisse
Green Beans with Goat Cheese Dressing

Apple Bread Pudding

A grand tureen of soup and a warming, homey dessert are still all it takes to make a comforting lunch or supper for an informal occasion. A fish soup, ruddy with bright tomatoes, spells summer but the rich flavors could make it winter fare as well. This fish soup is crafted along the lines of a classic bouillabaisse, a dish that incites argument and debate. Can it be made more than fifty miles from Marseilles? Is it still bouillabaisse without that hideous spiny denizen of the Mediterranean called *rascasse*? Is shellfish permitted? As long as you use only saltwater fish there is considerable leeway, and the more varieties of fish, the merrier the stew.

Châteauneuf-du-Pape Blanc

Selecting a wine for a soup can be a challenge. Whereas a light fish soup or a cream soup would call for a white wine and a hearty beef soup would insist on a robust red, for a rich stew flavored with tomatoes, garlic, and saffron such as bouillabaisse, the answer is less clear-cut. Provençal rosés are often suggested but I prefer white,

one with a good full bouquet and a crisp finish that I would also enjoy with the beans and goat cheese.

The bouillabaisse provides a clue. It hails from the region that produces the legendary sturdy red wine, Châteauneuf-du-Pape. The name means new castle of the popes, referring to the princes of the church who resided in Avignon during the fourteenth century and actually began planting the vines. The red Châteauneuf-du-Pape would be more appropriate with the Fillet of Beef (page 108), Butterflied Lamb (page 91), or Veal Ragout (page 34). But there is also a white Châteauneuf-du-Pape with a lovely floral scent and a lingering, complex flavor. There is no better white wine made in southern France and it is actually one of the finest white wines of the entire Mediterranean region.

Only about five percent of the total wine production of Châteauneuf-du-Pape (all of which has a papal seal embossed on the bottle) is white, made possible because among the thirteen varieties of grapes permitted in the blending of the red wine are several white varieties, included to provide some delicacy to the otherwise forceful red wine.

Assorted Olives

To nibble with a drink beforehand, present an assortment of savory European-cured olives—green, brown, purple, black—from the tiny Niçoise, steeped in herbs, to plump cracked green Sicilian ones, redolent of garlic and hot peppers.

Don't worry about buying more olives than you can use for this occasion; once refrigerated, they keep forever. But by all means, do avoid buying canned California black olives. These have been chemically treated to oxidize and turn black, and are devoid of flavor and texture.

Quick Bouillabaisse

Bouillabaisse is essentially fast food. From start to finish it can be clocked in at a flat thirty minutes. Ladle it over garlic croutons and serve it with rouille, a fiery condiment redolent of garlic, peppers, and olive oil. Many varieties of fish are suitable, including mackerel, monkfish, eel, striped bass, sea bass, croaker, porgy, whiting, mullet, haddock, flounder, blackfish, halibut, and tilefish; the more you use, the better the stew.

⅓ cup olive oil
½ cup finely chopped onions
½ cup finely chopped leeks
½ cup finely chopped fresh fennel
3 cloves garlic, minced
2 cups finely chopped drained tomato pulp (fresh or canned)
2 cups dry white wine
2 cups fish stock or water
3 tablespoons Pernod or Ricard
1 bay leaf, crushed
1 teaspoon dried oregano
2 teaspoons minced fresh thyme
¼ teaspoon powdered saffron
Salt and freshly ground black pepper
4 pounds cleaned fish cut into chunks
Garlic Croutons (see following recipe)
2 tablespoons chopped fresh parsley
Rouille for garnish (see following recipe)

In a large heavy pot or casserole heat the olive oil and sauté the onions, leeks, and fennel until soft but not brown. Add the garlic and sauté until soft. Stir in the tomatoes, wine, stock, and Pernod, and simmer 5 minutes.

Add the bay leaf, oregano, and thyme. Dissolve saffron in a small amount of the hot cooking liquid in a separate dish, then add it to the casserole. Season with salt and pepper.

With the casserole simmering slowly, add the fish pieces, starting with the fattier varieties such as eel, mackerel, and monkfish, and continuing with the lighter fish including striped bass, sea bass, mullet, and haddock. Finally add delicate fish or fillets such as flounder or whiting. Allow the fish to simmer very slowly another 6 to 8 minutes. Remove from heat and serve.

To serve place a crouton in each soup bowl. Using a slotted spoon distribute pieces of the fish over the crouton and then, with a ladle, add the soup. Sprinkle parsley over the top. Pass rouille and extra croutons on the side.

8 servings

Garlic Croutons

1 large loaf French or Italian white bread (about 12 ounces)
1 to 2 cloves garlic, peeled
⅓ cup extra-virgin olive oil

Slice the bread into ½-inch-thick slices. Toast the slices. Rub each slice with garlic, then brush lightly with olive oil.

Rouille

½ cup finely chopped sweet red peppers
1 teaspoon crushed dried hot red pepper flakes (or to taste)
½ cup water
½ cup soft fresh bread crumbs
4 cloves garlic
¾ cup extra-virgin olive oil

Combine the sweet and hot red peppers in a small saucepan, add the water, and simmer until the sweet peppers are tender and the water has evaporated.

Soak the bread crumbs briefly in warm water, then squeeze out excess water. Blend the bread crumbs, peppers, and garlic in a food processor. With the machine running, slowly drizzle in the olive oil and process until smooth.

Green Beans with Goat Cheese Dressing

2 pounds young green beans
Salt and freshly ground black pepper
3 tablespoons white wine vinegar
1 teaspoon Dijon mustard
½ cup extra-virgin olive oil
6 ounces goat cheese, such as Montrachet
1 tablespoon chopped fresh chervil or parsley

Steam the beans for 3 to 5 minutes, until bright green and crisp-tender. Rinse under cold water and drain well. Arrange on a platter and season with salt and pepper.

Beat the vinegar and mustard together until smooth. Beat in the olive oil. Just before serving, crumble the goat cheese over the beans and drizzle with the dressing. Sprinkle with chervil.

8 servings

Apple Bread Pudding

¼ cup dark rum
½ cup raisins—all dark or half light, half dark
6 tablespoons sweet butter
3 cups apples, peeled, cored, and sliced ¼ inch thick
3 tablespoons plus ½ cup sugar
3½ cups firm-textured white bread in ½-inch cubes
3 eggs
2 cups milk
1 teaspoon vanilla extract
Pinch nutmeg
Cider Sauce (see following recipe)

Butter a 6- to 8-cup mold, casserole, baking dish, or soufflé dish. Warm the rum and pour over the raisins in a medium-size bowl and set aside.

Melt 2 tablespoons of the butter in a large skillet over medium-high heat. When the foam subsides, add the apples, increase heat to high, and sauté, turning frequently, for about 5 minutes, until the apples begin to turn golden. Do not allow them to become soft and lose their shape. Add 3 tablespoons of the sugar and continue to sauté for another few minutes, until the sugar begins to caramelize. Transfer the apples to the bowl with the raisins.

Reduce heat to low, add the remaining 4 tablespoons of butter to the skillet, and when the butter has melted scrape the pan and add the bread cubes. Toss for 1 or 2 minutes until evenly coated with butter. Remove from heat. Scatter half the apple-raisin mixture over the bottom of the baking dish. Cover with half the bread cubes. Repeat the layers.

Preheat oven to 375 degrees. Lightly beat the eggs and the ½ cup sugar. Scald the milk. Slowly pour the scalded milk in a thin stream into the egg mixture, stirring constantly. Add the vanilla and the nutmeg. Pour this over the apples and bread in the baking dish. Set the dish in a pan and add boiling water to come halfway up the sides of the baking dish. Place in the middle of the oven and bake for 45 minutes, until the top is crusty and golden. Serve while still warm with cider sauce.

6 to 8 servings

Cider Sauce

2½ cups sweet cider or natural apple juice
½ cup sugar
2 teaspoons cornstarch
⅓ cup light rum

Boil all but 2 tablespoons of the cider until reduced to 1 cup. Add the sugar and cook over medium heat until the sugar is dissolved. Dissolve the cornstarch in the remaining 2 tablespoons of cider and stir into the hot cider mixture. Bring to a boil, stirring, and simmer until the sauce turns clear and thickens. Add the rum. Serve warm with bread pudding.

Makes 1½ cups

A
South-of-the-Border Spread

Chilean Sauvignon Blanc
Seviche

Argentine Cabernet Sauvignon

Stuffed Flank Steak
Baked Sweet Potatoes
Corn on the Cob

Coconut Kheer

This is what I call a "theme feast," a menu that incorporates, more or less accurately, the foods of a particular region. It is colorful, tasty, a bit unusual, and as more of the dishes lend themselves to advance preparation, a joy to serve. It's especially suited to the summer months since the main course—flank steak—does not have to be served hot, and because corn, which originated south of the border, is best in summer.

South American Sauvignon Blanc and Cabernet Sauvignon

South American wines have started attracting attention. Quality is high and prices are low. Although there is even a wine-producing vineyard of some repute in Peru, most of the South American production comes from Argentina and Chile. Argentina is, in fact, among the top five leading wine producing countries in the world.

Grapes were introduced to these countries in the sixteenth century by the Jesuit padres accompanying the Conquistadores. An influx of immigrants from Europe in the nineteenth century added new life to the wine indus-

tries and today they are thriving. A great deal of Argentinian and Chilean wines are sold in bulk for home consumption. Premium reds and whites are exported and available in wine shops in the United States.

The most successful reds by far are the cabernet sauvignons, some made in an elegant Bordelais style, especially coming from Chile. Argentine cabernet sauvignon, sometimes blended with malbec, can be more robust. Sauvignon blanc with a straightforward herbaceous bouquet and clean taste is the white wine to look for from Chile, whereas light chardonnays are the better whites from Argentina.

In both these countries the grapes are harvested around March, six months in advance of our calendar.

The menu for which I chose these wines has a decidedly South American flavor, more Argentine perhaps than Chilean. The pickled fish seviche is typical throughout the region and the stuffed flank steak is an Argentine dish called *matambre*. I prefer a sauvignon blanc with the seviche so I would serve a Chilean wine, to be followed by a cabernet sauvignon either from Chile or Argentina, for the main course.

Stuffed Flank Steak

If desired, this recipe can be prepared early in the day or even the day before; serve at room temperature or cold.

> 1 2-pound flank steak
> 2 cloves garlic, finely minced
> 1 teaspoon oregano
> ¼ cup raisins
> 4 tablespoons olive oil
> 1 medium onion, thinly sliced
> ¼ pound fresh spinach, rinsed, stemmed, and coarsely chopped
> 1-inch piece of fresh green chili pepper, seeded and finely chopped
> 3 tablespoons fresh parsley, finely chopped
> 2 cups stale white bread, finely diced
> 1 hard-cooked egg, chopped
> 1 tablespoon red wine vinegar
> Salt and freshly ground black pepper
> 2½ cups beef stock
> ½ cup dry red wine
> ½ tablespoon soft sweet butter
> ½ tablespoon flour

Trim any bits of fat from the edges of the flank steak. Place the steak on a cutting board and using a large, sharp knife, carefully slice it through the middle, parallel to the cutting surface, but not cutting completely through the meat at one of the long sides. You should be able to open the meat up like a book: this is called butterflying and it doubles the surface area of the meat. If you wish, you can ask your butcher to butterfly the flank steak for you.

Spread the meat out flat and rub the cut surface with the garlic and oregano; set aside while preparing the stuffing. Preheat oven to 350 degrees.

Place the raisins in a small dish, cover with hot water, and set aside to soften.

For the stuffing, heat 1 tablespoon of the oil in a large skillet. Add the onion and cook over medium-low heat until soft and just beginning to turn golden. Add the spinach (you should have about 2 cups of tightly packed fresh spinach leaves) and stir until it begins to wilt. Add the chili pepper, parsley, and bread, and continue cooking, stirring, until the spinach has wilted. Fold in the egg. Add vinegar and 1 tablespoon of olive oil. Mix well and season to taste with salt and freshly ground black pepper.

Spread the stuffing on the flank steak, leaving a border of about ½ inch around the edges. Tightly roll

Seviche

Begin preparation of this recipe at least a day in advance to permit the seafood to marinate in the lime juice overnight.

> 1 pound scallops or flounder fillets
> Juice of 2 limes
> 1 cup chopped ripe tomato
> 1 ripe avocado, peeled and diced
> ½ medium green pepper, finely chopped
> 3 tablespoons chopped scallions
> 2 tablespoons finely chopped onions
> 2 teaspoons finely minced coriander leaves
> 1 teaspoon (or to taste) finely minced fresh chili pepper (canned green chilis may be substituted)
> Salt and freshly ground black pepper

If you are using bay scallops, leave them whole. Sea scallops or flounder should be diced. Mix the fish with the lime juice in a glass or ceramic dish. Cover and refrigerate for at least 12 hours.

A few hours before serving, mix the remaining ingredients with the marinated fish. Season carefully to taste. Refrigerate. Reseason if necessary before serving. Serve cold.

6 servings

up the flank steak so that the grain of the meat runs the length of the roll, and tuck in the ends. Then using kitchen string, tie up the meat roll, first wrapping the string around the roll lengthwise and tying it securely so the ends stay closed. Then tie the meat at 1-inch intervals crossways.

Heat the remaining 2 tablespoons oil in an oven-proof casserole or large, deep skillet that has a cover. Brown the meat on all sides. Add the stock and wine, cover, and bake in the preheated oven for 1½ hours. Remove the meat from the pan and set aside to rest for 10 minutes before slicing.

Boil down the pan juices until they are reduced by about half and have intensified in flavor and thickened slightly. Make a beurre manié by working the soft butter and flour together with your fingertips; whisk bits of this into the sauce. Cook the sauce several minutes longer, until thickened and smooth. Check for seasoning and add salt and pepper, if necessary.

Carefully remove the trussing strings from the meat and with a thin, sharp knife, cut it into slices ½ to ¾ inch thick. Serve with sauce.

4 to 6 servings

Baked Sweet Potatoes

There is no difference between the sweet potatoes and yams in our markets. The true yam, a tropical tuber, is not grown here.

> 1 medium sweet potato per person
> Butter, salt, and pepper

Preheat oven to 450 degrees. Prick the sweet potatoes in a couple of places, place in the oven, and bake for 50 minutes. Serve with butter, salt, and pepper.

Corn on the Cob

> 1 to 2 ears corn on the cob per person
> Butter, salt, and pepper

Shuck the corn. Bring a large pot of water to a boil, and add the corn. When the water returns to the boil cover the pot, shut off the heat, and allow to stand for 8 minutes. The corn can continue to stand for another 15 to 20 minutes and remain hot without overcooking.

Drain, and serve with butter, salt, and pepper.

Coconut Kheer

Kheer is a type of creamy rice dessert served in India. This is my version, with a tropical twist.

> ½ cup long-grain rice
> 3 to 4 cups milk
> ⅓ cup sugar
> 1 vanilla bean
> 1 cup grated sweetened coconut
> 1 cup heavy cream
> 1 ripe papaya, peeled, seeded, and finely diced
> 1 banana, peeled and finely diced
> Juice of ½ lime
> 2 tablespoons Cointreau or triple sec
> 1 tablespoon light rum

Cover rice with cold water in a heavy saucepan, bring to a boil, and drain. Return rice to the saucepan with two cups of the milk, the sugar, and vanilla bean, and cook slowly, stirring from time to time, until the rice is very tender and thick, 45 minutes to 1 hour. Add additional milk, up to a total of 4 cups, to prevent the rice from sticking during cooking. Remove from heat, remove the vanilla bean, and fold in the coconut.

Set rice aside, covered, until cooled to room temperature; then refrigerate several hours until cold. Whip the cream and fold into the cold rice. Refrigerate until ready to serve.

Mix the papaya and banana with lime juice, Cointreau, and rum. Serve the fruit as a topping for the rice.

6 servings

An Alsatian Feast

Alsatian Gewürztraminer

Three-Onion Quiche
Choucroute Garnie
Beet and Watercress Salad

Grilled Pineapple with Kirsch

I have included choucroute garnie among the informal dinners but, truthfully, despite the fact that I'm talking about sauerkraut and sausages (deli food) this meal could easily be a menu for elegant entertaining. Begin with foie gras canapés (use imported canned foie gras if you wish), break open a bottle of sweet Champagne or late-harvest Alsatian wine with dessert, require your guests to come in black tie, and you have the makings for a splendid New Year's Eve dinner. I devised just such a game plan for a formal benefit for the New York Public Library. You'll discover the peasant tastes in every aristocrat, and vice-versa.

Alsatian Gewürztztraminer

One of the more felicitous marriages of a wine with a regional culinary specialty occurs in Alsace, the hilly, pine-forested, castled frontier province of France that has been indelibly marked by the physical and cultural influence of Germany. The wine is gewürztraminer, a fresh, pale golden balance of lively acidity and graceful fruit enhanced by an audacious spiciness characteristic of the grape. The name means "spicy traminer."

Unlike German wines, Alsatian white wines, unless they are late-harvest dessert wines, are bone-dry. But they are never austere: the ripeness of their bouquet and assertiveness of the fruit and spice flavors give them a lively vivacity. It is no accident that gewürztraminer is the partner of a rich yet strongly flavored dish like choucroute, with its tart edge and fragrant seasonings of bay and juniper.

Three-Onion Quiche

Basic Pastry for a one-crust 9-inch tart (page 55)
4 tablespoons sweet butter
2 cups thinly sliced onions
1 cup thinly sliced leeks
½ cup thinly sliced scallions (white part only)
3 eggs
1 cup milk
½ cup heavy cream
Salt and freshly ground white pepper

Preheat oven to 425 degrees. Roll out pastry, fit it into a tart pan, and line with foil. Weight the pastry with pastry weights or dried beans. Place in the oven and bake for about 6 to 8 minutes, until the pastry looks dry but has not begun to color. Remove from the oven, remove foil and weights, and set aside.

Heat the butter in a large, heavy skillet. Add onions, leeks, and scallions, and sauté over low heat, stirring from time to time, until the vegetables are very tender and turning golden. Spread the onion mixture in the prepared tart shell.

Beat the eggs with milk and cream until well blended but not frothy. Season to taste with salt and pepper. Pour this custard mixture over the onions, place the quiche in the oven, and lower temperature to 375 degrees. Bake for 35 to 40 minutes, until the quiche is puffed and lightly browned.

Allow to cool a few minutes before cutting and serving, or cool to room temperature before serving.

6 servings

Choucroute Garnie

An attractive garnish for the choucroute can be made with two apples—peel, core, and cut them into thick wedges, sauté them in butter, wrap the wedges in thin slices of Westphalian ham, secure them with toothpicks, and arrange them as a border on the platter.

2½ pounds bulk sauerkraut
2 ounces salt pork or slab bacon, diced
2 cups finely chopped onions
½ cup chopped carrots
1 large clove garlic, minced
1 tart apple, peeled, cored, and chopped
1½ cups chicken stock, preferably homemade (page 22)
2 cups dry white wine or Champagne
1 bay leaf
6 whole peppercorns
8 juniper berries or 2 tablespoons gin
Salt and freshly ground white pepper
1½ pounds garlic sausage, fresh or smoked (use French sausage, kielbasa, or knockwurst)
1½ pounds boneless smoked pork tenderloin, sliced
½ pound Black Forest ham or baked ham, in 6 slices about ⅛ inch thick
6 medium boiling potatoes, peeled and quartered
Dijon mustard

Drain sauerkraut, reserving the juice. Rinse in two changes of cold water, wring out well, and set aside. Preheat oven to 325 degrees.

In a large casserole (at least 5 quart), cook the salt pork over medium heat until golden. Drain well, leaving fat in the casserole, and set pork aside. In the fat sauté the onions and carrots over medium heat until soft but not brown. Add the garlic and apple and continue to cook for several minutes, until the ingredients are golden. Add the sauerkraut along with the salt pork. Stir in the chicken stock and wine and bring to a gentle simmer.

Add the bay leaf, peppercorns, juniper berries or gin, and salt and pepper to taste. Cover, place in the oven, and bake for 2 hours.

Add the sausage to the casserole, tucking it into the sauerkraut. There should still be some liquid in the casserole. If most of it has evaporated, add additional stock or wine, or both. Taste the sauerkraut. If you feel it should be sharper, add some of the reserved sauerkraut juice. Return to the oven and bake for 20 minutes.

Add the sliced pork and ham to the top of the cas-

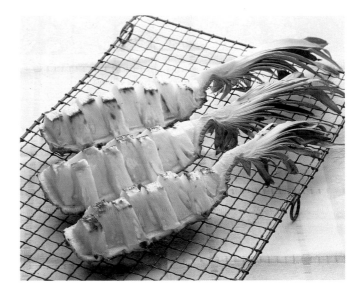

Grilled Pineapple with Kirsch

serole, place a piece of foil directly on the surface of the food, cover the casserole, and return to the oven for another 15 to 20 minutes.

While the meats are cooking, in a separate pan bring potatoes to a boil in salted water, cover, and simmer until tender, about 20 minutes.

Serve the choucroute directly from the casserole with the potatoes on the side, or transfer to a serving dish and surround it with the potatoes. You may want to slice the sausages into chunks before serving. Serve the choucroute with a sharp French mustard, or a selection of mustards.

6 servings

Beet and Watercress Salad

3 pounds beets
4 tablespoons red wine vinegar
1½ teaspoons Dijon mustard
⅔ cup extra-virgin olive oil
3 bunches watercress

Scrub beets and trim leaves to within 1 inch of the root. Place beets in a saucepan, cover with water, bring to a boil, and simmer until the beets are just tender when pierced with a sharp knife, about 30 to 45 minutes, depending on their size. The beets are also done when the skin feels as though it will slip off. Beets will hold their color best when simmered whole, uncut.

As soon as the beets are cooked and cool enough to handle, peel them. You may want to use rubber gloves or cover your hands with plastic bags to protect them from becoming stained. Cut the peeled beets into julienne strips.

Place beets in a bowl. Beat the vinegar, mustard, and olive oil together, and pour over the beets. Toss lightly. Allow to marinate until shortly before serving time.

Rinse watercress. Dry it and remove any heavy stems. Just before serving toss the watercress with the beets and dressing.

6 servings

Grilled Pineapple with Kirsch

Pineapples do not ripen after picking, so select a sweet one. Pulling out a leaf does not indicate ripeness, but the leaves should look fresh, the skin should be more russet than green, there should be no soft spots or bruises, and the fruit should have a nice, pineappley aroma at the bottom. Do not refrigerate pineapples.

1 large Hawaiian pineapple with an attractive crown of leaves
1½ tablespoons sugar
2 tablespoons kirsch

Slice the pineapple in half vertically, slicing right down through the leaves. Cut the rind off the end of each half so that it can stand upright. Next slice each half in thirds, vertically, still slicing through the leaves and keeping them attached. If necessary you can mark the thirds on the outside with toothpicks as a guide. (You can also use two smaller pineapples, cutting them in quarters.)

Slice away the tough central core that runs the length of each section. Using a sharp, flexible knife cut the flesh away from the rind at the bottom, keeping the flesh in a single piece for each section and leaving as little of it attached to the rind as possible. You should now have 6 shells, complete with leaves, and 6 solid pieces of pineapple.

Slice the pineapple flesh crosswise to make ½- to ¾-inch-thick slices. Shift slices alternately to the left and to the right for a decorative effect, as illustrated in the photograph.

Preheat broiler. Wrap the leaves of each section in foil and arrange the pineapple on a broiler pan. Dust with sugar. Broil until lightly browned, about 8 minutes. Remove foil, sprinkle with kirsch, and serve.

6 servings

A Hearty Belgian Menu

Belgian Beers

Cream of Endive Soup
Carbonnades à la Flamande
(***Belgian Beef Stew***)
Braised Potatoes, Turnips, and Carrots
Chicory Salad with Walnut Oil

Frozen Mandarin Mousse

Instead of the culinary mixed metaphors that characterize so much of our cooking today, I occasionally enjoy serving a culturally single-minded menu. This is one of several in the book.

Belgian food is earthy and hearty yet refined. A typical centerpiece for a Belgian dinner is naturally *carbonnades à la Flamande* which, after mussels and "French" fries (something the Belgians claim to have invented) might be called the national dish. I have been preparing it for informal dinner parties for decades, first from Craig Claiborne's *The New York Times Cook Book*, then gradually from a recipe that I evolved over the years. The dish was something of a showstopper in the days when everyone else was serving *boeuf bourguignon* and it remains a fine choice when the mood and the season call for filling, simple food.

Belgian Beers

In Belgium beer amounts to a tourist attraction. Cafés that ring the gilded, Gothic central market squares in Brussels, Bruges, Antwerp, Ghent, and Liège offer astonishing beer lists with dozens, sometimes hundreds of selections. The spectrum of colors can range from light gold to nearly black, with amber, russet, burgundy, and mahogany tones in between. The flavors run from light and refreshingly dry to a liqueur-like cherry sweetness. Some are still being made in monasteries, as they have been for centuries.

With a Belgian menu, beer is the libation of choice. Increasingly available, Belgian beer would be ideal, but a well-made deep gold to amber brew with a good yeasty flavor, whether imported or domestic, would also be suitable. What we call ale would be as appropriate as beer.

Strictly speaking, *beer* is the most general term referring to products brewed from fermented grain. What is usually called beer in the United States is actually lager, a type of beer called bottom-fermented because the sediment of the yeast falls to the bottom of the brewing tank. Ales are top-fermented beers, in which the sediment floats on top. Dark bottom-fermented beers are usually called bock whereas dark ales often bear the names porter or stout. Which you prefer is a matter of taste, but to accompany food with complex flavors a medium-weight beer is best.

Since the beef is cooked in beer, a good beer is especially suited for quaffing, but if wine is still your preference, a sturdy Burgundy would be my recommendation.

Cream of Endive Soup

1 pound endives
½ lemon
2 tablespoons sweet butter
3 cups chicken stock, preferably homemade (page 22)
1 cup heavy cream
Salt and freshly ground white pepper
1 tablespoon minced fresh chives

Wash, trim, and chop the endives. Put them in a saucepan and add the lemon juice and butter. Cover pan and cook over very low heat until the endives are tender. Add chicken stock. Continue to simmer for 15 minutes.

Purée soup in a blender or food processor. Return it to the saucepan, stir in cream, and simmer for another 5 minutes. Season to taste with salt and pepper, and dust with chives just before serving. Soup can be served cold.

4 to 6 servings

Carbonnades à la Flamande
(Belgian Beef Stew)

3 tablespoons sweet butter
5 cups thinly sliced onions
½ tablespoon sugar
2½ pounds lean chuck for stew, cut into 1½ inch cubes
2 tablespoons flour
12 ounces beer, preferably a full-bodied amber-colored beer (but not a *dark* beer)
2 bay leaves
Salt and freshly ground black pepper
2 tablespoons red wine vinegar
2 tablespoons minced fresh parsley for garnish

Heat 2 tablespoons of the butter in a heavy casserole. Add the onions and sauté over medium-low heat, stirring frequently. As the onions soften, but before they have begun to brown, add the sugar. Continue cooking the onions, stirring, until they are golden and just beginning to brown. Remove the onions from the pan and set aside.

Toss the beef with the flour to coat lightly. Add the remaining tablespoon of butter to the casserole and when it has melted, sauté the beef over medium-high heat, a few pieces at a time, until lightly browned. As the cubes brown, remove them from the casserole. When all the cubes have browned, stir in the beer, scraping the pan to release any particles clinging to the bottom and sides. Return the beef and onions to the casserole and add the bay leaves. Season to taste with salt and pepper. Cover and simmer for about 2 hours, until the beef is tender.

Stir in the vinegar, and continue to simmer 15 minutes longer. Serve sprinkled with parsley.

4 to 6 servings

Braised Potatoes, Turnips, and Carrots

1 pound small new potatoes
1 pound white turnips, as small as possible
½ pound carrots
4 tablespoons sweet butter
1 cup chicken stock, preferably homemade (page 22)
Salt and freshly ground black pepper

Peel the potatoes, turnips, and carrots. Halve or quarter the turnips so they are roughly the same size as the potatoes. Slant-cut the carrots in 1-inch-thick slices.

Heat the butter in a heavy saucepan or skillet large enough to hold the vegetables in one or two layers. Add the potatoes and cook over medium-high heat for 5 minutes, tossing them frequently, until they are coated with the butter. Add the turnips and carrots. Stir in the stock, and season with salt and pepper. Cover, and cook over very low heat for 20 to 25 minutes, shaking the pan from time to time.

Serve at once, or set aside and reheat briefly just before serving.

4 to 6 servings

Chicory Salad with Walnut Oil

The dark green chicory leaves are bitter, so they are not used for this salad.

2 large heads chicory (curly endive)
4 tablespoons chopped scallions
2 tablespoons white wine vinegar
1 teaspoon grainy mustard
5 tablespoons walnut oil
Salt and freshly ground black pepper

Trim the dark and light green outer leaves from the chicory. Rinse and dry the inner white, yellow, and very pale green leaves, and tear them into bite-size pieces. Mix with the scallions.

Combine vinegar and mustard and beat until well blended. Add oil and continue beating until the dressing is smooth. Toss the chicory and scallions with the dressing, season to taste with salt and pepper, and serve.

4 to 6 servings

Frozen Mandarin Mousse

What makes this a Belgian dessert? Using the tangerine liqueur, Mandarine Napoléon, which is produced in Brussels.

4 eggs, separated
1 cup plus 2 tablespoons sugar
6-ounce container frozen concentrate of tangerine juice, thawed (use orange juice if tangerine juice is not available)
5 tablespoons Mandarine Napoléon liqueur (Cointreau or triple sec may be substituted)
1½ cups heavy cream
Tangerine sections for garnish
Shaved bittersweet chocolate for garnish

Beat the egg yolks with 1 cup of the sugar until thick and light. Beat in tangerine concentrate. Transfer mixture to the top of a double boiler and continue to beat over simmering water until it becomes thickened, like a custard. Do not let the mixture boil. Remove from heat and stir in all but 1 tablespoon of the liqueur. Refrigerate until cooled.

Beat egg whites until stiff but not dry, and fold into the cooled custard. Then beat 1 cup of the cream until it falls in soft peaks. Add remaining 2 tablespoons sugar and 1 tablespoon liqueur and beat until nearly stiff. Fold the whipped cream into the mousse mixture and transfer to a 4-cup soufflé dish. Freeze for at least 12 hours.

Whip remaining ½ cup cream and decorate the top of the mousse with whipped cream, tangerine sections, and shaved chocolate.

4 to 6 servings

GRAND DINNERS

Elegance transforms a mere dinner into a grand event. This does not mean being pretentious (because pretension is the very antithesis of elegance), but recognizes the importance of finesse in creating a memorable evening. A grand dinner party for four or more is civilized entertainment. I feel a dinner party is successful if, despite the work, I find it rewarding, interesting, pleasant, and of course delicious. It should be a delight, both to plan and to serve.

Instead of relying on luxury ingredients—smoked salmon from Scotland or Beluga caviar—an elegant dinner depends upon quality and attention to detail. In this respect it should not differ from any other meal you prepare but it's the special nature of the evening that elevates it beyond the everyday. It does call for the flourish of an attractive garnish, several wines, cloth napkins in place of paper, and the appropriate stemware. I also try to stamp a dinner party with my personal touch. It is being impressive in a way I enjoy.

An Evening in Spring

Pouilly-Fumé or Pouilly-Fuissé

Asparagus Soup
Medallions of Veal Gremolata
Walnut Rice
Cherry Tomatoes with Sherry Vinegar

Strawberry Cheesecake

In the freshness of the spring season, the once harsh winter landscape is softened by tender green growth. Asparagus introduces this seasonal dinner, accompanied by a refreshing white wine. The menu is simple and easy to assemble—dinner can be on the table in less than an hour (with calories and preparation time trimmed) if you omit the cheesecake and serve juicy, ripe strawberries. Most efficient is first preparing the rice so that it cooks while you prepare the rest of the meal. Both the soup and tomatoes can hold while you cook the veal just before serving dinner.

Pouilly-Fumé or Pouilly-Fuissé—
A Tale of Two Pouillys

Pouilly-Fumé and Pouilly-Fuissé, two of the most popular French white wines in the United States, have surprisingly little in common beyond their color, country of origin, and similarity of names.

One borrows part of its name from Pouilly-sur-Loire in the château country of the Loire Valley, the other from an area in the Mâcon district of southern Burgundy. Pouilly-Fumé, the Loire wine made from the sauvignon blanc grape, is characteristically herbaceous and dry, with a crisp "gunflint" taste. Its name is said to derive from the smoky looking mists that rise from the vineyards in early morning. It is this wine that Robert Mondavi had in mind when he coined the name *fumé blanc* for sauvignon blanc wines in California.

Pouilly-Fuissé, on the other hand, is made from the chardonnay grape, like most proper white Burgundies. It is a graceful wine, lighter than the white wines from the heart of Burgundy to the north, but still the most full-bodied of the white Mâcon wines. It is richer than Pouilly-Fumé.

Either of these wines would suit the menu so the choice is up to you. If you decide to serve Pouilly-Fumé, look for a recent vintage. A fine Pouilly-Fuissé can improve with a few years of bottle age. In each case the wine has more freshness and bouquet than power, perfect for a springtime dinner. And although I generally prefer red wine with veal, the piquant and lemony seasoning on the Veal Gremolata suggests the service of a white wine.

Asparagus Soup

Asparagus herald the spring more truly than any other vegetable. Whether used for a soup or served simply steamed, the asparagus should be selected with care. The stem ends should be moist, the tips tightly furled. Slender spears, tender enough to nibble raw, will not require peeling. To make a deliciously rich soup, replace up to one cup of the milk with heavy cream.

- 2 bunches fresh asparagus, about 2 pounds, preferably slender spears
- 2 medium onions, coarsely chopped
- 1⅔ cups milk
- 1 teaspoon sugar
- Salt and freshly ground white pepper

Rinse the asparagus and snap off the very bottoms close to where the asparagus break naturally. Reserve a few of the tips for garnish, then cut the rest of the asparagus into 1-inch lengths.

Place the asparagus and onions in a large, heavy, nonaluminum saucepan, cover with water, and bring to a simmer. Cook until the asparagus are very tender, 15 to 20 minutes. Drain, reserving the liquid.

Purée the asparagus and onions in a blender, in two or three batches, adding about 1 cup of the cooking liquid to make a smooth purée. It is better to use a blender than a food processor because the purée will be smoother.

Return the soup to the saucepan and stir in the milk. Season with the sugar, and salt and pepper to taste. Heat through. The soup should not be very thick. Add more milk if it becomes thickened upon standing. It can also be chilled and served cold, but check seasonings again after it has chilled.

6 servings

Medallions of Veal Gremolata

Gremolata, the Italian term for the piquant mixture of minced parsley, lemon rind, and garlic that is usually served as a garnish for braised veal shanks (osso buco), adds lively seasoning to veal medallions.

- Grated rind of 1 lemon
- 3 tablespoons chopped fresh parsley
- 1 clove garlic, minced
- 3 tablespoons sweet butter
- 12 ½-inch-thick veal medallions, each 2 to 3 ounces, cut from the leg
- Salt and freshly ground black pepper
- 1 cup dry white wine

To prepare the gremolata, combine the lemon rind, parsley, and garlic, and chop together. Set aside.

Heat the butter in one large skillet or in two medium-size skillets. Add the veal and cook over medium-high heat, turning once, until nicely browned and cooked to the desired degree of doneness. It is best to serve the veal pink in the middle. Also, do not crowd the meat in one pan because it will not brown well. When the meat is done remove it to a warm serving platter or individual dinner plates. Season with salt and pepper.

Pour the wine into the skillet and cook rapidly, scraping the pan. When the liquid has turned syrupy and is reduced to about ⅓ cup, add the gremolata, stir briefly, and immediately divide this sauce among the veal medallions, topping each with a little of the sauce. Serve at once.

6 servings

Walnut Rice

- 1 tablespoon vegetable oil
- ½ cup chopped onions
- 1 cup chopped walnuts
- 1½ cups brown rice
- ½ teaspoon powdered ginger
- 1 teaspoon salt
- 3 cups water

Heat the oil in a heavy saucepan. Add the onions and sauté over medium heat until soft and just turning golden. Add the walnuts and sauté 2 to 3 minutes. Stir in the rice and cook a minute or two longer, until the grains are well coated with oil. Add the ginger, salt, and water.

Bring to a boil, and cook for 2 minutes. Lower heat and simmer, covered, for about 40 minutes or until the liquid is absorbed. Remove from heat and allow to stand, covered, for 5 minutes before serving.

6 servings

Cherry Tomatoes with Sherry Vinegar

1½ pints cherry tomatoes, stems removed
1 tablespoon olive oil
1 tablespoon sherry wine vinegar
Freshly ground black pepper

Preheat oven to 400 degrees. Toss the cherry tomatoes with olive oil. Arrange closely in a single layer in a baking dish. Bake for 10 to 12 minutes.

Remove from the oven, toss with the vinegar, and season with pepper.

6 servings

Strawberry Cheesecake

1½ cups graham cracker crumbs
4 tablespoons melted butter
¼ cup plus ⅔ cup sugar
16 ounces cream cheese, at room temperature
3 eggs
1 cup sour cream
1 teaspoon vanilla extract
1½ pints strawberries, hulled, rinsed, and dried
½ cup red currant jelly

Preheat oven to 350 degrees. Butter an 8-inch springform cake pan.

Combine the graham cracker crumbs, melted butter, and ¼ cup sugar. Press this mixture into the bottom of the pan, making a thick layer.

Beat the cream cheese with remaining ⅔ cup sugar and eggs. Stir in the sour cream and vanilla, and pour into prepared pan. Bake for 1 hour. Turn off oven and allow cake to cool in the oven, then refrigerate until chilled, about 4 hours longer.

Remove sides of springform pan. Arrange strawberries over the top of the cheesecake. Melt the red currant jelly, then brush the berries with the jelly to glaze them.

6 to 8 servings

A Zesty Summer Dinner

❦❦❦

Dry Orvieto Classico

Marinated Mushroom Salad
Grilled Chicken with Pesto
Pan-Seared Zucchini Spears and Tomato Slices

Sweet Orvieto
Honeyed Sponge Roll with Peaches

When the temperature soars, I like to create menus that can be prepared in advance, early in the day. Then entertaining, even with a dinner for six or eight, becomes sheer relaxation. A light menu that can be served with a chilled white wine is what most appeals to me. This one takes advantage of seasonal produce and features dishes highly seasoned with herbs and garlic to whet heat-dulled appetites.

To trim the calories in this menu substitute a green salad with some sliced raw mushrooms dressed simply with mellow balsamic vinegar, salt, and pepper; skin the chicken, and marinate it in lemon juice and mustard before grilling. For dessert serve fresh fruit.

Dry Orvieto Classico and Sweet Orvieto

Perched atop a typically precipitous Umbrian hill, Orvieto is a town of winding cobbled streets that still seem to echo with medieval footsteps. Its origins are Etruscan but its glory is its unique Gothic cathedral, the Duomo.

The historic wine of Orvieto is *abboccato*, or sweet,

made naturally, it is thought, since Etruscan times. The cool temperatures of ancient wine cellars cut deep into the rock beneath the town stopped the fermentation before all the sugar in the must (grape juice) converted to alcohol. The result was the sweet wine, until relatively recently the only one associated with Orvieto. Today, the *secco*, or dry, Orvieto dominates production.

To begin the dinner and up until dessert, the pale, straw-colored dry Orvieto is the choice. It is a delightful summer wine, clean and lighthearted yet gracefully balanced. The choice of Orvieto as the dry white wine to accompany this menu is not written in stone (or carved in marble). Other dry white Italian wines—Gavi from the Piedmont, pinot grigio from the regions near Venice, or a dry Italian tocai from the same area would also suit this Italian menu, as would a light, young fruity red wine from the Piedmont such as dolcetto or grignolino, served after a white wine aperitif.

The sweet Orvieto is a perfect match with honeyed cake and the fresh ripe peaches of the summer season. Asti spumante is a good substitute if the Orvieto is not available.

Marinated Mushroom Salad

- 4 tablespoons olive oil
- 1 large clove garlic, chopped
- 1 pound fresh mushrooms, sliced
- 1 large sweet red pepper, cored, seeded, and cut in slivers
- 4 tablespoons chopped red onion
- 1 teaspoon fresh rosemary or ½ teaspoon dried
- 2 tablespoons white wine vinegar
- ½ cup chopped imported black olives (do not use California black olives)
- Salt and freshly ground black pepper
- 1 tablespoon extra-virgin olive oil
- 6 slices French or Italian bread, ½ inch thick

Heat the olive oil in a large skillet. Add the garlic, sauté for a few seconds, then add the mushrooms. Sauté the mushrooms over high heat until the liquid they give off has evaporated, and the mushrooms begin to brown. Add the red pepper and onion, and sauté another couple of minutes.

Stir in the rosemary, vinegar, and olives, and remove from heat. Season to taste with salt and pepper.

Allow the mixture to cool to room temperature. Add extra-virgin olive oil.

Just before serving toast the bread. Serve the mushroom salad on the toasted bread croutons.

6 servings

Grilled Chicken with Pesto

Pesto, the seasoned basil and garlic purée, became firmly fixed in our culinary vocabulary in the 1970s. Its popularity remains undiminished. Here, instead of appearing as sauce for pasta (its usual role), it is used as a marinade and condiment for grilled chicken.

- ½ cup fresh basil
- ½ cup fresh Italian parsley
- ⅓ cup finely grated Italian Parmesan cheese
- ½ cup olive oil
- 1 tablespoon capers, drained
- Freshly ground black pepper
- 2 broiling chickens, 2½ to 3 pounds each, cut into serving pieces

Place basil and parsley in the bowl of a food processor or blender and process until very finely minced. Add the cheese and combine. Slowly pour in the olive oil with the machine running. When the olive oil has been blended in, add the capers and process until the pesto is a smooth purée. Season to taste with black pepper.

Spoon half the pesto mixture into a large bowl, add the chicken, and turn the pieces in the bowl to coat with the pesto mixture. Set aside to marinate for up to 2 hours. Refrigerate the remaining pesto.

Grill or broil the marinated chicken until done. Serve hot or at room temperature. Just before serving, stir 2 tablespoons boiling water into the remaining pesto and mix until smooth. Spoon a little of this pesto mixture alongside each serving of chicken.

6 to 8 servings

Pan-Seared Zucchini Spears and Tomato Slices

2½ pounds zucchini, the smaller the better
2 medium-large ripe tomatoes
1 tablespoon olive oil
Freshly ground black pepper

Trim the zucchini ends. Cut each zucchini lengthwise into eight wedges. If the zucchini are more than 5 inches long cut them in half as well. Core the tomatoes and cut them in thick slices.

Heat the oil in a large, cast-iron skillet until it just begins to smoke. Put as many of the zucchini spears in the pan as will fit comfortably, placing them with one of the cut sides down. Cook briefly over high heat until they begin to brown. Turn, and place the other cut side down and cook a moment or two longer. Remove from the pan.

If you were unable to fit all the zucchini in the pan at once, continue cooking them in several batches until they are all lightly seared. When the zucchini has been cooked, next sear the tomato slices, but on one side only.

Arrange zucchini and tomato slices (seared side up) attractively on a serving platter, dust with pepper, and serve hot, or cool to room temperature.

6 to 8 servings

Honeyed Sponge Roll with Peaches

½ cup cake flour
4 tablespoons finely ground almonds
¾ teaspoon baking powder
Pinch of salt
4 eggs, at room temperature
½ cup granulated sugar
Confectioner's sugar
¾ cup warm honey
5 to 6 peaches
½ cup sweet white wine such as Orvieto abboccato or Asti spumante
¾ cup heavy cream, whipped

Preheat oven to 350 degrees. Butter a 10-by-15-inch jelly roll pan; line it with a sheet of waxed paper cut to fit the width, but extending a few inches at either end. Butter the paper.

Sift together the flour, almonds, baking powder, and salt. Set aside.

Beat eggs at high speed until very thick and light, almost like softly whipped cream. Gradually beat in the granulated sugar, then fold in the flour mixture. Spread batter in the pan, and bake for about 20 minutes, until puffed and golden brown. When done, quickly run a knife around the edges of the pan.

Heavily dust a clean towel (not terry cloth) or a sheet of waxed paper with sifted confectioner's sugar and invert the cake, pan and all, onto the surface. Lift off the pan, peel off the waxed paper, and spread the cake with the warm honey. Next, using one end of the towel or waxed paper for leverage, roll up the cake from the narrow side and transfer it to a serving platter. Allow to cool.

While the cake is cooling, peel and slice the peaches and toss with white wine. Serve the peaches alongside the cake with the whipped cream.

6 to 8 servings

Grilling with Style

California Gewürztraminer
Spiced Shrimp

California Cabernet Sauvignon
Butterflied Lamb with Rainbow Peppers
Cauliflower Dauphinoise
Assorted Cheeses

Strawberry-Rhubarb Tart

Several years ago this menu could only have been considered for a summertime party. Although green bell peppers were a year-round staple, finding red ones, to say nothing of yellow, required serious searching. No longer. Imports from Europe plus increased production of domestic peppers have recently brightened our markets.

Similarly, grilling, once strictly reserved for summer, may be enjoyed in any season. The lamb in this menu can also be sizzled indoors in an oven broiler.

Like the lamb, the first-course shrimp is marinated and can be started the night before or the morning of the party. The cauliflower, after a brief preliminary cooking, doesn't require attention while it bakes. All in all, this is one of the more accommodating dinner menus.

With slight modification, this menu can satisfy dieters. Reduce the oil to a scant tablespoon in the marinades for both the shrimp and the lamb, steam the cauliflower, omit the cheese course, and serve fresh strawberries for dessert, with a topping of cottage cheese puréed in the blender, sweetened with but a sprinkling of sugar, and flavored with chopped fresh mint.

California Gewürtztraminer, California Cabernet Sauvignon

Cabernet sauvignon has emerged as the premier red wine grape of California. Its range, geographically, stylistically, and economically, is vast. In recent years winemakers have sought to produce wines characterized more by grace and elegance than power, wines that are attractive, accessible, endowed with softer fruit, and less tannin.

Although the argument is that these wines are more suitable for accompanying food than for winning state fair competitions, these are also wines that are ready to drink sooner, requiring less bottle age on the part of the winemaker or consumer. In an era such as ours, when the best wines are sold out long before they are ready to drink (and often purchased by consumers unwilling to wait five or more years to sample their cache), this is a sensible approach.

Except for a handful of top names—Beaulieu Vineyard Georges de Latour Private Reserve, Freemark Abbey, Clos du Val, Heitz, Stag's Leap, Joseph Phelps, and Mondavi—the aging potential for the majority of California cabernet sauvignons has yet to be established. Jordan Vineyards' cabernet sauvignon, a relative newcomer that earned high acclaim almost instantly, is ready to drink within only a few years of the vintage, but no one is certain how long the wine will last.

It is impossible to generalize about the style of the California cabernets. The wines vary from vineyard to vineyard, and sampling (or relying on a good wine shop) is the only means of becoming acquainted with them. This summer menu, with its grilled lamb, calls for a medium-weight cabernet sauvignon. The wine will also complement the cheese. If the cabernet is not too fleshy and lush, it would also do with the first course, but my preference there would be a white wine with some fruitiness and spice. A dry California Johannisberg riesling, a dry chenin blanc, or best of all, a California gewürztraminer that can stand up to the hot, fragrant pungency of shrimp laced with ginger, would be my choice.

Spiced Shrimp

Salting the shrimp is a Chinese technique that "crisps" and improves the texture.

2 pounds medium shrimp, shelled and deveined
1 tablespoon salt
4 teaspoons vegetable oil
½ tablespoon minced fresh ginger
1 small clove garlic, chopped
1 teaspoon minced fresh green chili pepper (canned jalapeno pepper can be substituted)
1 cup minced scallions
2 tablespoons Oriental sesame oil
2 tablespoons light soy sauce
2 tablespoons rice vinegar

Toss the shrimp with salt and set aside for one hour. Rinse shrimp thoroughly and pat dry.

Heat 1 teaspoon of the vegetable oil in a wok or large skillet. Brush or swirl the oil to coat the pan. When the pan is very hot add the shrimp and stir-fry, gently tossing the shrimp until they have turned pink and are beginning to char. Transfer shrimp to a bowl.

Add remaining 3 teaspoons vegetable oil to the wok or skillet, lower heat, and stir-fry the ginger, garlic, chili pepper, and scallions for a minute or two. Pour these ingredients over the shrimp and mix. Add the sesame oil, soy, and vinegar, stir to combine, and set aside at room temperature. Serve tepid or cooled.

6 to 8 servings

Butterflied Lamb with Rainbow Peppers

A thatch of finely slivered colorful peppers, quickly stir-fried, splashed with a touch of vinegar to sharpen the flavor, and piled on a platter is an excellent accompaniment to marinated grilled lamb. At farm stands in midsummer I have sometimes found pale celadon, salmon-colored, off white, and deep purple-brown "chocolate" peppers, all sweet, giving added range to the more available palette of green, red, and yellow peppers.

1 6- to 7-pound whole leg of lamb, butterflied
Juice of 2 lemons
⅓ cup olive oil
3 large cloves garlic, minced
Freshly ground black pepper
Fresh rosemary sprigs
2 large sweet red peppers, cored and cut in very thin strips
2 large sweet yellow peppers, cored and cut in very thin strips
2 large green peppers, cored and cut in very thin strips
2 tablespoons white wine vinegar

Place the leg of lamb in a large dish. Combine the lemon juice, ¼ cup of the olive oil, the garlic, pepper, and rosemary, and pour this mixture over the lamb. Marinate, turning the meat once or twice, for 4 to 6 hours at room temperature, or overnight in the refrigerator.

Prepare the grill or preheat broiler. Drain lamb, reserving the marinade. Grill or broil the lamb to desired degree of doneness (about 20 minutes for medium-rare), turning it once, and basting it with the marinade. Watch the lamb carefully. This is a cut of meat of uneven thickness so some sections may be done sooner than others. Cut the parts that are done away from the rest of the lamb and transfer them to a serving platter and keep warm.

While the lamb is cooking, heat remaining 2 tablespoons oil in a wok or large skillet and stir-fry the peppers until they are crisp-tender, about 5 minutes. Mix with vinegar and mound on a large platter. Slice lamb, cutting against the grain, and arrange slices on the platter with the peppers. Serve at once.

6 to 8 servings

Cauliflower Dauphinoise

2 tablespoons sweet butter
6 tablespoons dry bread crumbs
1½ to 2 heads cauliflower, cored and cut into
  small flowerets (8 to 10 cups flowerets)
2½ cups milk
1¼ cups heavy cream
3 cloves garlic, sliced
Salt and freshly ground black pepper

Preheat oven to 400 degrees. Butter a large baking dish with a little of the butter and coat with about 2 tablespoons of the bread crumbs.

Place cauliflower in a heavy saucepan with the milk, cream, and garlic. Bring to a boil, then simmer for 10 minutes. Season to taste with salt and pepper. Transfer cauliflower mixture to the baking dish, sprinkle with remaining bread crumbs, and dot with butter.

Bake for 45 minutes, until lightly browned.

6 to 8 servings

Strawberry-Rhubarb Tart

Rhubarb is a seasonal vegetable available from late spring through midsummer; frozen rhubarb can be substituted during the fall and winter months.

Strawberries and rhubarb are a combination that is a minor classic. The sweetness of the strawberries balances the acidity of the rhubarb. Since I am not fond of cooked strawberries—they become faded and watery—I cook only the rhubarb for the tart and top it with fresh berries.

Sweet Tart Pastry for a one-crust 9-inch tart (page 30)
2 cups diced fresh rhubarb
1 cup light brown sugar
1 tablespoon kirsch
¼ cup strawberry or red currant jelly
1 tablespoon granulated sugar
3 cups perfect whole strawberries, rinsed, hulled, and dried
¾ cup heavy cream, whipped

Preheat oven to 425 degrees. Roll out pastry and line a 9-inch straight-sided French tart or flan ring with the pastry. Prick the bottom, cover with foil, and weight with dried beans or pastry weights. Bake for 6 minutes. Remove foil, prick again, and bake 10 minutes longer, until the pastry is golden brown. Remove from oven.

Combine rhubarb and brown sugar in a saucepan. Cook, covered, over low heat, stirring occasionally, for 10 minutes. Uncover, increase heat to medium, and continue to cook about 20 minutes longer to make a thick purée. (If using frozen rhubarb, reduce cooking time to 10-15 minutes.) Stir frequently to prevent scorching. Stir in kirsch, remove from heat, and allow to cool.

Combine jelly and granulated sugar in a small saucepan and boil for 2 to 3 minutes. Paint a thin coating of this glaze on the bottom of the pastry shell and reserve the rest.

Spread cooled rhubarb purée over the glaze. Arrange strawberries closely, pointed ends up, over the top of the rhubarb; spread them with the remaining glaze. Serve the tart with whipped cream.

6 to 8 servings

A Dinner for a Chilly Evening

A Dinner for a Chilly Evening

California Sauvignon Blanc or Chardonnay
Scallop-Almond Chowder with Celery Root Chips

California Merlot

Sautéed Quail with Apples
Cornmeal Timbales
Spinach Salad with Fresh Chanterelles

Toblerone Mousse

This menu makes me think of a chilly evening in late autumn or in early winter with such seasonal clues as toasted nuts, celery root, apples, fresh chanterelles, bacon, and quail. (Strictly speaking, quail is not a game bird. These days they are raised on farms and are in the market all year.)

I would also serve this menu as a small Thanksgiving dinner, with the quail as a change from the inevitable turkey, and substituting the Two-Crust Pumpkin Pie (page 143) for the Toblerone Mousse.

California Sauvignon Blanc or Chardonnay, California Merlot

Back in 1960 when the wine boom was barely audible, a mere two acres of California soil were planted with merlot grapes. Two and a half decades later the cultivation of merlot has increased a thousandfold and merlot is beginning to emerge from the shadow of its impressive, well-known big brother, cabernet sauvignon.

Although it plays a major role in some areas of Bordeaux, notably St. Émilion and Pomerol, its use has been primarily as a blending grape in France to soften the sometime tannic harshness of cabernet sauvignon. Winemakers in California likewise use merlot effectively to blend with cabernet sauvignon, and have begun to discover that merlot also makes a fine bottle of wine on its own.

The full fruitiness of a good California merlot makes it an excellent foil for game, especially the little dark-fleshed quail in a sauce fortified with tart apples in this menu. However, merlot is not the ideal choice to accompany the creamy scallop soup. Instead, begin the dinner by opening a bottle of California sauvignon blanc or a light chardonnay that has not been intensified by oak-aging to serve with the soup. A French Chablis or a Mâcon blanc would be an excellent alternative, but be sure to select a recent vintage. There is really no ideal wine to serve with a chocolate dessert, but a snifter of Armagnac or Cognac might satisfy.

Scallop-Almond Chowder with Celery Root Chips

2 tablespoons sweet butter
1 cup chopped leeks
½ cup chopped onions
2 cups peeled, diced boiling potatoes
1 cup dry white wine
3½ cups milk
½ cup heavy cream
Salt and freshly ground white pepper
1 pound scallops, bay or sea (dice if sea scallops are used)
¼ cup ground blanched almonds
¼ cup toasted slivered almonds
Celery Root Chips (see following recipe)

Melt the butter in a large nonreactive saucepan (do not use iron or aluminum). Add the leeks and onions and sauté slowly until very tender but not brown. Add the potatoes and stir to coat them with butter. Add the wine. Cover and cook over low heat for 30 to 40 minutes, until the potatoes are very tender. Roughly mash the potatoes, leaving some in pieces.

Stir in milk and cream, and season to taste with salt and pepper. Heat until simmering. Add the scallops and ground almonds and continue to simmer for a few minutes, just until the scallops are cooked.

Readjust seasonings, and serve sprinkled with toasted almonds and the celery root chips on the side.

6 servings

Celery Root Chips

1 celery root (about 1 pound)
Vegetable oil for deep frying
Salt

Peel the celery root and cut it into long, thick pieces about 1½ inches square. Slice thin using a sharp knife or the slicing blade of a food processor. You should have about 2 cups of slices.

Pour oil to a depth of 1½ inches in a heavy skillet, wok, or electric skillet. Heat to 375 degrees. Fry the celery root chips until golden brown, and drain on absorbent paper. Dust with salt and serve with the soup.

6 servings

Sautéed Quail with Apples

The sauce for the quail is thickened according to a French technique which is useful to master—the butter liaison. Essentially, soft butter is swirled into a wine-based sauce over low heat to form a light emulsion. Care must be taken so the sauce does not overheat, or else it will break down.

2 cups fresh apple cider
⅔ cup Calvados
1 medium onion, chopped
1 teaspoon crushed black peppercorns
2 tablespoons minced fresh ginger
12 quail
5 tablespoons sweet butter
1½ tablespoons minced shallots
1 small apple, peeled, cored, and finely chopped
⅓ cup rich duck, chicken, or veal stock
Salt and freshly ground black pepper

Prepare a marinade with the cider, ½ cup of the Calvados, the onion, peppercorns, and 1 tablespoon of the ginger. Marinate the quail for 3 to 4 hours. Turn the quail a couple of times while they are marinating.

Remove the quail from the marinade and pat with paper towels to dry. Reserve marinade. Heat 1½ tablespoons of the butter in a large, heavy skillet, and sauté the shallots and the remaining tablespoon of ginger over medium heat until they are soft but not brown. Remove the shallots and ginger from the pan, draining as much butter as possible back into the pan; set the shallots and ginger aside. Add another tablespoon of butter to the pan and sauté the quail, turning several times to brown on all sides. If all the quail do not fit in one skillet, use two, dividing the butter between them. Total cooking time for the quail should be about 10 minutes. When done, remove quail to a platter and keep warm in an oven preheated to 150 degrees. Leave the remaining 2½ tablespoons of butter out to soften.

Return the shallots and ginger to the pan (use only one pan to make the sauce), add the apple, and cook over low heat, stirring for about 5 minutes until the apple is tender. Add the remaining Calvados, and increase heat to medium-high to reduce the sauce slightly. Add ⅔ cup of the marinade, strained, and continue to cook until the liquid is reduced by half. Strain the sauce through a fine sieve and return it to the pan.

Add the stock and cook a few minutes longer until the sauce is slightly thickened. Taste and season with salt and pepper.

Over low heat whisk in the remaining butter bit by bit until the sauce is further thickened. Do not allow it to boil. Arrange the quail on a warm serving platter or individual plates, spoon the sauce over them, and serve.

6 servings

Cornmeal Timbales

1 cup milk
½ cup heavy cream
½ cup yellow cornmeal
Salt and freshly ground black pepper
Pinch of sugar
⅔ cup corn kernels—fresh or frozen
1 tablespoon chopped fresh chives
2 tablespoons melted sweet butter
6 eggs, well beaten

Butter six ½-cup ovenproof ramekins. Preheat oven to 350 degrees.

Bring milk and cream to a boil in a heavy saucepan. Immediately transfer to a bowl and add the cornmeal in a thin stream, stirring constantly until the mixture is thickened and smooth. Season with salt, pepper, and sugar. Stir in the corn kernels, chives, and melted butter. Stir in beaten eggs.

Pour batter into prepared molds. Set the molds in a pan with enough boiling water to come about halfway up the sides of the molds. Bake for 30 minutes. Unmold the timbales to accompany the quail.

6 servings

Spinach Salad with Fresh Chanterelles

1 pound fresh spinach, trimmed of stems, well rinsed, dried, and torn into small pieces
3 tablespoons vegetable oil
6 ounces slab bacon, trimmed of rind and finely diced
6 ounces fresh chanterelles (or cultivated fresh mushrooms, sliced)
2 tablespoons chopped shallots
6 tablespoons red wine vinegar
Freshly ground black pepper

Place the spinach in a glass or ceramic bowl. (Avoid using a wooden salad bowl which will soak up the warm dressing.)

Heat oil in a skillet and sauté the bacon until golden. Remove the bacon from the pan, leaving as much fat in the pan as possible. Sauté the chanterelles and shallots in the skillet until tender. Remove from heat and return the bacon to the pan of chanterelles and set aside. If using cultivated mushrooms add them raw to the bowl of spinach.

Reheat the bacon with the chanterelles, shallots, and drippings in the skillet and pour over the salad. Add the vinegar. Toss thoroughly, then invert the skillet over the salad bowl for 30 seconds to wilt the spinach. Toss again, season with pepper, and serve.

6 servings

Toblerone Mousse

3 3-ounce Toblerone milk chocolate bars, broken in pieces
5 eggs, separated
½ teaspoon almond extract
1 cup heavy cream
1 3-ounce Toblerone bittersweet chocolate bar, finely chopped (milk chocolate Toblerone may be substituted)

Place the broken Toblerone bars in the top of a double boiler and heat over simmering water just until the chocolate melts. The mixture will not be smooth because of the nougat in the candy. Remove from heat. Beat the egg yolks until light and mix with the chocolate, stirring until the egg yolks are well blended. Transfer to a large bowl.

Beat the egg whites until stiff but still glossy and not dry. Fold one-fourth of them into the chocolate mixture and stir in the almond extract. Fold in the rest of the egg whites. Whip the cream until it holds its shape but is not completely stiff. Fold half of the whipped cream into the chocolate mixture along with the chopped bittersweet Toblerone. Transfer to a serving bowl or individual dishes and chill for at least 8 hours. Serve topped with remaining whipped cream.

6 to 8 servings

An Autumn Holiday Celebration

California White Zinfandel
Seafood with Pickled Ginger

California Red Zinfandel

Roast Duck Sauced with Cranberries
Sautéed Sugar Snap Peas
Wild Rice Pilaf with Carrots and Nutmeg
Honey Cornmeal-Wheat Bread

Maple Pecan Pie

This menu title is, frankly, a catchall. The holiday referred to could be Halloween as easily as it could be Columbus Day or Election Day. It suits Thanksgiving as well because so many of the ingredients are native American, and if the traditionalist has the upper hand and prefers turkey, that's fine too because the cranberry-red wine sauce could just as easily grace a turkey (or a goose for that matter) as duck.

California Zinfandels

In selecting wines I prefer to create regional partnerships such as Italian wine with an Italian menu. When it comes to an American menu, the choices are many. Why zinfandel?

In some respects I regard zinfandel as more uniquely American than the other grapes grown here largely because, except for some minimal attempts elsewhere (notably in Italy where a grape similar to zinfandel is called *primitivo*), zinfandel is only made here. It is an interesting wine to serve because it comes in various styles and, indeed, colors.

I have occasionally turned a dinner into a zinfandel tasting, beginning with a white zinfandel as an aperitif and with a first course, following with a red zinfandel (or two—there are light red zinfandels and sturdier, meatier ones, and which to serve depends on the food), and even ending the meal with a sweet, high-alcohol late-harvest port-like example.

This menu suggests a white (or rosé) zinfandel to begin, preferably one that is not particularly sweet. The rich main course with its spicy side dishes calls for a red zinfandel with good acidity, body, and fruit rather than a lighter one. You cannot go wrong with a zinfandel bearing the Ridge label, the winery that has made its reputation in zinfandel with excellent results.

Seafood with Pickled Ginger

Littleneck clams
Oysters
Jumbo shrimp
Crab claws
½ cup Japanese pickled ginger
½ cup Japanese rice vinegar

Select either an assortment of seafood or use one variety. Each serving should consist of 6 to 8 pieces, 4 to 5 dozen in all.

Clams and oysters should be opened and on the half shell. Shrimp should be cooked—put them in a pot of boiling water, and when the water returns to a boil and the shrimp turn pink (about 2 minutes), they are done. Remove and drain. Chill, shell, and devein the shrimp. Crab claws are usually purchased cooked. Keep all the seafood chilled.

Finely chop the ginger, then mix with the vinegar. Spoon a little of this mixture over the seafood or serve tiny cups of it as a dipping sauce.

8 servings

Roast Duck Sauced with Cranberries

Although cranberries are marketed only in fall and winter, assuring a year-round supply only takes an extra bag or two in the freezer. Cranberries freeze well and may be used without thawing.

If you wish to substitute a turkey for the duck, take care not to overcook it. Twelve minutes per pound at 375 degrees to an internal temperature of 160 degrees (regardless of what a pop-up timer or other cookbooks might say) will assure a bird that is moist and juicy. A small instant-read thermometer is useful to have on hand for checking a roast. Whatever poultry you choose, be sure it is at room temperature before going into the oven. After cooking, allow it to rest for 15 to 20 minutes before slicing or carving.

2 4½-pound ducks, preferably fresh
Salt and freshly ground black pepper
1 cup chopped onions
1 cup chopped celery
2 cloves garlic, minced

2 cups dry red wine (such as zinfandel)
2 cups water
A fresh thyme sprig or a pinch of dried
8 sprigs parsley
3 cups fresh cranberries
2 tablespoons red wine vinegar
⅔ cup sugar

Remove necks, gizzards, hearts, and livers from the ducks and reserve. Pull off as much fat as possible from the duck cavities, reserving a small amount. Drain inside and out. If there is time refrigerate the ducks, loosely covered with waxed paper, for 6 to 8 hours. This will dry the skin so that it will crisp better.

Preheat oven to 350 degrees. Lightly season the ducks with salt and pepper and place them breast side up on racks in a roasting pan. An adjustable v-shaped rack that cradles the birds is the best kind to use. Roast the ducks for 2 to 2½ hours, pricking the skin every 15 minutes to render the fat.

While the ducks are roasting, place a tablespoon of the fat removed from the ducks in a heavy saucepan. Mince the gizzards and hearts and add to the saucepan along with the onion and celery. (You could mince the livers and sauté them along with the scallions and carrots for the wild rice pilaf.) Sauté over medium heat for about 10 minutes, until the vegetables are lightly browned. Add the garlic, stir, then add 1 cup of the wine and cook, stirring to loosen any browned particles stuck to the pan. Add the water, duck necks, thyme, parsley, and salt and pepper to taste. Simmer this stock covered for 45 minutes. Strain into a clean saucepan.

Add the cranberries, vinegar, and sugar to the strained duck stock and cook over medium-high heat until the berries soften and pop. Lower heat and simmer until the sauce has thickened. Remove from heat.

When the ducks are done, transfer them to a platter. Pour off all but a couple of tablespoons of fat from the roasting pan. Add remaining cup of wine, stir over heat, if necessary, to loosen browned particles clinging to the roasting pan. Strain this mixture into the cranberry sauce.

Reheat the sauce and season to taste with salt and pepper. Carve the ducks or cut them in sections, and serve with the sauce.

6 to 8 servings

Note: This recipe can be divided in half to serve 4.

Sautéed Sugar Snap Peas

These are a relatively new hybrid, a cross between snow peas and ordinary garden peas and can be eaten raw or cooked, pod and all. If they are not available, substitute snow peas.

2 tablespoons vegetable oil
1 tablespoon sweet butter
2 pounds fresh Sugar Snap peas
1 tablespoon chopped fresh parsley
Salt and freshly ground black pepper

Heat oil and butter in a large skillet or a wok. Add the peas and sauté, stirring frequently, until they turn a very bright green and are crisp-tender. Dust with parsley, season with salt and pepper, and serve.

8 servings

Wild Rice Pilaf with Carrots and Nutmeg

In this recipe, the proportion of liquid to rice is less than usually recommended (you will find the same is true of my recipes for kasha, brown rice, and white rice). Wild rice is an extremely variable product, but look for the longest, largest grains you can find. Allowing a "rest period" after the rice is done, an Oriental technique, also gives the grain a better, lighter texture.

4 tablespoons sweet butter
½ cup chopped celery
2 cups sliced carrots
1 cup fresh mushroom caps, the smaller the better
1 teaspoon nutmeg, preferably grated fresh
1⅓ cups (about 8 ounces) wild rice
3 cups chicken stock, preferably homemade (page 22)
Salt and freshly ground black pepper

Preheat oven to 350 degrees. In a heavy saucepan or heatproof casserole melt the butter, add the celery, and sauté until tender. Stir in the carrots and mushrooms, and continue to sauté, coating them with the butter. Stir in the nutmeg.

Add the rice, stir briefly, then add the stock. Bring to a simmer. Season to taste with salt and pepper. Cover and place in the oven to bake for 1 hour and 15 minutes. When done the rice grains will have split open somewhat and become tender, and all of the liquid will have been absorbed. After baking set aside, covered, for 15 minutes before serving. If all the liquid had not been absorbed at the end of the cooking period, this rest period will take care of it. Fluff with a fork, check seasonings, and serve.

8 servings

Honey Cornmeal-Wheat Bread

2 cups milk
½ cup yellow cornmeal
2 packages active dry yeast
½ cup warm water
1 teaspoon sugar
1½ teaspoons salt
¼ cup honey
2 cups whole wheat flour
2½ to 3 cups all-purpose flour

Scald the milk in a heavy saucepan. Slowly stir in the cornmeal, mixing vigorously until the mixture is thick and smooth. Transfer to a large mixing bowl.

Dissolve the yeast in the warm water with the sugar. Set in a warm place to proof for about 5 minutes.

Add the yeast to the cornmeal mixture and blend in the salt and honey. Stir in the whole wheat flour. Stir in about 2 cups of the all-purpose flour, ½ cup at a time,

until a ball of dough forms that cleans the sides of the bowl.

Turn dough out onto a floured board and knead until the dough is smooth and elastic, kneading in additional flour as necessary to prevent sticking. Kneading should take about 8 minutes. The dough can be mixed in a mixer or a food processor.

Place the dough in a buttered bowl, turn to coat on all sides, cover, and set aside to rise until doubled in bulk, about 1 hour.

Punch the dough down and turn out onto a lightly floured board. Cut in half, shape into 2 loaves, and place in buttered baking tins 8½-by-4½ inches. Cover lightly and allow to rise again until doubled—dough should be level with the tops of the tins. Preheat oven to 425 degrees.

Bake in a preheated oven for 10 minutes. Lower oven temperature to 350 degrees and continue baking for 20 to 25 minutes, until the bread is nicely browned and the crust sounds hollow when tapped. Remove from pans and cool before slicing.

Makes two 8½-by-4½-inch loaves

Maple Pecan Pie

Basic Pastry for a 9-inch one-crust pie or tart (page 55)
1 cup pecan halves
¾ cup dark corn syrup
¾ cup pure maple syrup
4 tablespoons melted sweet butter
3 eggs, lightly beaten
1 teaspoon vanilla extract
½ cup chopped pecans
¾ cup heavy cream, whipped

Preheat oven to 425 degrees. Roll out pastry, line pie pan with pastry, prick all over, and line with foil. Weight it with dried beans or pastry weights. Bake for 6 to 8 minutes, until the pastry looks dry but has not colored. Remove foil.

Remove pastry from oven and lower heat to 350 degrees. Spread pecan halves over pastry. Combine remaining ingredients (except the cream), and pour into pie shell. Bake for 35 to 40 minutes, until filling is fairly firm. Cool and serve with whipped cream.

6 to 8 servings

An Eclectic Menu for Six

German, Alsatian, or American Rieslings

Hot and Sour Scallop Soup
Dilled Chicken in Riesling
Kasha with Onions
Broccoli with Sesame Oil Dressing

Dessert Soufflés:
Rum-Raisin Soufflé
or
Irish Coffee Soufflé

The ethnic smorgasbord that has become our contemporary American table is both intriguing and challenging. In the course of a meal one can proceed from foods that are Oriental to European to American and back, acknowledging trends such as healthful whole grains and desserts that cater to an unrepentant sweet tooth along the way. This eclectic menu is appropriate to serve dinner guests almost any season.

Do not be daunted by a dessert soufflé: it can be readied for baking in advance and placed in the oven when the chicken is ready to serve. Two soufflé recipes are included—the decision is yours.

German, Alsatian, or American Rieslings

Never cook with a wine you would not drink. That axiom serves a dual purpose. The wine meant for the saucepan can be enjoyed by the cook at work ("all good cooks drink," observed Whistler) and a decent wine will not pollute the dish with oddly sweet or sour flavors.

Well-made dry red or white wines are usually on hand in my kitchen, but occasionally a specific wine is appropriate. This chicken in riesling, for example, depends on the fruitiness of the wine to add depth to the cream and dill sauce. Chinese flavors in the first course and salad are also complemented by the evident fruit in a good riesling. Therefore, use the riesling for drinking with dinner as well as for preparing the chicken.

But which riesling? The premier wine grape of Germany is also cultivated in a number of other countries. A German riesling in a green bottle from the Mosel-Saar-Ruwer region (especially the Bernkastel and Piesort districts) will be lighter, more refreshing than the rieslings from the Rhine in a brown bottle. These are more full-bodied, with those from the Rheingau especially well balanced.

Rieslings from Alsace are dry, very lively, and fresh-tasting. California, New York State, and Washington rieslings can also be very good. Look for the term Johannisberg riesling to identify the proper grape. It refers to Schloss Johannisberg near Frankfurt, Germany, a famous estate owned by the family of Metternich which pioneered the development of riesling cultivation and selected late-harvest picking.

There is also the possibility of serving a sweet riesling with the dessert soufflé. Rieslings come in every shade of sweetness and those labeled *auslese, beerenauslese,* and *trockenbeerenauslese* from Germany; late harvest from the United States; or *vendange tardive* from France will be sweetest. The sweeter ones are too rich and nectarous to accompany any of the dishes on this menu except the dessert or perhaps an assertive cheese to precede it. But a dessert wine served at the end of dinner is a particularly luxurious finale.

Hot and Sour Scallop Soup

This is a variation on a popular Chinese soup. It can be prepared well in advance, up to the addition of the scallops.

8 dried Chinese tree ears (a type of dried black fungus)
½ cup hot water
4 cups chicken stock, preferably homemade (page 22)
4 tablespoons rice vinegar
1½ tablespoons light soy sauce
6 ounces sea scallops, sliced thin
1 tablespoon cornstarch
2 tablespoons cold water
1 egg, lightly beaten
¼ to ½ teaspoon chili oil
2 scallions, chopped

Place tree ears in hot water and allow to soak for 30 minutes. When they have softened, drain them, reserving the soaking liquid. Cut each tree ear in half.

Bring stock to a simmer in a saucepan, add the soaking liquid, vinegar, soy sauce, and tree ears. Bring to a boil and simmer for 5 minutes. Add the scallops and simmer a couple of minutes, just until the slices turn opaque. Remove soup from heat.

Dissolve cornstarch in cold water and stir into the soup. Return soup to the stove and allow it to come to a simmer, then gradually dribble the beaten egg into the soup. The egg will cook when it comes in contact with the hot soup and form egg strands. Season soup with chili oil to taste, add scallions, and serve at once.

6 servings

Dilled Chicken in Riesling

Simmer the chicken in the same wine you pour to drink; the fruity riesling adds an extra dimension that balances the fragrance of the fresh dill. The riesling should be dry or only slightly sweet. Chenin blanc or sylvaner may be substituted. This dish can be finished in advance and reheated at serving time.

2 small broiling chickens, about 2½ pounds each, cut up
½ tablespoon sweet butter
½ tablespoon vegetable oil
3 tablespoons finely minced shallots
1 teaspoon minced garlic
1 cup riesling
½ cup well-flavored chicken stock, preferably homemade (page 22)
Salt and freshly ground white pepper
2 tablespoons finely minced fresh dill
1 cup heavy cream
Several drops of fresh lemon juice
Dill sprigs for garnish

For this recipe I recommend removing the backbone and wing tips since they provide very little meat. (Save them for the stockpot, or simmer them with water and a small onion to make the stock for this recipe.) Pat the chicken pieces dry on paper towels.

Heat the butter and oil in a large ovenproof skillet or casserole. (The pan must have a nonreactive finish.) Sauté the chicken pieces over medium-high heat until they are golden brown, turning them once. If they do not all fit in the pan without crowding, sauté in several shifts, adding more butter and oil if necessary. Remove the chicken, set it aside, and pour all but a thin film of fat from the pan. Preheat oven to 350 degrees.

Add the shallots to the pan and cook over low heat until soft but not brown. Add the garlic and cook for a few seconds longer.

Pour in the wine, raise the heat to high, and deglaze the pan by scraping up all the little particles that cling to the bottom. Cook until the wine is reduced to about ½ cup. Add stock and lower heat to simmering.

Return the chicken to the pan, season with salt and pepper, and baste with the pan juices. Cover and place in the preheated oven for about 20 minutes, until the juices from the drumsticks run clear when pricked with a sharp fork. Remove from oven.

Transfer chicken to a serving platter and keep warm. Add dill to the cooking liquid in the pan and boil until the liquid has reduced to about one-third the original volume, 5 to 8 minutes. You should have about ½ cup. Add cream. Cook over high heat, stirring until somewhat reduced and thickened, about 5 minutes. Stir in lemon juice. Taste sauce and reseason if necessary.

Pour sauce over chicken, garnish with dill sprigs, and serve.

6 servings

Kasha with Onions

Package directions for kasha invariably call for 2 cups of liquid to 1 cup of the grain, but I have found these proportions make the kasha too soft. Use 1½ cups of water to 1 cup of grain for kasha that is still tender, but light and fluffy.

    1 cup kasha (buckwheat groats), preferably whole
        or coarse grain
    1 large egg, lightly beaten
    1½ cups stock or boiling water
    1 teaspoon salt
    2 tablespoons vegetable oil or sweet butter
    2 cups thinly sliced onions

Mix kasha with the egg in a heavy 1-quart saucepan. Place over medium heat and stir with a fork for 2 to 3 minutes, until the grains are separate.

Add the liquid and salt. Stir. Cover and cook over very low heat for 10 to 15 minutes, until the liquid has been absorbed. Fine- or medium-grain kasha will cook faster than whole or coarse groats.

While the kasha is cooking, heat the oil or butter in a large skillet. Sauté onions over medium heat until they are just beginning to brown. Add cooked kasha to the pan, toss lightly with the onions, and serve.

6 servings

Broccoli with Sesame Oil Dressing

Like the soup, this recipe calls for some Chinese ingredients that have become widely available. The salad can be prepared in advance, but should not sit in its dressing for more than an hour before serving. Any longer and the vinegar in the dressing will dull the bright green color of the broccoli.

    1 large bunch broccoli or a medium head of cauli-
        flower or half broccoli, half cauliflower
    2 tablespoons sesame seeds
    Salt and freshly ground black pepper
    ½ cup Oriental sesame oil
    ¼ cup rice vinegar
    1 tablespoon soy sauce
    ½ teaspoon sugar
    Pinch red pepper flakes (optional)

Separate broccoli into small flowerets; peel, and slant-cut the stems. You should have 3 to 4 cups. Rinse well. Steam until crisp-tender, about 6 to 8 minutes. Allow to cool in a colander, then transfer to a bowl.

Sprinkle sesame seeds in a dry, heavy skillet and toast over medium heat, mixing once or twice, until golden, about 5 minutes. Set aside.

Season vegetable with salt and pepper. Combine remaining ingredients and beat to mix well. Pour over broccoli and toss. Sprinkle with toasted sesame seeds and red pepper flakes if using, and serve.

6 servings

Dessert Soufflés

The egg whites that lighten and puff a soufflé are fragile, and especially so once the soufflé has been baked. Julia Child has proven that a soufflé can be assembled and wait, ready to bake, for up to two hours in a warm kitchen with a large bowl inverted over the soufflé dish to protect it. However, be sure to serve the soufflé as soon as it is baked.

Rum-Raisin Soufflé

    ⅓ cup light rum, warmed
    ½ cup golden raisins
    3 tablespoons sweet butter
    ½ cup sugar
    ½ teaspoon freshly grated nutmeg
    3½ tablespoons flour
    ¾ cup milk
    4 egg yolks
    5 egg whites, at room temperature
    Confectioner's sugar, sifted
    1 cup heavy cream whipped with 2 tablespoons
        confectioner's sugar, 1 tablespoon light rum, and
        a pinch of nutmeg

Combine the rum and raisins and set aside. Fit a 6-cup soufflé dish with a collar of aluminum foil extending one inch above the rim—double a long strip of foil about 2 inches wide, and secure it with straight pins. Butter the dish and the foil collar with 1 tablespoon of the butter. Combine 2 tablespoons sugar with a pinch of nutmeg and dust the inside of the dish and collar with this mixture. Set aside.

Heat the remaining 2 tablespoons butter in a heavy saucepan. Add the flour, blending with a whisk, and continue cooking the flour and butter for a couple of minutes. Scald the milk and add, whisking constantly. The mixture will be very thick. Whisk in the remaining sugar and the nutmeg.

Remove this mixture from heat and beat in the egg yolks, one at a time, blending well after each addition. Stir in the rum and raisins. The soufflé mixture can be prepared in advance up to this point. If not being used immediately, cover by placing a piece of plastic wrap directly on the surface.

Preheat oven to 400 degrees. Whip the egg whites until they hold peaks, but are still glossy and not dry. Stir one-fourth of the egg white mixture into the egg yolk mixture to lighten it, then gently fold in the remaining egg whites. Do not overmix. Pour into prepared soufflé dish. About one inch from the outer circumference, run a knife or spatula around the soufflé to a depth of about 2 inches.

Place the soufflé in the lower third of the oven and reduce heat to 375 degrees. Bake for 25 to 30 minutes, until puffed and golden. Dust top of soufflé with sifted confectioner's sugar and serve at once with flavored whipped cream.

6 servings

Irish Coffee Soufflé

    5 tablespoons sweet butter
    4 tablespoons flour
    1 cup milk
    ⅔ cup sugar (plus additional sugar for dusting
        baking dish and top of soufflé)
    3 tablespoons instant coffee
    Pinch of cinnamon
    4 egg yolks
    ¼ cup Irish whiskey (Scotch or bourbon can be
        substituted)
    6 egg whites, at room temperature
    ⅔ cup heavy cream, whipped

Prepare an 8-cup soufflé dish with a collar of aluminum foil extending one inch above the rim—double a long strip of foil about 2 inches wide, and secure it with straight pins. Heavily butter the dish and the collar with 1 tablespoon of butter and dust both with sugar.

Melt remaining 4 tablespoons butter in a heavy saucepan. Add the flour and cook for about 3 minutes, until the flour is golden. Scald the milk, and stir in the sugar, instant coffee, and cinnamon until they dissolve. Slowly pour the hot milk mixture into the flour mixture, whisking constantly. Cook over low heat, stirring, until thickened and smooth. Off heat beat in the egg yolks, one at a time. Stir in the whiskey. Transfer to a large bowl. The soufflé may be prepared in advance up to this point. If so, cover by placing a piece of plastic wrap directly on the surface.

Preheat oven to 400 degrees. Whip the egg whites until stiff but not dry. Stir about one-fourth of the egg whites into the coffee mixture. Gently and quickly fold in the rest. Pour the mixture into the prepared soufflé dish, smooth the top, and sprinkle with about 2 tablespoons sugar. About one inch from the outer circumference run a knife around the soufflé to a depth of about 2 inches.

Place soufflé in the lower third of the oven, lower heat to 375 degrees, and bake for 35 minutes. Serve at once with whipped cream. If desired, the Dark Caramel Sauce (page 35) can be served on the side.

6 to 8 servings

A Grand Dinner Party
for a Special Occasion

❧

Champagne
Cucumber and Golden Caviar Canapés

White Burgundy
Penne with Fennel and Shiitake Mushrooms

Red Burgundy

Fillet of Beef with Peppered Onion Confit
Buttered Haricots Verts
Classic Green Salad
Assorted Cheeses

Raspberry Tortoni
Chocolate Thins

This is a major menu. Fine wines and several presentations elevate the evening to a high plane of convivial dining. Though traditional in its outline, telling details announce that this is not everyday fare.

Organize your preparation of this dinner from the end to the beginning, starting with the dessert. A brief stint in the kitchen to cook the pasta, consign the beef to the oven, and reheat the sauce will be the only time required away from your guests before dinner is served.

White and Red Burgundies

The entire Côte d'Or, the "golden slope" of Burgundy, is not more than forty miles long. Yet it is dotted with some of the world's greatest vineyards.

White wines—chardonnays—of harmonious golden richness, some capable of aging many years in the bottle, share Burgundy's great reputation for reds—pinot noirs—of noble structure cloaked in velvet. The Côte d'Or is divided into two subdistricts; the northern half, the Côte de Nuits, produces red wines almost exclusively whereas the Côte de Beaune, to the south, is a source of both reds and whites. The reds of the Côte de Beaune tend to be lighter than those of the Côte de Nuits.

Burgundy also includes Chablis, the white wine district further north, as well as Chalonnais and Mâconnais south of Beaune, bordering the Beaujolais.

But it is from the heart of Burgundy that I would select wines for a grand dinner. The first course of pasta with exotic mushrooms is fine with a lush white, a Chassagne-Montrachet, for example, but one of the lighter reds such as a Santenay or a Volnay could also handle it with ease. Such a red wine could accompany the entire menu. I would be sorely tempted to begin with a white Chassagne-Montrachet followed by the red of the same name, a lovely wine that is produced in relatively small quantities even for the tiny vineyards of Burgundy.

Burgundy is such a mosaic of little patches of vineyards and communes that keeping all the names straight is not easy. Buy Burgundies labeled "premier cru" if you can, and look for wines of the major négociants, or shippers: Joseph Drouhin, Louis Jadot, Louis Latour, Bouchard Père et Fils, and Faiveley. These are often the most consistent and reliable. And if the prices of red wines from the famous Burgundian slopes are too steep, consider a wine called Mercurey, from the Chalonnais, a charming and highly palatable red wine with the combination of fruit and structure that suits this menu.

White and Red Chassagne-Montrachets

Cucumber and Golden Caviar Canapés

Penne with Fennel and Shiitake Mushrooms

Cucumber and Golden Caviar Canapés

Caviar is a luxury but the golden whitefish variety makes it affordable, and it is available in supermarkets. The aperitif of choice with these elegant tidbits is a glass of Champagne. (For more about Champagne, see page 155.)

    1 medium cucumber
    ½ cup sour cream
    ¼ cup golden whitefish caviar
    Dill sprigs

Peel the cucumber and trim the ends. Using a small, sharp knife score the cucumber vertically at equal intervals, making about six shallow scores so that when the cucumber is sliced horizontally it will have a scalloped design. Or, you can score the flesh with the tines of a fork. Cut the cucumber into thin slices.

Place a small dab of sour cream (a scant half teaspoon) in the center of each cucumber slice, and top with a smaller dab of golden caviar. Tuck a tiny sprig of dill into the sour cream next to the caviar. Arrange the canapés on a platter and serve.

32 to 40 canapés

Penne with Fennel and Shiitake Mushrooms

In the past few years, shiitake mushrooms have been cultivated in many parts of the country and are now widely available fresh. In preparing this recipe be sure to allow ample time for the pasta water to come to a boil.

    4 tablespoons olive oil
    ¾ pound shiitake mushrooms, sliced (cultivated mushrooms can be substituted)
    2 large cloves garlic, minced
    4 cups very thinly sliced fennel bulb
    ½ teaspoon fennel seeds, crushed
    1 pound penne
    2 tablespoons finely slivered sun-dried tomatoes
    ¾ cup heavy cream
    1 tablespoon minced fennel tops
    Salt and freshly ground black pepper
    Freshly grated Italian Parmesan cheese

Heat oil in a large skillet. Add the mushrooms and cook over medium heat until they begin to wilt. Add the garlic and cook a moment or two longer. Stir in the fennel and fennel seeds. Continue to cook, stirring, until the fennel begins to soften, about 5 minutes. Cover the pan, lower heat, and cook very slowly for 10 minutes longer.

Meanwhile bring at least 4 quarts of salted water to a boil and cook the penne until al dente, about 7 minutes. Drain well and transfer to a warm serving dish.

Uncover the mushroom-and-fennel mixture, add the sun-dried tomatoes, cream, fennel tops, and salt and pepper to taste. Cook over high heat a minute or so to combine the flavors; spoon the sauce over the cooked pasta, toss lightly, and serve dusted with cheese.

8 first-course servings

Fillet of Beef with Peppered Onion Confit

Fillet of beef is a reliably tender cut of beef, even when you purchase choice instead of prime grade. Instead of the usual roasting method, the meat is braised on a flavorful bed of onions that later becomes its condiment. To expand the menu to serve twelve or more, use one and one-half to two whole fillets.

    1 whole fillet of beef, well trimmed and with the narrow end tied under, about 3½ pounds
    2 tablespoons vegetable oil
    5 tablespoons sweet butter
    6 cups very thinly sliced onions
    ¼ cup Cognac
    ¼ cup water
    Freshly ground black pepper
    Watercress for garnish

Be sure the fillet is trimmed of as much fat as possible and that its silvery membrane has been peeled off. Tie the meat at one-inch intervals with butcher's string. Cut the beef in half if you do not have a casserole large enough to hold it in one piece. Preheat oven to 400 degrees.

Heat the oil in the casserole and brown the meat on all sides over medium-high heat. When the meat is browned remove it from the casserole and set aside on a platter. Add 1 tablespoon of the butter and all of the onions to the casserole; cook the onions over very low heat until they are golden and tender. Stir in the Cognac and water, scraping any bits up from the bottom of the casserole.

Return the meat to the casserole, setting it on the bed of onions. Cover and place the casserole in the oven. If you are braising the meat in one piece, time it for about 20 minutes for medium-rare. If it was cut in two, it will require only 13 to 15 minutes. The best way to check for doneness is by using a small, instant-read thermometer. For medium-rare it should register 120 degrees.

Remove the meat from the casserole and allow to rest 10 minutes before carving. (It can rest longer.)

Return the casserole to the top of the stove and cook the onions over medium heat until the liquid has evaporated. Stir in the remaining 4 tablespoons butter and season liberally with freshly ground black pepper. If you wish to hold the meat, return it to the casserole and cover. It will keep warm, but not continue to cook, for 20 to 30 minutes.

To serve, remove the string, cut the meat into ½-inch-thick slices, and arrange them on a platter. Stir the onion confit to incorporate any juices released from the meat, reheat briefly, and spoon onto the platter, either in the center surrounded by the beef slices, or around the edges. Some watercress sprigs will add a touch of color. Serve immediately.

8 servings

Buttered Haricots Verts

Haricots verts are very slender, dark green beans that are sometimes sold in fancy greengrocers.

    2 pounds haricots verts or young, tender green
        beans
    Salt and freshly ground black pepper
    3 tablespoons sweet butter

Trim the beans. Steam over boiling water until the color intensifies and the beans are crisp-tender. Haricots verts will require 3 to 4 minutes, green beans about 5 to 6 minutes.

Immediately rinse beans with cold water. Drain and set aside. Season with salt and pepper.

A few minutes before serving reheat the beans, tossing them lightly in a large skillet with the butter and 3 tablespoons water. Cook only until they are heated through, then serve.

8 servings

Classic Green Salad and Vinaigrette

The Greens: As an interlude between the main course and dessert (or cheese) approximately one and one-half cups of salad greens provide a nice serving. If the main course does not include many vegetables, I would increase that quantity to two cups. An assortment of lettuces and other greens is always interesting, but a fine salad can also be limited to Bibb lettuce or Boston lettuce when dressed with a good vinaigrette.

The Vinaigrette: Proportions are a matter of taste, but using a good white or red wine vinegar and olive oil, I prefer three parts oil to one of vinegar. The amount of oil can be decreased if you are using an assertive, heavier oil such as Italian extra-virgin olive oil or hazelnut oil, or with a mellower acid such as lemon juice, balsamic vinegar, rice vinegar, or fruit vinegar.

Among the salads in this book that would be suitable for this menu are the Bibb and Watercress Salad, page 22, and the Arugula, Radicchio, and Endive Salad, page 35.

Right: Fillet of Beef with Peppered Onion Confit

Below: Chocolate Thins

Below right: Raspberry Tortoni with snifters of raspberry eau de vie

Raspberry Tortoni

So impressive, so irresistible, and yet so simple to make, this raspberry tortoni can remain in the freezer for up to three or four days before serving.

¾ cup granulated sugar
¼ cup water
3 egg whites, at room temperature
7 tablespoons *eau de vie de framboise* (raspberry spirits)
2 cups well-chilled heavy cream
3 pints fresh raspberries
Super-fine sugar
Mint sprigs for garnish

Line the bottom and the long sides of a 6-cup metal loaf pan with waxed paper. (You can use a fluted 6-cup mold without waxed paper if you wish, but removing the tortoni will become more complicated.) Allow enough paper to extend beyond the pan so that it will cover the top. Place the pan in the freezer.

Mix the granulated sugar and water in a small saucepan, bring to a boil, and cook until the mixture registers 237 to 239 degrees on a candy thermometer which is the soft-ball stage. While the sugar is cooking, beat the egg whites until soft peaks form. If you have a standing mixer use it; a hand-held mixer or whisk will not be as efficient in this recipe.

Now slowly drizzle the hot sugar syrup into the egg whites, beating constantly. Continue beating for at least 5 minutes until the egg whites are stiff and glossy. This is called an Italian meringue. Add 3 tablespoons of the framboise, 1 tablespoon at a time, beating for 30 seconds after each addition. Refrigerate this mixture.

Whip the cream with chilled beaters in a chilled bowl until soft peaks form; add 1 tablespoon of the framboise and beat until stiff. Fold the whipped cream into the meringue, spread in the prepared pan, cover the top with waxed paper, and freeze at least 6 hours. Tortoni may be kept frozen for several days before using.

Purée 1 pint of the raspberries. Strain out the seeds, sweeten to taste with super-fine sugar, and add 1½ tablespoons of the framboise. Refrigerate. Sweeten remaining 2 pints whole berries with super-fine sugar if necessary, and sprinkle with remaining 1½ tablespoons framboise. These berries should not be prepared more than 2 or 3 hours before serving. Refrigerate until ready to use.

Refrigerate the serving platter and the dessert plates you will use for the tortoni.

Just before serving run a knife along the *short* sides of the mold (without the waxed paper). Lift off the paper covering the top and unmold the tortoni onto the chilled platter. Peel off the waxed paper. If you used a fancy mold, wring out a dish towel in hot water and place the towel over the mold to loosen the tortoni; or quickly dip the bottom of the mold in hot water, then unmold the tortoni onto a serving platter. Doing this may cause some melting of the outer surface of the dessert so place it immediately in the freezer to firm it.

Pour the raspberry purée around the tortoni in the platter, spoon some of the whole berries on the top of the tortoni, and nestle the rest in the purée. Decorate with mint sprigs. Serve at once.

10 servings

Chocolate Thins

8 tablespoons sweet butter, at room temperature
¾ cup sugar
1 egg yolk
1 teaspoon vanilla extract
⅔ cup sifted flour
⅓ cup cocoa
1 egg white
1 teaspoon cinnamon

Preheat oven to 400 degrees. Butter a 14-by-18-inch cookie sheet with 1 tablespoon of the butter. Do not use a pan that has sides.

Cream the remaining butter with ½ cup of the sugar until light and fluffy. Beat in egg yolk and vanilla. Together sift in the flour and cocoa and stir well. Repeatedly dipping a slender spatula or a large knife into cold water, spread the batter over the cookie sheet, completely covering it out to the edges.

Beat the egg white until stiff and spread it over the batter. Combine the cinnamon with the remaining ¼ cup sugar, and sprinkle it over the egg white. Bake for about 10 minutes.

Immediately cut pastry into diamond, square, or oblong shapes; carefully remove shapes from the cookie sheet with a spatula and cool. The cookies will keep a long time in an air-tight container, particularly a locked one.

About 4 dozen cookies

Lunches, Brunches,

From A Holiday Buffet (pages 155–161), clockwise from top left: Cocktail Party Mussels, Pasta Salad with Tomato Concassé, Fine Liver Pâté, Lemon-Soy Chicken Wings

Picnics, and Parties

WARM WEATHER LUNCHES

Cold soups and salads dominate the warm weather lunch menu, with particular attention paid to fruit. These are often menus suitable to serve out-of-doors—on a lawn, the deck, or a terrace—and they take advantage of seasonal produce. Because mid-day, especially in summer, can be stifling, most of the preparation can take place in the morning or the night before.

The wines suggested are white, or the kind of light reds that can stand a bit of cooling. And in most instances, the food and the wine are suitable for a light supper as well as a luncheon.

A Spring Luncheon

Muscadet

Asparagus and Morels in Mushroom Beurre Blanc
Scallops in White Wine and Cream
Goat Cheeses

Lace Cookies
Fresh Cherries

Light, but so luxurious are the flavors of spring. Slender asparagus, the quintessential vegetable of the season, is married with regal morel mushrooms, another seasonal specialty. The scallops, quick and simple to prepare, are a last minute dish like the asparagus. Following these riches, the acidity of goat cheese puts the palate back in focus. A bowl of shiny, wine-red cherries and delicate lacy cookies are all that are needed for dessert. Purchase firm, plump cherries, if possible by picking them out one by one.

Muscadet—A Breton Wine

Brittany, the seacoast province in the north of France that juts defiantly into the stern Atlantic, is better known for its seafood, its crêpes, and the high starched lace *coiffed* headdresses of the traditional Breton costume than for its wine. Muscadet, made from grapes planted in vineyards that encircle the city of Nantes near the mouth of the Loire River, is a white wine that deserves serious consideration. Little attention is paid to the Breton origin of this Loire wine.

Glinting pale gold in the glass, Muscadet at its best is dry and fresh. The better Muscadets are from the district identified as Sèvres-et-Maine and are also marked *sur lie* meaning that the wine was fermented, then left for several months in contact with the sediment or lees, thereby adding a dimension of complexity to the traditionally light, crisp wine. And if a young Muscadet has a touch of sparkle or *pétillance*, that is alright.

Muscadet is delightful with the fresh asparagus, the plump scallops in white wine sauce, and tangy, snow white goat cheeses—it emphasizes the freshness of a springtime luncheon.

Asparagus and Morels in Mushroom Beurre Blanc

Although fresh morels are a springtime luxury, the dried ones, easier to find and excellent, are used in this recipe because the soaking liquid is essential for the sauce.

1 ounce dried morels
1 cup boiling water
1½ pounds pencil-slim asparagus
10 tablespoons sweet butter, in small pats
Salt
1 tablespoon white wine vinegar
2 tablespoons dry white wine
Freshly ground black pepper
1 tablespoon chopped fresh chervil

Place morels in a dish, cover with the water, and set aside to soak for 1 hour. Drain, pat dry, and spread on paper towels. Boil the soaking liquid in a small saucepan until it is reduced to about 2 tablespoons and set aside.

Snap off the ends of the asparagus where they naturally break. Slant-cut the asparagus in 1½- to 2-inch lengths.

Heat 2 tablespoons of the butter in a large skillet or a wok. Add the asparagus, sprinkle with salt, and stir-fry for about 4 minutes. Add the morels and stir-fry until the asparagus are fairly tender, another 4 to 5 minutes. Divide the asparagus and morels among four salad-size plates and keep warm.

Add vinegar and wine to the mushroom liquid and cook briefly to reduce to 2 tablespoons. Begin to whisk in the remaining 8 tablespoons butter, about a tablespoon at a time, over very low heat, until the sauce has thickened and is creamy. Season with pepper, pour over the asparagus and morels, and dust with chervil. Serve at once.

4 servings

Scallops in White Wine and Cream

2 tablespoons sweet butter
1 small leek (white part only) sliced in fine julienne strips, about 2 inches long
1 small carrot sliced in fine julienne strips, about 2 inches long
1 rib celery sliced in fine julienne strips, about 2 inches long
2 tablespoons minced shallots
1½ pounds sea scallops
1 cup dry white wine
½ teaspoon salt
Freshly ground white pepper
3 egg yolks
1 cup heavy cream
1 teaspoon lemon juice
½ tablespoon finely minced fresh chives

Melt 1 tablespoon of the butter in a heavy 10-inch nonreactive pan. Add the leek, carrot, and celery—there should be at least 1½ cups of these vegetables—to the pan and sauté over medium-low heat until the vegetables are just tender, about 5 minutes. Do not allow them to brown. With a slotted spoon, remove the vegetables from the pan, leaving behind as much butter as possible. Set the vegetables aside in a dish.

Add the remaining tablespoon of butter and the shallots to the pan. Sauté the shallots over medium-low heat until they are soft and translucent, but not brown.

If any of the scallops are particularly large, cut them in half so that the pieces are uniform in size. Add the scallops to the pan and increase the heat. Sauté the scallops, turning them gently but constantly, over medium-high heat until they begin to turn opaque, about 3 minutes. Add the wine, salt, and pepper, lower the heat so the liquid is just barely simmering, and poach the

scallops in the wine until they are cooked through, about 3 to 5 minutes longer. The scallops will be white and show signs of cracking around the edges. Do not overcook.

Using a slotted spoon, remove the scallops from the pan and set aside. Increase heat and cook the wine in the pan until it has reduced by half. The recipe can be prepared in advance up to this point. Beat the egg yolks and cream together, and stir some of the hot cooking liquid into the cream mixture.

Slowly add the cream mixture to the pan, stirring constantly. Cook over low heat, stirring until the sauce has heated through and thickened. Do not allow the sauce to boil or the egg yolks will curdle. Stir in the lemon juice and recheck seasonings.

Return the scallops and the vegetables to the pan and stir gently over low heat just long enough to heat through. Dust with chives and serve.

4 servings

Lace Cookies

¼ cup dark corn syrup
5 tablespoons sweet butter
⅓ cup light brown sugar
½ cup flour
½ cup unsweetened wheat germ
1 teaspoon grated orange zest
½ cup golden raisins

Preheat oven to 325 degrees. Line a baking sheet with parchment paper.

In a heavy saucepan combine the corn syrup, butter, and brown sugar. Bring to a boil, then remove pan from heat.

Combine the flour, wheat germ, and orange zest in a bowl. Add butter mixture and stir until the ingredients are well blended. Stir in raisins. Drop by scant teaspoonfuls onto the prepared baking sheet, leaving at least 2 inches of space between each cookie. You will probably not be able to fit more than 12 to 16 cookies on a sheet.

Bake for 10 minutes, until cookies are light brown around the edges. Slide parchment with cookies onto a smooth surface such as a countertop, and allow to cool for 2 to 3 minutes. Lift cookies off with a spatula and continue cooling on a wire rack.

Makes 24 to 30 cookies

Cool Italian Classics

Pinot Grigio

Tomatoes and Mozzarella
Vitello Tonnato
Roasted Peppers
Summer Rice Salad

Mango Mousse

This menu, an array of cold dishes *al'Italiano*, satisfies the summer appetite. Bright colors and sharp flavors beat the heat.

It is essentially a collection of antipasto items, expanded in quantity to become an alfresco lunch. The annual harvest of scarlet tomatoes and verdant basil, the ripe red and glossy green peppers, and herb-flecked rice take advantage of the season. The classic vitello tonnato, delicate veal poached in white wine (use the pinot grigio), chilled, and sliced with a piquant sauce of tuna fish, anchovies, lemon, and capers in mayonnaise is both mellow and forceful, smoothly textured but sharp in flavor, and as well balanced as the wine. Moreover, it must be made in advance, a blessing in summer.

The dessert is a cool confection, not Italian, but refreshing.

Pinot Grigio

Gray is not the color of summer. A blazing palette of primary reds, vibrant yellows, brilliant blues of sea and sky, the rich greens of foliage, dazzling orange tones of flowers in bloom, and the royal purple of late summer fruits paints a lush season. But pinot grigio—for grigio means gray—is a fine summer wine. In fact, it is a clear golden wine, with an occasional suggestion of coppery tones perhaps, but never gray in color or taste. It is one of the first of the varietal Italian white wines, simply named for the grape.

Landscapes of mountain lakes and Alpine vistas, of Venice's pastel palaces and sparkling strand, of hills and plains that border Yugoslavia and edge the Adriatic in the regions of Trentino–Alto Adige, Veneto, and Friuli–Venezia Giulia are the sources of pinot grigio.

A lightly chilled glass of pinot grigio reveals a bouquet that suggests the vine and a clean, dry flavor touched with fruit. Enough acid provides a lively balance and the aftertaste lingers with a hint of pleasant quenching bitterness. The vitello tonnato, with its briny purée of tuna, calls for a white wine with just these qualities.

Tomatoes and Mozzarella

Fresh, snowy, moist mozzarella bears little resemblance to the waxy supermarket variety and is the only acceptable mozzarella for this classic southern Italian appetizer, also called caprese. *And by fresh I mean no more than one day old.*

1 pound fresh mozzarella (do not use pre-packaged supermarket mozzarella)
3 ripe beefsteak tomatoes
Basil leaves
Extra-virgin olive oil
Freshly ground black pepper

Slice the mozzarella and tomatoes, and arrange on a platter. Adorn with basil leaves. Drizzle with olive oil and season with freshly ground pepper. Serve at room temperature.

6 servings

Vitello Tonnato

Vitello tonnato may be prepared up to several days in advance and refrigerated until ready to serve. It should be removed from the refrigerator and brought almost to room temperature before serving.

2½ pounds boneless veal roast, preferably rump
2 tablespoons olive oil
2 carrots, sliced in thick rounds
2 stalks celery, cut in chunks
1 small onion, quartered
½ cup dry white wine
Sprig of parsley
2 bay leaves
1 clove garlic, peeled and crushed
Salt and freshly ground black pepper
6 anchovy fillets, drained
1 7-ounce can tuna fish, preferably the imported variety packed in oil, drained
2 tablespoons lemon juice
1¼ cups mayonnaise, preferably homemade, made with olive oil (page 58)
1 tablespoon capers, drained
Lemon slices, rolled or flat anchovy fillets, and capers for garnish

Lightly brown the veal roast on all sides in the oil in a heavy casserole. Remove veal from casserole.

Add the carrots, celery, and onion, toss lightly in the oil, then add wine and bring to a simmer. Add parsley, bay leaves, garlic, and salt and pepper to taste. Return meat to casserole, cover tightly, and simmer gently for about 45 minutes, turning once or twice during cooking. The meat should register 150 degrees on an instant-read thermometer and the juices should be very faintly tinged with pink when the meat is done. Do not overcook. Allow the meat to cool to room temperature, covered, in the cooking liquid.

When the meat is cool, remove it from the liquid. Strain the cooking liquid and reserve ½ cup. Tightly wrap the veal and refrigerate until ready to serve.

Place the anchovies, tuna, and lemon juice in a blender or food processor along with the reserved cooking liquid and combine until smooth and creamy.

Stir mayonnaise until smooth and gradually stir in the tuna mixture. Fold in the capers. The sauce should not need any salt.

Slice the veal and arrange on a serving platter. Spoon the sauce over the veal slices, covering them completely. Decorate the platter with lemon slices, anchovies, and capers.

6 servings

Roasted Peppers

2 large sweet red peppers
2 large green peppers
Extra-virgin olive oil
Salt and freshly ground black pepper

Roast the peppers either under a broiler or by holding them with a long fork over a flame until the skin is completely charred. Place the charred peppers in a brown paper bag, close the bag, and set aside for 10 minutes. The skins can now be rubbed off. Rinse the peppers.

Cut the peppers into strips, drizzle with olive oil, season to taste with salt and pepper, and serve.

6 servings

Cool Italian Classics: *Roasted Peppers, Vitello Tonnato,*
Tomatoes with Mozzarella

Summer Rice Salad

Incorporating chopped tomatoes and cucumbers in a rice salad keeps the texture nice and moist.

2 cups water
1⅓ cups long-grain rice
¼ cup olive oil
1 cup chopped onions
1½ cups peeled, seeded, and chopped ripe
   tomatoes
½ cup peeled, seeded, and chopped cucumber
½ cup mayonnaise, preferably homemade (page
   58)
3 tablespoons white wine vinegar
Salt and freshly ground black pepper
2 tablespoons minced fresh herbs
2 tablespoons drained capers

Combine water and rice in a heavy saucepan. Bring to a simmer, cover, and continue to cook until the rice is tender and water is absorbed, about 17 minutes. Set aside, covered, 5 to 10 minutes.

Meanwhile, heat the oil in a skillet, add the onions, and cook over medium heat until soft but not brown. Fold the onion mixture into the cooked rice and set aside. loosely covered, until cooled to room temperature. Fold tomatoes and cucumbers into the salad. Combine the mayonnaise and vinegar, and add it along with some salt and pepper, herbs, and capers to the rice.

6 to 8 servings

Mango Mousse

4 eggs, separated
⅓ cup fresh lime juice
⅔ cup sugar
1 cup mango purée, strained (about 1 ripe mango)
1 tablespoon rum
1 cup heavy cream
Pinch of salt
Pinch of nutmeg

Combine egg yolks and lime juice in the top of a double boiler. Gradually beat in the sugar. Cook over simmering water, stirring slowly, until the mixture thickens enough to coat a spoon. This may take 15 to 20 minutes. When the mixture has thickened, remove it from the heat and stir in the mango purée and the rum. Allow to cool 2 hours in the refrigerator. You can speed up the cooling by placing the mixture in a metal bowl set inside a larger one filled with ice.

Whip the cream. Whip the egg whites with a pinch of salt until stiff and still glossy, but not dry. Fold the egg whites into the mango custard, and then fold in the whipped cream. Pour into a 4-cup soufflé dish, sprinkle with nutmeg, and freeze for at least 4 hours.

Allow to stand at room temperature for 5 to 10 minutes before serving.

6 servings

A Casual Summer Lunch or Supper

Red Table Wine

Bronson's Baked Clams
Chili-Fried Chicken
Sweet Potato Chips
Tossed Salad with Sprouts

Lemon Tart

Fried chicken is casual food for a weekend lunch, a picnic, or an early dinner as the season warms at the solstice. Served out-of-doors if the weather permits, it anchors any convivial occasion. It is a particularly felicitous choice if the party includes children, the universal appeal of fried chicken having long been proven (and it is a dish by no means exclusively American).

Instead of regular fries I slice sweet potatoes in sticks or rounds, plunge them quickly in hot oil to brown lightly, and make sweet potato chips.

The first course of baked clams, a tossed salad fortified with assorted sprouts and seasoned with a yogurt dressing, and a silken textured *tart* lemon tart round out this menu.

Red Table Wine

At first glance a lunch that begins with clams and continues with chicken might suggest a white wine, but I would serve a red. First of all, the clams have a meaty bacon topping and the chicken, assertively seasoned with chili powder, also provides enough richness to support a red wine. Red wine is often preferable to white with poultry.

In keeping with the informal nature of this menu, the wine should be undemanding, pleasant, designed for easy drinking at a very reasonable price. You could offer a white table wine as well for those who might prefer it.

California red table wines have been steadily improving in recent years and many of them, labeled simply red table wine or basic red, or terms to that effect, are serious but moderately priced blends. They bear vintage dates but are usually consistent from year to year.

A Beaujolais-Villages of recent vintage (but not a nouveau), a generic red Burgundy (from France, not California) or Bordeaux, a fruity Côtes du Rhône, a young Chianti or Rioja, or a light, fruity red California zinfandel would all be on my list of enjoyable red wines. Serve them a bit cool, at what might be cellar rather than room temperature.

Bronson's Baked Clams

This is the most delicious and simplest method I know for baking clams, first shown to me by an old friend.

36 littleneck clams on the half shell
4 scallions, chopped
½ pound bacon

Preheat broiler. Arrange the clams on a baking sheet. Scatter scallions evenly over the clams. Cut the bacon into 36 pieces, about 1 inch square. Place a piece of bacon on each clam. Broil clams until bacon is crisp. Serve at once.

6 servings

Chili-Fried Chicken

Try to obtain good quality chili powder, without added salt.

2 frying chickens, 2½ to 3 pounds each
Juice of 1 lemon
1½ cups whole wheat flour
1½ tablespoons chili powder
1½ teaspoons salt, or to taste
1½ cups milk
1 egg, lightly beaten
Vegetable oil for frying

Cut the chicken into serving pieces (or have the butcher do it). The pieces should be fairly uniform in size, so each of the breast pieces should also be cut in half. Remove the wing tips and discard or reserve for making stock. You may also want to remove the backbone section—there is not much meat on it, and it can be frozen for later use in a soup or stock. Skin the chicken pieces and rub them with the lemon juice. Set aside while mixing batter.

Combine the flour, chili powder, and salt in a large bowl. Beat the milk and egg together and stir into flour mixture to make a smooth batter. Add chicken pieces, turning them to coat evenly.

Heat oil to a depth of about ¾ inch in one or more heavy skillets. When the oil is medium-hot (this will register 325 degrees in an electric skillet) add as many pieces of the chicken as will fit in the pan without crowding. Lower heat to medium and fry until the coating becomes a deep nut brown, turning the chicken once. White meat should be done in 20 to 25 minutes, dark meat in about 35 minutes. Juices should run clear when the chicken is pricked with a fork.

Drain chicken on paper towels. Serve at once or keep warm in a 200 degree oven. Chicken can also be served at room temperature.

6 to 8 servings

Sweet Potato Chips

2 pounds sweet potatoes
Vegetable oil for deep frying
Salt and freshly ground pepper

Peel the sweet potatoes and cut into thin sticks or slice into thin rounds. Deep-fry in vegetable oil until lightly browned. Drain on paper towels, season, and serve.

6 servings

Tossed Salad with Sprouts

1 medium head romaine lettuce
1 head red leaf lettuce
1 bunch watercress
1 cup mung bean sprouts
½ cup alfalfa sprouts
½ cup radish sprouts
3 tablespoons rice vinegar
3 tablespoons peanut oil
½ cup plain yogurt
Salt and freshly ground black pepper

Rinse and thoroughly dry the lettuces, remove cores, and tear into bite-size pieces. Rinse and dry the watercress, remove any heavy stems, and combine with the lettuces in a salad bowl. Toss with the mung bean, alfalfa, and radish sprouts.

Beat the vinegar and oil together until thickened and well blended. Stir into yogurt. Season to taste. Toss salad with dressing.

6 servings

Lemon Tart

Sweet Tart Pastry for a 8- or 9-inch tart (page 30)
2 tablespoons orange or lemon marmalade
4 eggs
¾ cup sugar
⅓ cup fresh lemon juice
6 tablespoons cooled melted sweet butter
1 whole lemon
¾ cup heavy cream, whipped

Preheat oven to 425 degrees. Prepare pastry and line a straight-sided 8- or 9-inch tart pan. Prick the bottom. Line with foil and cover with pastry weights or dried beans. Bake for 6 to 8 minutes, until the pastry looks dry but has not begun to color. Remove foil and weights. Do not turn off oven. Spread the partially baked shell with the marmalade.

Beat the eggs with sugar and lemon juice. Stir in the melted butter. Peel all the skin and white pith from the lemon, thus exposing the flesh, and slice it into 9 thin slices; remove any seeds.

Pour the custard mixture into the prepared tart shell and carefully arrange the lemon slices in a circle on the custard, with 1 slice in the center. Bake the tart for 25 to 30 minutes, until the custard is set and the pastry is lightly browned. Cool to room temperature. Serve with unsweetened whipped cream.

6 to 8 servings

Clockwise, top right: Tossed Salad with Sprouts, Chili-Fried Chicken with Sweet Potato Chips, Lemon Tart, Bronson's Baked Clams

Lunch Alfresco

Above: Tofu and Vegetable Salad
Below: Bluefish in Soy Marinade with Buckwheat Pasta

Lunch Alfresco

❀

New York State White Wine

Tofu and Vegetable Salad
Mackerel or Bluefish in Soy Marinade with Buckwheat Pasta

Pink Grapefruit Sorbet

A mélange of bright fresh vegetables with snowy cubes of tofu, and fillets of fresh fish with satiny buckwheat noodles followed by grapefruit sorbet are the elements of a fine summer lunch, many of which are prepared in advance. Oriental flavorings—soy sauce, sesame oil, rice vinegar, and ginger—so appropriate for the tofu, also enhance the fish and noodles.

Prepare this menu a day in advance because several of the dishes require chilling overnight. It is also a menu to satisfy the calorie counters, especially if you omit the final addition of sesame oil to the fish and dress the pasta with a little of the fish sauce instead of oil.

New York State White Wine

New York is the second largest grape-growing state in the nation after California. But when vinifera, or European varietal grapes are considered, it ranks third, behind Washington. For the serious wine drinker, vinifera grapes are the only ones worth considering.

In recent years, New York State wineries have increased production of vinifera wines. These are whites—chardonnay, sauvignon blanc, and riesling, for the most part—because except for an atypical Southeastern corner of the state on Long Island, the winters are too severe and the growing season too short to permit the cultivation of red varietals such as merlot, cabernet sauvignon, and pinot noir.

A category of grapes called European hybrids, which are a cross between vinifera and native American grapes, have been grown successfully upstate, especially in the Hudson Valley. The most interesting of these is the crisp, white seyval blanc. The red European hybrids might satisfy the chauvinistic Empire Stater but they do not have the finesse of the European varietals.

Look for lightly fruited New York rieslings and chardonnays to accompany this fish lunch with its complex, spicy flavors. My second choice? A Washington State riesling.

Tofu and Vegetable Salad

1 cup slant-cut carrot slices
½ pound firm tofu, diced
¾ cup sliced mushrooms
3 red radishes, sliced
1 green pepper, thinly sliced
1 sweet red pepper, thinly sliced
¼ cup chopped scallions
1 teaspoon minced fresh ginger
2 tablespoons rice vinegar
1 teaspoon Dijon mustard
1 tablespoon light soy sauce
¼ cup vegetable oil
A few drops Chinese hot oil
¼ cup parsley sprigs

Steam the carrots for about 5 minutes, until crisp-tender. Rinse under cold water and drain well. Place in a bowl with the tofu, mushrooms, radishes, green and red peppers, scallions, and ginger.

Mix the vinegar with the mustard and soy sauce. Beat in the oils until well blended. Pour dressing over salad, add parsley, and toss lightly.

4 servings

Mackerel or Bluefish in Soy Marinade with Buckwheat Pasta

½ tablespoon minced fresh ginger
1 clove garlic, chopped
1 medium onion, thinly sliced
1 tablespoon peanut oil
1½ pounds mackerel or bluefish fillets
¼ cup rice vinegar
3 tablespoons sugar
½ cup light soy sauce
½ teaspoon Chinese five-spice powder
1 cup water (approximately)
3 tablespoons Oriental sesame oil
½ pound Japanese buckwheat noodles (soba)
3 tablespoons chopped scallions

In a large skillet sauté the ginger, garlic, and onion in peanut oil until very lightly browned.

Place the fish fillets skin side down in a single layer on top of the vegetables. Mix the rice vinegar, sugar, and soy sauce together, then stir in the five-spice powder,

and pour this mixture over the fish. Add a cup or slightly more than a cup of water so the liquid covers the fish.

Bring to a simmer, and simmer until the fish is just cooked, about 8 minutes. Remove from heat.

Using a large spatula, transfer the fish to a shallow glass or ceramic dish, draining as much of the liquid as possible back into the pan.

Reheat the liquid in the pan and boil it down until it is reduced to barely a cup and is somewhat syrupy. Stir in 1 tablespoon of the sesame oil. Pour the reduced liquid over the fish and refrigerate the fish overnight. The liquid will jell.

Just before serving, bring 2 to 3 quarts of salted water to a boil and cook the pasta until al dente, 4 to 5 minutes. Drain, rinse in cold water, and drain again thoroughly. Mix pasta with remaining 2 tablespoons sesame oil. Scatter the chopped scallions over the fish in its aspic and serve with pasta on the side.

4 servings

Pink Grapefruit Sorbet

1 6-ounce can frozen pink grapefruit concentrate
1½ cans (9 ounces) cold water
1 tablespoon vodka
2 tablespoons super-fine sugar
½ pint ripe strawberries, halved

Mix the frozen pink grapefruit concentrate with the water, vodka, and sugar. To prepare sorbet without an ice cream maker, freeze the mixture in a shallow metal pan (or in ice cube trays) until firm. With a sharp knife, cut it into blocks about 1 inch square and place them in the bowl of a food processor. Process until the sorbet is uniformly smooth. Return the sorbet immediately to the freezer container and freeze again for at least 2 hours.

If you have an ice cream machine or a sorbet maker, transfer the concentrate, water, vodka, and sugar mixture into it and freeze according to manufacturer's directions. Serve at once or transfer to a freezer container and freeze until ready to serve.

Place the sorbet in the refrigerator for 15 minutes before serving to allow it to soften slightly.

To serve, divide half the strawberry slices evenly among 4 chilled stemmed goblets. Scoop sorbet over the strawberries, then cover with the remaining berries.

4 servings

COOL WEATHER
LUNCHES

W hen the weather acquires a seasonal nip, a lunch or brunch should be designed to satisfy appetites. Instead of white wine we prefer red, instead of cold pasta salad our tastes run to hot, and a hearty soup is in order. Dessert can be rich. Two of these lunch menus focus on pasta, another is a colorful and highly flavored spread of Hispanic inspiration, and yet another is anchored by a thick and savory soup.

An Autumn Lunch

Chianti Classico

Calamari Salad
Eggplant Lasagne
Green Beans with Garlic

Individual Fig Tartlets

Our understanding of Italian cuisine has certainly changed and become enlightened. Travel, restaurants, and cookbooks have revealed that Italian food does not begin and end with pasta in red sauce sealed beneath a melt of cheese. The prominent role that vegetables play has been made evident. In fact, by substituting the marinated mushrooms on page 88 for the first-course Calamari Salad, this menu becomes vegetarian.

Lasagne, once given an exclusively Neapolitan-American interpretation with macaroni pasta, ricotta cheese, and sausages is also a Northern Italian specialty. The lasagne in this menu is made with sheets of egg pasta, homemade if possible, layered with eggplant, parsley, Parmesan cheese, and two sauces.

The repast opens with a cold calamari salad. Calamari, or squid, is a vastly underutilized variety of seafood in this country, but adored by Italians. Instead of a traditional salad, green beans are glossed with warm, garlic-infused olive oil, and served on the side. The rich fig tartlets are quickly assembled on rounds of pastry and served at once for a lush, sophisticated dessert to suit a *new* Italian menu.

Chianti Classico—The New Chianti

Red-and-white checked tablecloths. Straw-covered bottles filled with sharp red wine. More of the same bottles hold flickering candles that illuminate the charming little restaurant. Plates of steaming pasta bathed in basic red are served. A familiar flashback? Remember the round bottles wrapped in straw and containing a harsh red wine called Chianti?

That Chianti and those bottles have become memories. The peasant wine in the romantic flask that symbolized Chianti for an entire generation of Americans has grown up and matured. Nostalgia buffs may be disappointed but wine lovers appreciate the change.

All Chianti is still made basically from the dark, sturdy sangiovese grape that flourishes in the russet Tuscan countryside around Florence and southward to Siena. Some lush red canaiolo is blended in to soften the wine. White grapes are also added to lighten the wine but the percentage allowed has been reduced considerably. Moreover, atypical red grapes such as cabernet sauvignon are now permitted in the blend.

These changes have gradually allowed producers to achieve a more consistently stylish and elegant Chianti, without harshness and deserving a high-shouldered Bordeaux bottle. Many of the Chiantis that reflect the new style are labeled *Classico*, the area at the heart of the seven zones of the Chianti district. Chianti styles vary from youthful and fruity to bigger and more complex.

The new, elegant Chianti suits a refined version of lasagne, both illustrating an enlighened attitude toward Italian dining. A Tuscan white wine could begin this autumn lunch (or supper) with the calamari salad. Since this is a party for six to eight, you will require more than one bottle of wine so it makes sense to begin with a white.

Eggplant Lasagne

1½ pound eggplant
6 tablespoons olive oil
2 cloves garlic, finely chopped
⅓ cup chopped onions
3 cups fresh ripe or Italian canned tomatoes, peeled and chopped
½ teaspoon oregano
Salt and freshly ground black pepper
3 tablespoons fresh parsley
8 tablespoons butter
6 tablespoons flour
4 cups milk
¾ pound fresh egg pasta, in sheets or wide strips (*see note*)
3 tablespoons dry bread crumbs
¾ cup freshly grated Italian Parmesan cheese

Cut off the ends of the eggplant, and slice it into thin horizontal slices. Oil a baking sheet with some of the olive oil, and arrange the eggplant slices in a single layer. You may have to do this in two batches. Brush the eggplant with more of the olive oil and place under the broiler. Broil until lightly browned, turn, and broil on the other side. Repeat with remaining eggplant slices. Set aside.

Heat the remaining olive oil (about 2 tablespoons) in a heavy saucepan. Add the garlic and onions, and sauté them until soft but not browned. Add the tomatoes and oregano, and salt and pepper to taste. Simmer sauce for 15 minutes. Stir in parsley and set aside.

To make a béchamel sauce, melt the butter over low heat in a heavy saucepan. Add the flour and stir with a whisk until well blended, then increase the heat to medium. Whisk in the milk. Cook, stirring constantly, until the sauce is thick and smooth. Season to taste with salt. Cover and set aside.

Preheat oven to 350 degrees. Cut the pasta into large, manageable squares or rectangles to fit a baking pan 8- or 9-by-13 inches.

Bring a pot of salted water to a boil and cook the pieces of pasta, 1 or 2 at a time, for just 1 minute. Drain briefly on paper towels. Spread a little tomato sauce, just to film the bottom of the baking pan. Place a layer of pasta over the sauce. Arrange a single layer of eggplant over the pasta, and sprinkle with one-third of the bread crumbs. Spread half the remaining tomato sauce over the eggplant, then spread with one-third of the béchamel, and sprinkle with one-third of the cheese.

Calamari Salad

2 pounds squid, cleaned
⅔ cup extra-virgin olive oil
4 tablespoons white wine vinegar
Juice of 2 lemons
⅔ cup finely chopped red onion
2 large cloves garlic, minced
The heart plus 3 to 4 center stalks of 1 bunch of celery, chopped
1 teaspoon oregano
½ teaspoon salt, or to taste
Generous grinding of fresh black pepper
1 lemon, in thin slices

Boil the squid in 3 quarts of boiling water just until it turns opaque and firms up, about 3 minutes. Drain and rinse with cold water. Slice the bodies into thin rings, and chop the triangular fins and tentacles. Place in a glass or ceramic bowl.

Add the remaining ingredients, mix well, and refrigerate for at least 30 minutes before serving. The squid may be allowed to marinate for several days. Garnish each serving with lemon slices.

6 to 8 servings

Repeat these layers in the same order, ending with a layer of pasta. Spread the top pasta layer with the remaining béchamel, sprinkle on the remaining cheese and bread crumbs, and place in the oven to bake for 30 to 40 minutes, until the top is lightly browned. Allow to sit for 5 minutes or so before cutting and serving.

6 servings

Note: To make fresh pasta, blend 2 cups of flour, 3 eggs, 1 tablespoon of olive oil, and a pinch of salt; roll the pasta by hand or machine. Fresh pasta can also be purchased in sheets for lasagne in Italian specialty shops. The dried lasagne strips that come in boxes can also be used if necessary but they have a completely different texture and require longer boiling.

Green Beans with Garlic

1½ pounds fresh green beans, trimmed
¼ cup extra-virgin olive oil
2 large cloves garlic, sliced
Salt and freshly ground black pepper
2 tablespoons chopped flat leaf parsley

Blanch or steam beans for 5 to 6 minutes, until they are crisp-tender but still bright green. Refresh under cold water and drain well.

Heat the oil in a saucepan or skillet. Add the garlic and cook over low heat until the garlic is tender but not brown. Cool the oil briefly, then pour it, still warm, over the beans. Allow the beans to marinate for at least 1 hour.

Season to taste with salt and pepper, and sprinkle with parsley before serving.

6 to 8 servings

Individual Fig Tartlets

The season for fresh figs extends from midsummer through October. If figs are not available, other good desserts with this menu are the Pears in Red Wine (page 42) or the Pear-Almond Cake (page 35).

½ cup all-purpose flour
½ cup whole wheat flour
½ teaspoon salt
4 ounces cream cheese, in small pieces
8 tablespoons sweet butter, in small pieces
3 tablespoons sugar
8 to 10 fresh figs
1½ tablespoons finely chopped pecans
Vanilla ice cream

Preheat oven to 500 degrees. Mix flours and salt together. Using a pastry blender, two knives, or your fingertips, blend the cream cheese and butter into the flour until a dough can be formed. This pastry does not come out well in a food processor.

Roll the pastry on a floured board to ¼ inch thickness. Cut six to eight 5-inch rounds (the cover of a 1-pint plastic container makes a good template). Reroll the pastry scraps if necessary. Transfer pastry rounds to a foil-lined baking sheet. Sprinkle each one with ½ teaspoon of the sugar. Slice the figs and arrange them in a pattern on the pastry. Sprinkle again with remaining sugar and the pecans. Bake for 10 minutes. Serve warm or cool, with vanilla ice cream on the side.

6 to 8 servings

A Pasta Menu for Lunch or Supper

Barbaresco

Smoked Fish Spread
Rigatoni with Hot Sausage and Broccoli

Fresh Pears and Gorgonzola

Prune Cake

Lunches (or suppers) are less elaborate than dinners and, as such, should make less severe demands on the cook's available time. This menu is a case in point. Except for the cake, which requires about half an hour to mix and over an hour to bake and cool, this might be the speediest menu in the book.

Its inspiration is Italian but not unremittingly so. The fish spread appetizer, served with country bread or rough-hewn toast, is merely a savory starter of no particular ethnic allegiance. But the pasta is very Italian, prepared in a trice and providing the bright crunch of broccoli, the rich mellowness of cream, and the mouth-filling spiciness of hot sausage over big, textured pasta.

Gorgonzola imported from Italy and ripe pears to follow is a classic combination, and the prune cake, rich without being overly sweet, becomes an excellent accompaniment for cups of inky espresso. Omit the cake (or substitute some purchased baked goods) and you can have this meal on the table in thirty minutes.

Barbaresco

With but a few exceptions, red wine is more suited to pasta than white. But unless the pasta is prepared in a lusty meat or game sauce, the red should be light to medium-bodied rather than robust. In the traditional format, with the pasta preceding a main course, this combination is logical because it permits a bigger red wine to follow. When pasta is the focus of a lunch, there is greater flexibility in the choice of a wine.

With a pasta I would be most inclined to select an Italian wine. This pasta dish, spiked with hot sausages and followed by pungent Gorgonzola, is complemented by a nebbiolo red, made from the noble red grape of northern Italy. These wines range from hugely magistral to light and relatively austere, including the sturdy, long-lived Barolos, the somewhat lighter Barbarescos, and the graceful Gattinaras and Spannas of the Piedmont, as well as the smoothly elegant, often delicate reds of the Valtellina.

My choice would be a Barbaresco, well structured and endowed with fruit and yet less powerful than a Barolo. It will stand up to the sausage yet not overwhelm the pasta, and is superb with the cheese. A good aperitif with the fish would be a bottle of *brut* (bone-dry) Italian sparkling wine, a Gavi (the premier white wine of the Piedmont), or a pinot grigio.

Smoked Fish Spread

1½ cups smoked bluefish, mackerel, eel, or trout, skinned and shredded
½ cup sour cream
1 tablespoon lemon juice
¼ cup finely minced scallions
Freshly ground black pepper

Mash the fish with the sour cream until it is uniformly finely textured. Work in the lemon juice and scallions and season with pepper.

Mold into a dome or loaf, or pack into a crock. Serve as a cocktail spread with bread, toast, or crackers.

About 2 cups

Rigatoni with Hot Sausage and Broccoli

1 pound Italian hot sausage
1 large bunch broccoli
1 pound rigatoni
1½ cups heavy cream
Salt and freshly ground black pepper
Freshly grated Italian Parmesan cheese

Divide the sausages into separate links, prick them lightly, and place in a skillet with water to a depth of ½ inch. Simmer, pricking from time to time, until the water evaporates. Continue cooking the sausages in the pan, turning them from time to time, until they are lightly browned on all sides. Remove from heat and slice.

Cut the broccoli into small flowerets. You should have about 4 cups of broccoli flowerets (reserve the stems for another use such as making soup). Steam the flowerets for 2 to 3 minutes, until bright green and crisp-tender. Set aside, uncovered.

Meanwhile bring 6 quarts of salted water to a boil, boil the rigatoni until al dente (about 8 minutes), and drain.

Place the sausage rounds in a very large skillet. Cook briefly to reheat, then add the cream. Add the broccoli and the drained rigatoni and cook, stirring, until the cream has thickened somewhat and coats the pasta, and the other ingredients are heated through. Season to taste with salt and pepper and serve, dusted with Parmesan.

4 to 6 servings

Fresh Pears and Gorgonzola

Fresh pears ripen from the inside out and they will ripen better, to peak flavor and texture, off the tree. Buy those that are unblemished and firm, and allow them to ripen for a few days at room temperature. Except for Bartletts, which turn yellow, most pear varieties do not change color as they ripen. The Bartlett is an excellent all-purpose eating pear (and there is now a red variety as well). Anjou, in season late in the winter, is also very good. The most succulent (and fragile) of pears is the Comice. Brown Bosc pears have a pleasantly grainy texture.

As with pears, there are several types of Gorgonzola cheese, some sharper, some mellower, with the latter called *Dolcelatte*. Above all, be sure that the Gorgonzola you purchase is imported from Italy.

Prune Cake

1 cup pitted prunes
2 cups whole wheat pastry flour
2 teaspoons baking powder
½ teaspoon baking soda
½ teaspoon mace
¼ teaspoon ground cardamom
8 tablespoons sweet butter, at room temperature
1⅓ cups sugar
2 eggs
1 cup milk
3 tablespoons Armagnac or Cognac
1 teaspoon vanilla extract

Preheat oven to 350 degrees. Butter and flour an 8-inch springform cake pan or a 9-by-5-by-3-inch loaf pan.

Quarter the prunes and toss with 1 tablespoon of the flour. Set aside. Sift remaining flour with the baking powder, baking soda, mace, and cardamom.

Cream the butter. Add 1 cup of the sugar and beat until fluffy. Beat in eggs one at a time. Stir in dry ingredients alternately with the milk, mixing just until ingredients are blended. Lightly fold in prunes. Spread batter in prepared pan and bake until a cake tester comes out clean, about 1 hour and 10 minutes.

Dissolve remaining ⅓ cup sugar in Armagnac or Cognac, and simmer for a couple of minutes in a small saucepan. Spoon this glaze over the warm cake. Allow cake to cool completely before removing from pan.

8 servings

Lunch, Brunch, or Supper for Twelve

Red and White Riojas, or Beer

Grilled Cumin Shrimp
Gazpacho Salad
Picadillo
Sherried Black Beans
Saffron Rice

Oranges in Wine
Spice Squares

I find that once a party expands beyond eight, the nature of the food that I serve changes. Stews and casseroles become preferable, because with a group of this size you enter the realm of quantity cooking. The casserole dish works best for another reason: it is easier to serve buffet style. And for larger groups that sort of informality seems preferable. It is also excellent for lap service or sitting on the floor because it does not require knives, just forks.

Picadillo, a minced meat dish of Cuban or South American origin, is an excellent buffet preparation. Not only is it tasty but with its garnish of bacon-wrapped bananas and sprinkling of nuts and chili, its side dishes of yellow rice and black beans, it is simply stunning. Picadillo is a triumph for lowly hamburger meat. This threesome is fine prepared early in the day and reheated.

Red and White Riojas, or Beer

The hearty, rustic, assertive flavors of a picadillo call for red wine in my book, even though you could serve beer.

And since the menu has a Hispanic tone, the wines of Rioja, the major Spanish region producing quality table wines, are appropriate.

Most Riojas are red. White wine accounts for a relatively small production. A given winery, called a bodega in Spain, usually makes both white and red. The whites are light, pleasant, and at their best are fresh and fruity. Select a recent vintage to pour as an aperitif, or if this menu is served as a lunch for those guests who would prefer to sip white wine throughout.

Red Riojas are elegant wines, full-bodied and fruity, displaying a youthful charm that often belies extensive aging. They are usually blends of several grapes, dominated by a variety called *tempranillo*, which seems uniquely suited to the chalky, uninviting soil of the hilly terrain in the north of Spain.

Young Riojas, gentle of tariff, provide extremely appealing drinking, and older vintages labeled *Reserva* or *Gran Reserva*, also very reasonably priced, would add a sumptuous touch to a party such as this.

Grilled Cumin Shrimp

8 tablespoons sweet butter
2 teaspoons ground turmeric
1½ teaspoons ground cumin
1 teaspoon ground coriander
1½ teaspoons salt
Juice of 2 lemons
2 pounds large shrimp, shelled and deveined

Preheat broiler. Melt the butter in a saucepan. Stir in the turmeric, cumin, coriander, salt, and lemon juice.

Arrange the shrimp in a single layer in a shallow baking dish. Spread the butter mixture over them. Broil in a very hot broiler until the shrimp are glazed and golden brown, about 8 minutes. Skewer with toothpicks and serve at once.

12 hors d'oeuvre servings

Gazpacho Salad

1¼ cups extra-virgin olive oil
An 8-inch piece of Italian bread, in ½-inch-thick slices
3 cloves garlic
3 pounds ripe tomatoes, peeled, seeded, and chopped
1 small green pepper, seeded and chopped
1 small sweet red pepper, seeded and chopped
1 cup chopped scallions
4 cucumbers, peeled, seeded, and chopped
4 tablespoons chopped fresh parsley
½ cup red wine vinegar
Salt and freshly ground black pepper

Heat ½ cup of the oil in a heavy skillet and sauté the bread slices, turning once, until they are golden. Add a little more oil if necessary. Drain croutons on paper towels. When drained and crisp, rub them thoroughly on both sides with garlic. Discard the garlic.

Combine the tomatoes, peppers, scallions, cucumbers, and parsley in a bowl. Break the croutons into ½ inch pieces and add them. Stir in the vinegar and remaining ¾ cup oil, season to taste, and refrigerate until ready to serve.

12 servings

Picadillo

3 pounds ground beef round
1 cup dry sherry
4 tablespoons olive oil
2 cups chopped onions
2 cups chopped green pepper
2 large cloves garlic, minced
1 cup sliced and pitted California olives
2 tablespoons capers
1 cup raisins
1 teaspoon oregano
1 teaspoon ground cumin
½ teaspoon cayenne pepper, or to taste
2 teaspoons salt, or to taste
½ cup tomato paste
2 bay leaves
¼ cup finely chopped and seeded fresh green chili pepper
½ cup slivered blanched almonds
4 medium bananas
8 strips bacon

Using a fork, mix the meat with the sherry in a bowl and set aside.

Heat the olive oil in a large skillet. Add the onions and green pepper and sauté over low heat until they are tender and just beginning to brown. Stir in the garlic and continue cooking for another minute. Stir in the olives, capers, and raisins. Increase heat to medium. Gradually stir in the meat, mixing well to break it up and incorporate it with the other ingredients. Be sure to add any juices from the meat. Continue to cook the meat, stirring, until it has lost its color. Stir in the oregano, cumin, cayenne pepper, salt, tomato paste, bay leaves, and chili pepper. Cover and cook over low heat for 45 minutes. (This part may be prepared in advance and reheated before serving.)

Just before serving the picadillo, toast the almonds in the oven or by stirring them in a dry skillet over medium heat until they are light brown. Set aside. Peel the bananas and cut each into six pieces. Cut the bacon strips in thirds. Wrap a piece of bacon around each of the banana chunks, secure with a toothpick, and broil, turning once, until the bacon is crisp.

Spoon the picadillo into a large platter or shallow serving dish (or you can serve it right from the skillet in which it is cooked). Garnish with a sprinkling of toasted almonds and a border of broiled bananas and bacon.

12 servings

Sherried Black Beans

   2 cups dried black beans
   ½ cup finely diced salt pork
   1 cup chopped onions
   1 cup chopped green pepper
   2 cloves garlic, minced
   2 teaspoons salt
   2 tablespoons dry sherry

Rinse beans and place in a bowl. Cover with boiling water and set aside. In a saucepan of at least 4-quart capacity, sauté the salt pork just until it begins to brown. Add the onions and green pepper and continue to cook over medium heat until soft. Add garlic and continue to cook, stirring, for another minute or so.

Drain beans and add them to the saucepan along with 3 cups water. Bring to a boil, lower heat, and simmer, covered, for 1½ hours, or just until tender. Add salt and simmer uncovered for another 30 minutes. Watch the beans carefully, and stir once or twice to be sure they do not stick to the bottom of the pan.

Remove 1 cup of the beans, mash them, and stir them back in along with the sherry. The beans should be in a thick liquid, but not soupy. (If there is too much liquid, simmer a little longer.) Check seasonings and serve. If not served at once, keep at room temperature and then gently reheat, covered, for about 10 minutes.

12 servings

Saffron Rice

   4 tablespoons olive oil
   3 cups long-grain rice
   3 teaspoons salt
   ¼ teaspoon powdered saffron
   5⅓ cups boiling water

Heat the oil in a saucepan or heatproof casserole. Add the rice and stir over low heat until the grains are coated with oil and have turned milky. Do not allow rice to brown. Stir in the salt and saffron, and slowly pour in the water. Stir once more, cover tightly, and cook over low heat until all the liquid has been absorbed and the rice is tender, 15 to 18 minutes. Set aside, covered, for 10 minutes before serving.

12 servings

Oranges in Wine

If clementines, the tiny seedless tangerines imported from Morocco, are in season you can use thirty-six of them, peeled and sectioned, instead of oranges. This greatly simplifies the preparation, especially since clementines are seedless. But you will still need the cup of grated orange peel.

    20 juice oranges
    1⅓ cups sugar
    2   cups orange juice
    2   cups slightly sweet white wine
    1   cup Grand Marnier

Grate 1 cup orange peel. Combine with ⅓ cup of the sugar and ⅔ cup of the orange juice in a saucepan. Bring to a simmer, and simmer until the orange peel turns translucent and the liquid is syrupy. Remove from heat and set aside.

Peel the oranges down to the flesh with a sharp knife. Be careful to remove all the white pith. With a small, sharp knife, separate each orange segment from the membrane, cutting as close to the membrane as possible. Remove any seeds. Place the orange segments in a heavy saucepan with the remaining 1 cup sugar, 1⅓ cups orange juice, the wine, and Grand Marnier.

Bring to a simmer, and then immediately remove the orange segments with a slotted spoon and transfer them to a bowl. Boil down the cooking liquid until it becomes syrupy. Mix with the orange peel and its syrup. Pour this mixture over the orange segments and refrigerate until ready to serve.

12 servings

Spice Squares

This unusual cake is made without eggs. I don't know the origin of the recipe but I can remember my mother baking it.

    2   teaspoons baking soda
    ¼   cup warm water
    2   cups unsweetened applesauce
    2   cups sugar
    3   cups flour
    1   cup vegetable oil
    2   teaspoons cinnamon
    ½   teaspoon ground cloves
    1   teaspoon nutmeg
    1   teaspoon grated orange peel
    Pinch of salt
    1   cup chopped pecans
    1   cup raisins
    ½   cup chopped dates

Preheat oven to 300 degrees. Grease and flour a 9-by-13-inch baking pan. Dissolve baking soda in warm water. Set aside.

In a large bowl mix the remaining ingredients except the pecans, raisins, and dates. Stir in the baking soda mixture, then add the pecans, raisins, and dates. Spread the batter in the prepared pan and bake for 1 hour. Cut into squares when cooled.

12 to 16 servings

Brunch with a Portuguese Touch

Vinho Verde

Caldo Verde
(*Portuguese Vegetable Soup*)
Frittata of Sturgeon and Onions
Carottes Rapées

Two-Crust Pumpkin Pie

The central attraction of a winter brunch is a satisfying caldo verde, a thick Portuguese potato soup with finely shredded greens and nuggets of garlic sausage added to it for flavor and color. Like most soups, this one can be prepared in advance and reheated, a strategy that actually improves the flavor.

Following, a frittata or open-face omelet with a filling of smoked sturgeon and onions is served, for what is a brunch without some kind of smoked fish? Be sure to provide plenty of good bread to accompany the soup and frittata. Either the Walnut Wheat Bread, page 66, or the Honey Cornmeal-Wheat Bread, page 100, would be excellent.

Dessert is an unusual double-crust pumpkin pie served warm, with a wedge of Cheddar cheese.

Vinho Verde

Green soup matched with a green wine? That's one way of looking at it. *Vinho verde* means green wine but the greenness refers to its youth. The wine is made from grapes that are barely ripe. It is light, easy to sip on a Sunday afternoon when friends gather at brunch time, or for an early supper, with one eye on gridiron strategies unfolding on the TV screen, perhaps.

Vinho verde sounds green but actually comes in normal wine colors, red and white. More red than white is made in Portugal but more of the white is exported to the United States. Because of the name one might be tempted to detect a glint of green in the delicate white wine but the white vinho verdes are actually among the palest wines produced anywhere.

Light and refreshing, it is a delightful sipping wine to accompany casual dining on an afternoon warmed by a glowing hearth, team spirit, or rays of winter sunshine. The soup comes from the same northern region of Portugal as the wine. And although a Portuguese red wine might marry nicely with the soup, the frittata requires a fairly austere white wine.

When it comes to dessert, a glass of mellow, nut-sweet port or Madeira, Portugal's illustrious fortified wines and the jewels in her winemaking crown, would not be a mistake.

Caldo Verde
(Portuguese Vegetable Soup)

Kale or cabbage leaves, the greener the better, are the traditional greens for this soup. Savory cabbage is likewise excellent. Spinach, Swiss chard, collards, or turnip greens may be used, or in combination. About ten ounces of greens, well washed and trimmed of all heavy spines and ribs, should be enough.

½ pound smoked garlic sausage, preferably Portuguese linguica, although chorizo or kielbasa may be used
½ cup extra-virgin olive oil
1 large onion, diced
4 to 5 medium boiling potatoes (about 1½ pounds), peeled and sliced about ½ inch thick
1 tablespoon salt, or to taste
Freshly ground black pepper
5 cups packed very finely shredded greens

Place the sausage in a heavy 3- to 4-quart saucepan, add ⅓ cup water, and cook until the water has evaporated. Add 2 tablespoons of the olive oil and sauté the sausage over medium heat until it is just beginning to brown. Drain the sausage, leaving the oil in the pan. Set the sausage aside, and slice into rounds.

Add the onion and sauté over low heat until soft but not brown. Add the potatoes and 8 cups of water. Bring to a boil, add salt, and cook until the potatoes are very soft, about 15 minutes.

Drain the potatoes and mash them with a fork or a potato masher. You can use a food processor, but the texture will not be as grainy. Return the mashed potatoes to the pot and stir to dissolve them in the cooking liquid. Season with pepper.

Add the greens, sausage, and 4 tablespoons of the olive oil to the soup. Bring to a boil and simmer for 5 minutes. Drizzle about a teaspoon of oil on top of each serving of soup.

8 servings

Frittata of Sturgeon and Onions

This recipe is for one omelet serving four. To serve eight according to the brunch menu, make two frittatas in two skillets. Be sure the skillet or skillets are well oiled and that you have loosened the frittata before you turn it.

3 to 4 tablespoons olive oil
2 large onions, chopped
6 eggs, beaten
½ pound smoked sturgeon, diced
1 tablespoon chopped fresh parsley
Salt and freshly ground black pepper

Heat 3 tablespoons of the oil in a heavy 9-inch skillet, preferably cast iron. Add the onions and cook very slowly, covered, until they are tender but not brown.

Meanwhile mix the eggs with the sturgeon and parsley. Season to taste with salt and pepper (go easy on the salt because the fish may be salty). When the onions are tender remove them from the skillet with a slotted spoon, leaving as much of the oil as possible in the skillet. Add the onions to the egg mixture.

Add additional oil to coat the bottom and sides of the skillet if necessary. Reheat the skillet. When it is quite hot, pour in the egg mixture, filling the pan evenly, and cook over medium heat until the eggs have set on the bottom and are golden brown but the mixture is still creamy on top, 5 to 7 minutes. Loosen the omelet around the sides, and if necessary, along the bottom with a spatula.

Position a large platter over the skillet. Using pot holders, hold the plate and skillet tightly together and invert the omelet onto the plate, then quickly slide it back into the skillet. Continue cooking the underside until it is golden brown, another 3 to 5 minutes.

Serve directly from the skillet, or transfer to a serving platter.

4 servings; double recipe to serve 8

Caldo Verde

Carottes Rapées

1½ pounds carrots, scraped and grated
¼ cup finely chopped flat leaf parsley
3 tablespoons minced fresh chives
2 tablespoons white wine vinegar
3 tablespoons olive oil
Freshly ground black pepper

Combine all the ingredients and allow to marinate for at least 30 minutes.

8 servings

Two-Crust Pumpkin Pie

My family does not care for the traditional creamy, ginger-flavored pumpkin pie made with pumpkin purée. So one Thanksgiving I tried baking a pie using chunks of pumpkin, along with raisins, brown sugar, nutmeg, and lemon juice, as if it were an apple pie. The double-crust pumpkin pie was an astonishing success. Serve it warm for this brunch, with wedges of Cheddar cheese.

5 cups pumpkin, peeled and cut in 1-inch cubes
⅔ cup raisins
1 cup light brown sugar
3 tablespoons flour
2 tablespoons lemon juice
½ teaspoon ground ginger
¼ teaspoon nutmeg
¼ teaspoon ground cloves
Basic Pastry for a two-crust, 9-inch pie (page 55)
2 tablespoons sweet butter
Cheddar cheese

Preheat oven to 425 degrees. Combine the pumpkin, raisins, brown sugar, flour, lemon juice, and spices in a large bowl.

Line a 9-inch pie pan with pastry for the bottom crust. Spoon filling mixture into the pastry. Dot with butter. Cover with the top crust. Seal and crimp edges. Cut a few decorative slits in the top to allow steam to escape.

Bake for 15 minutes. Reduce heat to 350 degrees and bake until crust is golden brown, about 1 hour longer.

Serve warm or cooled to room temperature, with Cheddar cheese.

8 servings

Fresh eggs, onions, and smoked sturgeon for frittata

A TRIO OF PICNICS

Spread a magic carpet, rub a lamp, and produce a feast. An adventure on a moment's notice on a warm but not sultry afternoon takes place beneath an azure sky in a grassy meadow perfumed with wild flowers, alongside a gently rolling surf, or in the shade of a bosky glade. It is delivered on request.

It requires more than storybook planning to produce a storybook picnic setting. Some imagination, organization, and wit replace a fairy tale. Plan an exotic picnic of a hamper filled to overflowing with surprises, not tuna on white. Rummage the attic and around the house. Gather accessories by the armload to inspire the menu. Create a mood.

An Indian picnic fit for the Raj is arrayed on trays and in baskets on a floral-printed spread borrowed for the day from the bed in the spare room. An open-air Mexican buffet is set out in pottery bowls on a brightly woven blanket, that beachside bargain lugged home from vacation years ago. An assortment of Greek *meze* (traditional hors d'oeuvres) is served on a curly flokati rug on loan from the foyer. With the theme thus established, the decorating done, so to speak, the food and drink are coordinated to match.

Ideal foods for a picnic are those that are most appealing halfway between hot and cold. ("Room temperature" would have to describe picnic food only in the most unfortunate meteorological circumstances, but it does give you the idea.) Many cuisines, notably Indian, Mexican, and Greek, depend largely on foods like this. They do not strain the limited confines of the cooler or require the bother of lighting a fire. Lemon, lime, vinegar, and yogurt marinades keep the food appetizing and fresh.

Reserve insulated bags and jugs for maintaining drinks, fruit, and a few other items such as an Indian-style cold soup at their most refreshing. Plan to have trays, plates, and baskets for serving. Stemware is not a requirement but glasses rather than flimsy plastic tumblers add elegance. So do good quality plastic dishes (or better still, earthenware), metal flatware, and cloth napkins. Miscellaneous necessities include a corkscrew, a small cutting board and bread knife, a pepper mill, and some ample plastic bags for trash. And of course that the sun will shine is a necessary ingredient.

Picnic Quaffs—Rosé Wines, Sangria, Beer

Providing quenching refreshment is the paramount consideration when it comes to selecting a picnic quaff. Cold beer, soft drinks, lemonade, and iced tea (the latter pair made from scratch, not mixes) are the obvious, traditional choices. They would be appropriate with the Mexican, Greek, and Indian picnic menus.

As for wine there are numerous options. I remember spending part of an early summer afternoon lazing in a rowboat on the Moselle in the city of Metz in eastern France. We had a bottle of Alsatian muscat, given to us the night before by the Haeberlins, owners of the Auberge de l'Ill, a three-star restaurant in Alsace. We put the bottle in a string bag and hung it in the water. When it was cool enough we drank it with quiches and sandwiches we had purchased in a bakery. Is it any wonder that I love to sip Alsatian muscat with a picnic? Unfortunately the wine is difficult to find.

The argument for red wine is that it does not require chilling. But there are so many handy insulated bottle holders available that the proper temperature of the wine should not influence the decision. I prefer a chilled wine for a picnic, a white and especially a rosé.

Every country that makes red wine produces rosés. By allowing the skins of the pressed grapes, which contain most of the color, to be in contact with the juice only briefly, the wine will only be pinkish rather than deep red or purple. Despite their frivolous pastel appearance, many rosés are worthy of appreciation—especially on a summer afternoon.

Some rosés are on the sweet side, not inappropriate for highly spiced picnic menus, but the best are dry. Tavel from Provence and rosé d'Anjou from the Loire Valley are outstanding examples, to be drunk young and chilled, so their freshness can shine through. Bandol is another to recommend, as are some of the so-called blush wines coming from California, notably the blancs de noirs made from pinot noir grapes, which tend to be less sweet than many of the "white" zinfandels.

Other suitable quenchers at picnic time include beer and sangria—a glorified spritzer made with fruit juice, in addition to club soda and red or white wine, and sweetened if you like. A container of homemade lemonade with fresh lemon juice, or brewed iced tea flavored with lemon and mint are two welcome drinks. The point is to provide an ample supply of beverages at a picnic.

Mexican Picnic

~~~~~~~~~~

Guacamole
Seviche
Jalapeño Cornbread
Mexican Chicken Salad

Killer Brownies
Watermelon

Guacamole

Prepare Asparagus Guacamole according to the recipe on page 45. To make a traditional guacamole, substitute two ripe avocados—peeled, pitted, and mashed—for the asparagus. The best avocados are the Haas variety, with a pebbly black skin.

Seviche

Prepare Seviche according to the recipe on page 73.

Jalapeño Cornbread

- 4 tablespoons vegetable oil
- 1 cup chopped onions
- ⅓ cup finely minced fresh or canned seeded jalapeño peppers
- 1½ cups yellow cornmeal
- 1 cup flour
- 1½ teaspoons baking soda
- 1 teaspoon salt
- 1½ cups buttermilk
- 1 egg, beaten
- 2 tablespoons melted sweet butter

Preheat oven to 400 degrees. Butter a 9- or 10-inch round baking pan.

Lightly sauté the onions in 2 tablespoons of the oil. Mix in the peppers and set aside. In a large bowl blend the cornmeal, flour, baking soda, and salt. Add the buttermilk, egg, the onion-green pepper mixture, and remaining 2 tablespoons vegetable oil. Spread batter in prepared pan and bake for 30 minutes. Brush with melted butter and serve warm or at room temperature.

6 to 8 servings

Mexican Chicken Salad

- 3 tablespoons Dijon mustard
- 6 tablespoons sherry wine vinegar
- ½ cup extra-virgin olive oil
- 2 whole boned and skinned chicken breasts (about 1½ pounds)
- 2 sweet red peppers
- 1 large green pepper
- 1 teaspoon minced fresh green chili pepper
- 3 tablespoons minced scallions
- 2 tablespoons minced fresh coriander
- ½ cup cooked corn kernels (fresh, frozen, or vacuum-packed)

½ cup cooked kidney beans (if using canned, rinse first)

Salt and freshly ground black pepper

Mix the mustard with 2 tablespoons of the vinegar and 1 tablespoon of the oil. Brush this mixture on the chicken and allow to marinate at room temperature for 15 minutes.

Core and seed the peppers, and quarter them lengthwise. Brush with a little of the oil.

Preheat grill or oven broiler, and grill the chicken and peppers for about 20 minutes, turning them once, until nicely browned and cooked through. Do not place them too close to the heat source so that they char before they are cooked through.

Slice the chicken against the grain in ½-inch-thick slices. Slice the peppers in strips ½ inch wide.

Separately mix remaining 4 tablespoons vinegar and remaining oil together. Combine chicken and peppers with the chilis, scallions, coriander, corn, and kidney beans. Toss with the vinaigrette, season with salt and pepper, and serve.

6 servings

Killer Brownies

4 ounces unsweetened chocolate
2 ounces semisweet chocolate
½ pound sweet butter, at room temperature
3 eggs
1½ cups sugar
⅔ cup flour
1 teaspoon vanilla extract
1 cup chopped walnuts

Preheat oven to 350 degrees. Butter a 9-by-13-inch baking pan.

Melt the chocolates and butter over low heat in a saucepan. Set aside to cool slightly. Beat the eggs and sugar together until light. Stir in the chocolate mixture and the flour. Add the vanilla and walnuts, and spread the batter in the prepared pan. Bake for 20 to 25 minutes, until the brownies just begin to shrink around the edges and a cake tester comes out clean.

Remove from oven, allow to cool, then cut into squares.

Makes 24 to 30 brownies

Clockwise, top left: Mexican Chicken Salad, Jalapeño Cornbread, sangria, Seviche, Guacamole, tortilla chips

Greek Picnic

Eggplant Caviar with Garlic
Marinated Artichokes, Peppers, and Olives
Vine Leaves Stuffed with Brown Rice
Meat, Spinach, and Cheese Pies
Tomatoes and Feta Cheese

Walnut Butter Cookies
Grapes

Eggplant Caviar with Garlic

1½ pound eggplant
1 large clove garlic, finely minced
¼ cup finely chopped onions
Juice of 1 lemon
2 to 3 tablespoons plain yogurt
1 tablespoon olive oil
2 tablespoons toasted sesame seeds

Cook the eggplant in the oven or directly over a flame until brown all over and soft. Set aside to cool.

When the eggplant is cool enough to handle, split it, scrape the pulp from the skin, and mash it to a purée. Mix it with the garlic, onions, lemon juice, and 2 to 3 tablespoons yogurt depending on the consistency you like. Stir in the olive oil and sesame seeds. Refrigerate until a half hour before serving.

Makes about 2 cups

Vine Leaves Stuffed with Brown Rice

⅔ cup olive oil
1 cup finely chopped onions
½ cup finely chopped scallions
1 cup brown rice
3 tablespoons dried currants
½ teaspoon salt
1 tablespoon chopped fresh mint
1 tablespoon chopped fresh dill
Freshly ground black pepper
1 pound vine leaves in brine
Juice of 2 lemons

Heat 3 tablespoons of the oil in a heavy saucepan. Add the onions and scallions and sauté for about 5 minutes over medium heat, until soft but not brown. Add the rice and sauté, stirring, 3 minutes longer. Stir in the currants, and add ½ cup of water. Cover and cook over low heat until the water is absorbed, about 10 minutes. The rice will not be tender yet. Stir in the salt, mint, dill, and pepper; set aside.

While the rice is cooking, rinse the leaves in several changes of cold water. Cut away any tough little stem ends. Allow the leaves to soak in cold water until ready to use.

Place a heaping teaspoon of the rice filling on the underside of each vine leaf (the side where the ribs are more prominent) near the bottom. Fold in the sides and roll up the leaf to enclose the filling completely. Do not roll the leaf too tight because the filling will expand as it cooks. Fill about 36 leaves (some leaves will be left over). Use uniform, undamaged leaves. Extremely large ones can be cut in half, and any that are torn can be patched with a piece from another leaf. No filling should be exposed.

Coarsely shred any unused leaves and place them in the bottom of a heavy saucepan. Mix half the lemon juice with the remaining olive oil. Arrange the filled vine leaves seam side down, packed closely together, over the shredded vine leaves. Pour half the lemon-oil mixture over them. Repeat with another layer of filled vine leaves and cover with the rest of the lemon-oil mixture. Pour 1⅓ cups water into the pan. Weight the filled vine leaves with a plate or a saucepan lid that will fit directly into the saucepan. Cover the saucepan and simmer for 1 hour and 15 minutes. The liquid in the pan should be absorbed by the vine leaves.

Remove the stuffed vine leaves from the pan and arrange in a serving dish. Pour the remaining lemon juice over them and allow to cool. Refrigerate until ready to serve, or serve as soon as they have cooled.

Makes 3 dozen stuffed vine leaves

Meat, Spinach, and Cheese Pies

These baked pies can also be frozen. To reheat, bake in a 400 degree oven for 15 to 20 minutes.

    3 tablespoons olive oil
    1 cup finely chopped onions
    10 ounces spinach, rinsed well, stems removed,
        chopped
    3 tablespoons chopped scallions
    1 pound lean ground beef or lamb
    1 clove garlic
    3 tablespoons tomato paste
    ¼ teaspoon cinnamon
    1 tablespoon minced fresh parsley
    ½ teaspoon oregano
    Salt and freshly ground black pepper
    3 eggs
    1 cup feta cheese, crumbled

    12 to 16 ounces frozen phyllo leaves, defrosted
    6 ounces sweet butter, melted
    ¼ cup grated Italian Parmesan cheese

Heat 2 tablespoons of the oil in a large skillet, add the onions, and sauté until soft but not brown. Remove the onions from the pan and set aside. Add the spinach to the pan, cover, and cook over low heat for about 10 minutes, until the spinach is wilted. Uncover and cook long enough to evaporate any moisture in the pan. Remove the spinach to a bowl.

Heat the remaining tablespoon of oil in the skillet, add the scallions and beef or lamb, and sauté over medium heat until the meat loses its redness. Break the meat up with a fork as it cooks so the texture is evenly crumbly. Add the garlic, tomato paste, cinnamon, parsley, oregano, and salt and pepper to taste. Cook briefly, then transfer to a bowl. Beat 2 of the eggs with the spinach mixture, and beat 1 egg into the meat. Mix the feta with the spinach mixture.

Now you are ready to assemble the pies. Spread the phyllo leaves out on a work surface and cover them with a sheet of aluminum foil draped with a damp towel. Lightly butter a baking sheet. Preheat oven to 400 degrees.

Take one sheet of phyllo, brush it lightly with the melted butter, and place another sheet of phyllo on top of it. Then fold the sheets over like closing a book to form a sheet nearly square and four thicknesses thick. Place a tablespoon of the meat in the center at the bottom edge of the pastry, place a tablespoon of the spinach on the meat, and sprinkle with some of the Parmesan. Fold the phyllo lengthwise over the meat, in thirds, much like folding a letter. Brush the top of the phyllo with butter. Now fold the filled part of the pastry over itself about three times to form a neatly enclosed square of pastry with the filling tucked inside. Brush the top with butter and place on the baking sheet, seam side down. (You can also fold triangles which are a little fancier but more complicated to do—it's like folding a flag.)

Repeat with the remaining phyllo and filling. You should have enough to make 12 pies.

Bake the pies until lightly browned, about 20 minutes. Serve at room temperature (or, for a picnic, at outdoor temperature).

6 servings

Clockwise: Vine Leaves Stuffed with Brown Rice, grapes, Greek pastry; Meat, Cheese, and Spinach Pies with olives, marinated artichoke hearts and peppers, tomatoes and feta cheese

Walnut Butter Cookies

If you grind the walnuts in a food processor or blender, first mix them with 2 tablespoons of the sugar. This will prevent them from turning into a paste.

¼ pound sweet butter, at room temperature
½ cup sugar
½ cup finely ground walnuts
1½ cups sifted flour
Confectioner's sugar

Preheat oven to 350 degrees. Cream the butter and sugar together until well blended. Mix in the nuts and flour to make a soft dough. Break off walnut-size pieces of the dough, roll slightly, and curve into crescent shapes.

Bake on an ungreased pan until very lightly browned, 10 to 12 minutes. Allow to cool completely, then dust with confectioner's sugar.

Makes 3 dozen small cookies

Indian Picnic

Cold Curry Tomato Soup
Tandoori-Style Chicken
Puri
(*Indian Fried Bread*)
Cold Spiced Pilaf
Cauliflower and Chilis
Cucumber Raita

Fresh Melon

Clockwise, top left: Puri with Tandoori-Style Chicken, melon, Cold Curry Tomato Soup,
iced tea, Cucumber Raita, Cauliflower and Chilis, Cold Spiced Pilaf, cashew nuts

Cold Curry Tomato Soup

Chill the soup thoroughly and transport it to a picnic in a thermos.

2 tablespoons vegetable oil
1 large onion, finely chopped
2 cloves garlic, minced
½ tart apple, peeled, cored, and chopped
1½ teaspoons ground cumin
½ teaspoon ground coriander
½ teaspoon ground turmeric
1 teaspoon curry powder
½ pound potatoes, peeled and diced
2 cups chicken stock, preferably homemade (page 22)
1 cup peeled and chopped ripe tomatoes
1 teaspoon salt, or more to taste
Generous pinch cayenne pepper
¾ cup plain yogurt
¾ cup heavy cream

Heat the oil in a heavy saucepan, add the onion, and sauté over low heat until the onion begins to soften. Add the garlic, apple, cumin, coriander, turmeric, and curry powder and cook, stirring, for 2 to 3 minutes. Add the potatoes, chicken stock, and tomatoes. Stir in the salt and pepper. (Since this soup will be served cold, do not be afraid to overseason it.) Cover and simmer for about 30 minutes, until the potatoes are tender.

Purée the soup in a blender or food processor. Add the yogurt and blend. Stir in the cream and chill thoroughly. Recheck seasonings before serving.

6 servings

Tandoori-Style Chicken

½ sweet red pepper, finely chopped
1 tablespoon minced fresh ginger
1 large clove garlic, minced
1 teaspoon paprika
1 teaspoon ground cumin
½ teaspoon ground coriander
½ teaspoon turmeric
⅛ teaspoon ground cloves
½ teaspoon salt
½ teaspoon cayenne pepper, or to taste

Juice of 3 lemons
3 2½-pound broiling chickens, cut into serving pieces and skinned
½ cup plain yogurt
3 tablespoons vegetable oil

Cover the pepper with water in a small saucepan and simmer for about 10 minutes until tender. Drain and place in a blender jar with the ginger, garlic, paprika, cumin, coriander, turmeric, cloves, salt, pepper, and about 1 tablespoon of the lemon juice. Blend to make a smooth purée. Add remaining lemon juice.

Place the chicken in a bowl and pour this mixture over it, along with the yogurt and vegetable oil. Mix well to coat the chicken. Refrigerate and allow to marinate overnight.

Light a barbecue grill or broiler. Oil grill racks or broiling pan and cook the chicken until it is done, about 30 minutes.

6 to 8 servings

Puri
(Indian Fried Bread)

1 cup whole wheat flour
¾ cup all-purpose flour
¾ cup vegetable oil (approximately)
¼ teaspoon salt
¼ teaspoon freshly ground black pepper
½ cup warm water

Combine ¾ cup of the whole wheat flour with the all-purpose flour in the work bowl of a food processor. With the machine running add 2 tablespoons of the oil and process a few seconds until blended. Add the salt and pepper and process briefly again.

With the machine running, slowly add the water and continue to process until a ball of dough forms. Process for about 1 minute longer until the dough feels satiny. Remove the dough from the food processor and wrap in plastic wrap. Allow it to rest for 30 minutes.

The dough can be mixed by hand instead of in a food processor: combine both flours and toss with a fork, add the oil and seasonings, and stir until well blended. Mix in the water and knead for about 10 minutes, then allow to rest for 30 minutes.

Divide the dough in half, then cut each half into 8

equal portions. Roll each piece of dough into a smooth ball. Toss the balls of dough with some of the remaining whole wheat flour in a bowl. Dust a work surface with the flour.

Heat remaining vegetable oil in a heavy 8-inch skillet until it is nearly smoking. The breads are to be made and fried one at a time. Roll a circle of dough very thin, to a diameter of 5 to 6 inches. Place it in the hot oil, fry for about 10 seconds until it starts to puff, turn it with tongs, and fry for 5 to 10 seconds on the other side until puffed and lightly browned. Drain on paper towels. Repeat with remaining balls of dough.

Next wrap the fried breads in aluminum foil, taking care not to compress them tightly. They will deflate, but will retain an airy, tender quality.

6 to 8 servings

Cold Spiced Pilaf

    1 cup long-grain rice, preferably Indian basmati
    2 cups cold water, if using basmati rice
    4 tablespoons vegetable oil
    ¾ teaspoon cumin seeds
    ½ cup finely chopped onions
    1 clove garlic, minced
    1 cinnamon stick
    1 bay leaf
    4 whole cloves
    1 teaspoon turmeric
    8 black peppercorns
    1 teaspoon salt
  1½ teaspoons finely chopped fresh ginger
    ¼ cup raisins
    ½ teaspoon ground cardamom

Rinse the rice in several changes of cold water until the water runs clear. If using basmati rice place it in the 2 cups of cold water to soak for 30 minutes. (Reserve soaking water.) With plain long-grain rice this step is not necessary.

Heat the oil in a heavy casserole. Add cumin seeds and fry until they begin to brown, about 10 seconds. Add the onions and garlic and sauté over medium heat, stirring constantly, until they are golden.

Add cinnamon stick, bay leaf, cloves, turmeric, and peppercorns and sauté, stirring, for two minutes. Stir in rice, salt, ginger, raisins, and cardamom. Add either the

soaking water from the basmati rice or add 1¾ cups cold water if using long-grain rice. Bring to a boil. Cook, covered, over low heat until the liquid is absorbed, about 10 to 15 minutes for basmati rice, a trifle longer for long-grain rice. Keep covered and allow to stand for 20 minutes, then cool to room temperature. Fluff and toss the pilaf and serve at room temperature.

6 servings

Cauliflower and Chilis

    5 tablespoons vegetable oil
    1 teaspoon mustard seeds
    1 fresh green chili, seeded and very finely minced, about 1 tablespoon
    1 head cauliflower, cored and cut into small flowerets
        Salt to taste
    1 tablespoon rice vinegar

Heat 3 tablespoons of the oil in a wok or skillet. Add the mustard seeds and cook until they begin to "dance" around. Add the chili and cauliflower and stir-fry until the cauliflower loses its raw quality, about 3 minutes. It is alright if the cauliflower begins to brown slightly.

Lower heat to medium, stir in salt to taste, cover, and steam for about 1 minute, until the cauliflower is crisp-tender. Stir in remaining 2 tablespoons oil and the rice vinegar, remove from heat, and set aside to cool, stirring from time to time. Serve at room temperature.

6 servings

Cucumber Raita

    3 medium cucumbers, peeled, seeded, and finely chopped
    2 cups plain yogurt
    3 tablespoons chopped fresh mint
        Salt and freshly ground black pepper

Combine the ingredients and refrigerate until ready to serve.

6 servings

A HOLIDAY BUFFET

Unlike the preceding picnics or the picadillo brunch for twelve, this holiday buffet has not been crafted along ethnic lines. Buffets that are all Chinese, all French, or all Italian (conceived like the expanded antipasto menu suggested for a summer lunch, page 119) are delightful, and many of the "theme" menus in this book could be doubled or tripled as a buffet to serve a large crowd.

This buffet menu borrows from several cuisines however, with dishes that marry well together, lend themselves to quantity preparation and service, do not make impossible demands on refrigeration, ovens, or time, and require a minimum of last minute attention. This is not a cocktail party menu but a buffet suitable for a supper or an open house at which guests stay and mingle, rather than having a drink and a nibble before going off to the next activity.

A successful holiday buffet party for twenty or more guests is a serious undertaking to be planned with care and coordinated with precision only a shade less exacting than the Normandy landings. But since good times depend on good food, good wine, and good friends, the formula cannot miss.

The supper array is colorful and balanced among meat, poultry, vegetable, starch, and seafood items, none of which require more than a fork for convenient consumption. I have omitted a green salad as it tends to take over the plate already crowded with half a dozen delicious tastes. There is no "hot" dish, but several are fine at room temperature so special buffet warmers are not necessary.

As appetites wind down the desserts and coffee replace the other dishes or may be set out on a separate table. At that time you might consolidate leftovers in smaller bowls and keep them available for latecomers. Many of the other desserts in this book—the Apple Bread Pudding, Prune Cake, Strawberry Cheesecake and Spice Squares as well as any of the cookies—would also be suitable. Although the Raspberry Tortoni is a magnificent dessert for a crowd, it is too perishable for buffet service.

The menu has been designed so that only three of the dishes, the mussels, the Cold Seafood Mousse, and the Toblerone Mousse, need last minute refrigeration.

The Leek Tartlets and Christmas Stollen can be made in advance and frozen. The Seafood Mousse, Lentil and Sausage Salad, cucumbers with dill, pâté, mussels, and Toblerone Mousse should be made the day before. The remainder of the menu should be made early in the day and does not require refrigeration.

Prepare two lists, one a game plan and schedule for cooking and serving, the other a detailed shopping list that covers everything from lemons and limes and cocktail napkins to dishwashing detergent. Make a duplicate of each. There is no worse crisis than to lose such a list. Keep your serving utensils and dinnerware in mind. In addition to plates, flatware, napkins, glassware, cups and saucers, be sure you have enough bread, coffee, and tea. What is the size of your coffee maker? Where will the guests park their coats? Are there fresh towels in the bathroom? Enough ashtrays on the tables?

Attend to all these details and you will enjoy the party along with the guests. You deserve it!

Champagne and Sparkling Wine

When the occasion is festive, Champagne is poured filling glasses with lustrous, flickering pale gold. Champagne is the wine for all happy occasions, times for greeting, gathering, and toasting.

Although there is a tendency to refer to all sparkling wines as Champagne, strictly speaking, authentic Champagne comes from France and from a confined region east of Paris. This Champagne, made from white chardonnay grapes and pinot noir and perhaps pinot meunier grapes (the typical blend—when made only from chardonnay Champagne is "blanc de blancs") accounts for less than five percent of total sparkling wine sales. The chalky slopes around Épernay and the cathedral city of Reims would be incapable of supplying all the grapes necessary to quench the thirst for sparkling wine, a thirst that increases every year.

Which Champagne or sparkling wine you select will depend on both taste and pocketbook. But with any you plan to pour as an aperitif or with food, look for the term *brut* on the bottle. That means the Champagne or sparkling wine will be dry. Sweeter Champagnes and sparkling wines are labeled *sec* or *demi-sec* (dry or semi-dry), and are more suited to serve with dessert.

Each of the French Champagne houses follows a particular style—some are lighter, others more full bodied. The nonvintage blend (always the least expensive) reflects this style. In addition, the various houses produce vintage Champagnes in good years and top-of-the-line specialty bottlings, called *têtes de cuvée*, which are the most costly. Recently, there has been an increase in the production of rosé Champagnes, usually made by blending a little red wine (pinot noir) from the region into the Champagne before bottling. The best of non-Champagne sparkling wines that come from France, Italy, Spain, Germany, Australia, New Zealand, and the United States are made from the same types of grapes and according to the same method (*méthode champenoise*, usually indicated on the label) as French Champagne. Despite these similarities, these wines are usually less costly than Champagne, nor are they likely to have its finesse.

For all sparkling wines, certain time-honored notions about pouring and serving are best ignored. The cork should never be shot out of the bottle with a "pop" that results in the loss of wine and possible injury to bystanders, but should be eased out by turning it slowly. Shallow, saucer-shaped glasses are not recommended unless you want the fizz to fizzle. Slender flute glasses are best but a good all-purpose wineglass can also be used. Pour a small amount of the sparkling wine into the glass and when the foam subsides, fill the glass about two-thirds full.

Although I might plan to serve only Champagne or sparkling wine at a holiday buffet, I also offer bar spirits, still white and red wine, soft drinks, and sparkling water for those guests who might prefer them. Both alcoholic and nonalcoholic beers are good additions. And if a festive punch bowl is your preference, a rum and citrus punch recipe has been included. Another punch, quick and colorful, can be made by combining cranberry juice and sparkling wine in equal parts, and adding a touch of vodka to give it an extra kick.

Estimate a minimum half-bottle of sparkling wine per guest for a party, if that is all you are serving. Eighteen ounces, or two bottles for every three guests would provide a comfortable margin.

A Holiday Buffet

Champagne or Sparkling Wine

Cocktail Party Mussels
Fine Liver Pâté
Individual Leek Tartlets
Cold Seafood Mousse
Lemon-Soy Chicken Wings
Pasta Salad with Tomato Concassé
Lentil and Sausage Salad
Cucumber-Dill Salad
Cheese Platter

Lee Haiken's Praline Roulade
Christmas Stollen
Toblerone Mousse
Tropical Citrus Punch

Cocktail Party Mussels

6 pounds mussels, scrubbed and debearded
1½ cups dry white wine
1 cup mayonnaise, preferably homemade (page 58)
½ cup plain yogurt
2 tablespoons Dijon mustard
¼ cup capers
2 tablespoons lemon juice
1 tablespoon anchovy paste

Steam the mussels in wine in a large kettle until they open, 10 to 15 minutes. Drain mussels and chill, in their shells, several hours or overnight.

Combine the remaining ingredients, blending well. Serve chilled mussels in their shells with the mayonnaise sauce on the side for dipping.

20 servings

Fine Liver Pâté

1 pound chicken livers
⅓ cup milk
10 tablespoons sweet butter, softened
1 medium onion, finely chopped
½ cup chicken stock, preferably homemade (page 22)
3 tablespoons Cognac
4 tablespoons heavy cream
Salt and freshly ground white pepper
½ tablespoon minced black truffle (optional)
2 tablespoons clarified sweet butter

Trim the livers of all bits of fat, membrane, or green spots. Cut them into quarters and place in a bowl with the milk. Cover and refrigerate for 2 hours. Drain and dry the livers on paper towels.

In a large skillet (do not use aluminum or iron) heat 2 tablespoons of the butter. Add the onion and sauté gently over low heat until soft but not brown. Add another tablespoon of butter plus the livers and cook over low heat just until they lose their redness. Add the chicken stock and simmer until the livers are cooked but still pink inside, about 5 minutes. Using a slotted spoon, remove the livers and set aside.

Add the Cognac and 2 tablespoons of the cream to the skillet and cook quickly until the mixture has thickened and is reduced to about ½ cup.

Place the livers and the cooking liquid in a blender and purée until smooth, adding the additional 2 tablespoons of cream. Remove from blender and beat in the remaining butter 1 tablespoon at a time. Season with salt and freshly ground pepper. Do not be afraid to overseason slightly because chilling will dull the flavor. Fold in the truffles if using.

Transfer the pâté to a 2½- to 3-cup crock and cover with clarified butter. Refrigerate for at least 4 hours, but remove from the refrigerator 30 to 40 minutes before serving. Serve with thin slices of lightly toasted brioche.

18 to 20 servings

Individual Leek Tartlets

Double recipe for *Basic Pastry* (page 55) made
   with 2½ cups flour
3 tablespoons sweet butter
5 cups thinly sliced leeks
1 cup grated Gruyère cheese
3 eggs
1 cup milk
1 cup heavy cream
Salt and freshly ground black pepper

Preheat oven to 425 degrees. Roll out pastry and fit it into tartlet pans and line them with foil. Weight the foil with pastry weights or dried beans. Place in the oven and bake for about 6 to 8 minutes, until the pastry looks dry. Remove from the oven and set aside.

Heat the butter in a very large, heavy skillet. Add the leeks and sauté them over low heat, stirring from time to time, until the leeks are tender and golden. Spread a little of the leek mixture in each tartlet shell. Sprinkle with a little cheese.

Beat the eggs with the milk and cream until well blended but not frothy. Season to taste with salt and pepper. Pour this mixture into each of the tartlet shells and place in the oven. Lower heat to 375 degrees and bake until puffed and browned, 25 to 30 minutes.

24–30 2½-inch tartlets or 50 mini-tartlets

Cold Seafood Mousse

¼ pound snow peas
½ pound sea scallops
½ cup finely chopped sweet red pepper
1 teaspoon lemon juice
1½ pounds medium shrimp, shelled and deveined
4 large egg whites
2½ cups heavy cream
1 tablespoon minced fresh parsley
2 tablespoons minced fresh dill
¼ cup finely chopped onions
⅓ cup dry sherry
Salt and freshly ground white pepper
Large pinch cayenne pepper
Italian flat leaf parsley for garnish
2 cups homemade mayonnaise seasoned with 1
   tablespoon tomato paste (page 58)

Trim the tops from the snow peas. Drop them into a pan of simmering water for 30 to 40 seconds, just until they turn bright green. Drain and rinse in cold water. Pat the snow peas dry and cut them into thin vertical slivers, using a sharp knife or a Chinese cleaver. Set aside. Finely chop half the sea scallops, mix them with the red pepper and the lemon juice, and set aside.

Place the rest of the sea scallops along with the shrimp in the bowl of a food processor and process until a smooth purée. This will take several minutes and you may have to stop the machine once or twice to scrape down the mixture. Add the egg whites and process for about 30 seconds. With the machine running, add the cream and process just until blended.

Add the parsley, dill, onions, sherry, salt (at least a teaspoon will probably be necessary), pepper, and cayenne pepper. Process until blended. Taste the mixture for seasoning. If you do not wish to taste the raw seafood, poach a bit of it in simmering water just until it turns opaque, then taste it. Adjust the seasonings before you bake the mousse, because there will be no way to correct them after baking.

Preheat oven to 325 degrees. Oil an 8-cup mold, preferably an oblong or a ring mold. Spoon half the mousse mixture into the mold, then make a slight depression down the middle of the mixture. Spread half the snow pea strips running lengthwise in the depression, arranging them to within about ½-inch of the edge of the mold on either side. Spoon the minced scallop and red pepper mixture over the snow peas, then cover the scallops with the remaining snow pea strips. Spread the remaining mousse mixture into the mold, and smooth the top.

Cover the mold tightly with oiled aluminum foil. Place the mold in a slightly larger pan that will hold it comfortably and set in the middle of the oven. Pour boiling water into the pan to come at least ⅓ the way up the sides of the mold. Bake for one hour.

Remove mold from the oven and allow to cool at room temperature. Refrigerate overnight. To serve, drain any excess fluid from the mold, run a knife around the edge, then invert onto a chilled serving platter. Decorate the top with Italian parsley and serve with rosy-colored mayonnaise.

10 to 12 servings

Lemon-Soy Chicken Wings

Juice of 5 lemons
3 tablespoons Dijon mustard
4 tablespoons light soy sauce
40 chicken wings
¼ cup chopped scallions for garnish

Combine the lemon juice, mustard, and soy sauce in a large bowl.

Remove the small end joint of the chicken wings and discard, or reserve for making stock. Divide the wings at the remaining joint in two sections. Mix wings with the marinade and allow to marinate for at least 2 hours.

Arrange the wings on a foil-lined broiling pan. Broil close to the source of heat, turning once, until the wings are nicely browned. Allow to cool to room temperature before serving. Arrange on a platter and scatter scallions on top.

20 servings

Pasta Salad with Tomato Concassé

4 pounds peeled, seeded, chopped ripe tomatoes (about 6 cups—well-drained canned tomatoes can be substituted)
2 teaspoons finely minced garlic
Juice and grated rind of 2 lemons
Salt and freshly ground black pepper
6 tablespoons white wine vinegar
⅔ cup extra-virgin olive oil
⅓ cup minced fresh basil
2 tablespoons minced flat leaf parsley
2 pounds rotelle, fusilli, or other corkscrew pasta

About 1 hour before serving mix the tomatoes, garlic, lemon juice and rind, salt and pepper to taste, vinegar, ⅓ cup olive oil, basil, and parsley. Set aside to marinate.

Bring at least 8 quarts of water to a boil, add the pasta, stir to separate the pieces, and boil until the pasta is al dente, about 8 minutes. Drain and rinse in cold water; drain again.

Mix the pasta with the sauce, check seasonings, and stir in remaining ⅓ cup olive oil. Serve at room temperature.

20 buffet servings

Lentil and Sausage Salad

3 cups dried lentils
12 cups water
1 pound smoked kielbasa, thinly sliced
1½ cups chopped red onions
1 cup pitted, coarsely chopped black Greek or Italian olives
¾ cup chopped fresh parsley
2 tablespoons Dijon mustard
⅓ cup red wine vinegar
1 cup olive oil
1 tablespoon salt, or to taste
Freshly ground black pepper

Bring the lentils and water to a boil in a large kettle. Lower heat and simmer until lentils are just tender, about 45 minutes. Drain and set aside, covered.

Combine the sausage, onions, olives, and parsley in a large bowl.

In a separate container combine the mustard and vinegar, stirring until smooth, then beat in the oil. Mix this dressing with the sausage mixture. Fold in the lentils and season to taste with salt and pepper. Serve at room temperature.

18 to 20 servings

Cucumber-Dill Salad

9 cucumbers, peeled, seeded, and thinly sliced
3 cups thinly sliced onions
3 cups rice vinegar
2 teaspoons sugar
1 tablespoon salt
Freshly ground black pepper
⅔ cup minced fresh dill

Combine all the ingredients in a bowl. Allow to sit for at least 30 minutes before serving.

20 to 24 servings

Lee Haiken's Praline Roulade

Would you believe this dessert comes from the editor of Weight Watchers Magazine?

6 eggs
1½ cups sugar
1 cup sifted cake flour
8 tablespoons sweet butter, melted and cooled
1 teaspoon vanilla extract
Confectioner's sugar
¼ cup kirsch
1½ cups black currant jam, heated
1 cup sliced almonds

Grease a jelly roll pan 10½-by-15½-by-1 inch deep and line with parchment or waxed paper. Grease the paper. Preheat oven to 350 degrees. Place the bowl of an electric mixer over, not in, a pan of gently simmering water. Place the eggs and 1 cup of the sugar in the bowl and stir to combine. Warm gently for 15 minutes, stirring from time to time.

Remove bowl to the mixer and beat at high speed for about 15 minutes, until the mixture resembles whipped cream. (If your mixer has a hot water jacket you can use it without prewarming the mixture.) Reduce speed to low. Sift in the flour and pour in the melted butter through a fine strainer. Add the vanilla.

Spread batter into prepared pan and even the top with a spatula. Bake for 25 minutes, until golden brown and springy to the touch. Spread a sheet of waxed paper large enough to hold the cake on a work surface. Dust liberally with sifted confectioner's sugar. Run a knife around the edges of the pan and turn the cake out onto the paper. Peel off the liner and sprinkle the cake with kirsch.

Spread the cake with 1 cup of the warm jam and roll the cake from the long side, using the waxed paper as a guide. Spread the outside of the cake with the remaining warm jam.

Turn oven to 375 degrees. Spread the almonds and remaining ½ cup sugar onto a clean, large baking sheet and place in the oven. Turn this mixture frequently until the sugar begins to caramelize and the almonds are toasted, 10 to 15 minutes. Allow to cool in the pan.

Spread another sheet of waxed paper on the work surface. Scrape the almond mixture out of the pan, chopping up any large, hardened pieces. Spread the praline on the waxed paper.

Place the roulade at one edge of the paper and carefully roll it over the praline so that the nut mixture adheres to the jam coating. Dust roulade liberally with confectioner's sugar and place on a serving platter. Cut a small diagonal slice from each end and slice the cake at an angle when serving.

12 to 16 servings

Christmas Stollen

½ cup dark seedless raisins
½ cup golden (sultana) raisins
¼ cup brandy
1 package active dry yeast
1 teaspoon sugar plus ⅓ cup sugar
¼ cup warm water
⅔ cup milk
8 tablespoons sweet butter, at room temperature
1 egg
¾ teaspoon salt
½ teaspoon cinnamon
¼ teaspoon mace
⅛ teaspoon cardamom
1 teaspoon grated orange peel
4 to 4½ cups flour
⅓ cup blanched slivered almonds or shelled, unsalted pistachios
2 tablespoons melted butter
¼ teaspoon cinnamon mixed with 1 tablespoon sugar
Confectioner's sugar, or a combination of confectioner's sugar, milk, and almond extract for glaze

Combine the raisins and brandy in a small bowl and set aside. Mix the yeast and the teaspoon of sugar with warm water. Set in a warm place to proof. Scald the milk and stir in the butter and ⅓ cup sugar until dissolved.

Beat the egg in a large bowl. Gradually add the milk mixture, beating until smooth. Stir in the yeast mixture and add the salt, cinnamon, mace, cardamom, and orange peel. Drain the raisins, reserving the brandy, and set them on paper towels to dry. Stir the brandy into the egg-milk mixture.

Add about 3 cups of flour, 1 cup at a time, beating for several minutes after each addition. (An electric mixer comes in handy here.) Add just enough flour so that the dough may be gathered in a ball. Be sure you have beaten the dough at least 5 minutes in total.

Turn the dough out onto a floured board and begin to knead. Dust the raisins with flour and knead them in, along with the nuts. Knead for about 10 minutes, until the dough is very elastic and has lost its stickiness, but is still quite soft.

Place in a buttered bowl, turn to butter the top, cover, and put in a warm place to rise until doubled,

1 hour or more. Punch the dough down and shape into 1 large or 2 small rectangles. Using 1 tablespoon of melted butter, brush two stripes lengthwise down the rectangles, leaving a 1-inch border and a strip about 1½ inches wide down the center unbuttered.

Dust the buttered areas with cinnamon-sugar. Fold one long edge of the dough over to just past the center. Fold the second long edge over to just overlap the first and pinch the seams closed, at the ends as well as down the middle. Cover and set in a warm place to rise until doubled. Preheat oven to 375 degrees.

Place the stollen on a buttered baking sheet and bake until golden brown and sounds hollow when tapped, about 45 minutes. Cool on a rack. Before serving, dust heavily with confectioner's sugar or glaze with confectioner's sugar mixed with milk and a dash of almond extract until the consistency of thick cream.

Makes 1 large or 2 small stollen

Toblerone Mousse

Double the recipe on page 96 and serve it in a large bowl with whipped cream on the side.

Other dishes in this book which could be used for the buffet include Fillet of Beef with Peppered Onion Confit served at room temperature (page 108), Cucumber and Golden Caviar Canapés (page 108), Broccoli with Sesame Oil Dressing (page 104), Seviche (page 73), Spiced Shrimp (page 91), Apple Bread Pudding (page 71), Spice Squares (page 139), and Walnut Butter Cookies (page 150).

Tropical Citrus Punch

2 tablespoons black tea leaves
4 cups boiling water
⅔ cup sugar
2 to 4 cups golden or dark rum
4 cups orange juice, preferably freshly squeezed
½ cup Cointreau
¼ cup fresh lemon juice
¼ cup fresh lime juice
Slices of lemon, lime, and orange for garnish

Place the tea in a pitcher, pour boiling water over it, and allow it to steep for 5 minutes. Strain the tea into a bowl or other container with a capacity of at least 4 quarts. Stir in the sugar until it dissolves. Allow this mixture to cool, stir in the remaining ingredients (adjusting the amount of rum according to how strong you want the punch), chill thoroughly, and serve.

About 24 4-ounce servings

About Cheese

The European custom of serving a cheese course or fruit and cheese before dessert, or even instead of it, has not been adopted by Americans. Cheese is most often served as an hors d'oeuvre here. Recently cheeses, especially chèvres, are being served with or on salad, melted or warmed.

My preference remains the traditional European style however, for a number of good reasons. First of all, with the exception of chèvre, the majority of cheeses are best with red wine, and a good, round, full-bodied red wine at that, not the wine one usually serves as an aperitif. A wine such as this is a particularly poor match with a salad, especially one with a vinegar-based dressing, so serving the cheese and salad together, aside from being difficult to manage, represents a definite conflict of interest in my view. A separate cheese course, with a choice of cheeses or even just a single superb example, good bread, and a wine that suits extends the dinner in such a civilized fashion.

Chèvres, the snowy, tangy goat cheeses, are excellent with white wines and might be considered with a first course or post-main course when only a white wine is being served. Mozzarella dressed in olive oil is another first-course cheese, good with either white or red wine.

Select cheese with care from a reliable shop. Remember that cheeses do not ripen once they have been cut. And before serving, leave them out of the refrigerator for about an hour to allow them to come to room temperature where they will have more flavor and a richer texture.

Just Dessert ... and Dessert Wines

〜

There are occasions when I only serve dessert. After theater is one example. But instead of merely putting out doughnuts and coffee, I give it some grandeur. A towering dessert torte, ready to serve as soon as guests arrive, preceded, if you wish, by some cheese, can bring an evening to a close on a festive note.

The Almond-Apricot Torte is such a dessert. And nobody but you has to know how easy it is. This confection can be served almost at a moment's notice if you have prepared the cake layers in advance and stored them in your freezer. Then all you need is some apricot preserves from the pantry shelf, and to whip some heavy cream.

Despite the popularity of chocolate, a chocolate dessert is not my recommendation because it makes wine selection a problem. There is no wine that is a suitable, felicitous match with chocolate. My husband contends that cold milk is best and he may be right. My preference is for coffee, accompanied by a fine Armagnac or Cognac, but not wine.

Sweet wines, called dessert wines because they are most appropriate with dessert (or instead of it), are truly one of the greatest pleasures of the table. Ripe, honeyed, and intense, a concentration of scents and flavors such as peaches and apricots, and suggesting a rich toastiness as well, they are best complemented by fruit and nut tastes, buttery or creamy, but not overly sweet. They are the pride of a number of countries. The French have their Sauternes, of which the most esteemed is Château d'Yquem, but Barsac, Muscat de Beaumes-de-Venise, and sweet Vouvray are others of note. In the United States a label stating late harvest means the wine, made from overripe grapes, is sweet. The best of these, from California, are Johannisberg riesling. Hungary's Tokay

aszú or Eszencia, Italy's Asti spumante, vin santo, and picolit are also dessert wines.

Germany's excellent dessert wines are identified by tongue twisting terms like *auslese, beerenauslese, trockenbeerenauslese* (*tba* for short), and the less daunting but no less delicious *eiswein*. These are wines made from selected pickings of grapes left on the vine past the point of full maturity so they dehydrate and shrivel, thereby concentrating their sweetness. Under optimum conditions the grapes are affected by a beneficial mold, *botrytis cinerea* (noble rot) that enhances the process, not only in the German vineyard but in those of France and other countries. Eiswein is made only when ripe grapes are affected by a sudden frost.

Unlike most white wines, dessert wines stand up to long aging. Time in the bottle further concentrates their already syrupy richness, a richness at best balanced by lively acidity to keep the wine from cloying. Serve sweet wines cool but not ice cold, in smaller glasses than you might use for red or white table wines.

Certain cheeses, notably blue-veined varieties such as Roquefort or pungent soft-ripening cheeses like Vacherin au Mont d'Or, are excellent served with sweet wine. Unctuous foie gras is another classic partner.

Finally, a point should be made about serving Champagne for dessert, a celebratory custom that exists worldwide. For me, Champagnes (or sparkling wines) labeled brut (the driest) are not suited to the sweet tastes of most desserts and are tantamount to being undrinkable with anything chocolate. A *brut* Champagne is a superior aperitif which can be thoroughly enjoyable with the main meal, but when it comes to dessert it is time to switch. At the very least select a fruitier rosé Champagne or, better still, a *demi-sec*. Instead of a dry sparkling wine pour Asti spumante or Vouvray.

Almond-Apricot Torte

The moist almond-flavored cake layers in this recipe are excellent plain as a quick dessert to serve with fresh fruit. All they require is a dusting of confectioner's sugar.

1½ cups flour
1 teaspoon baking powder
Pinch of salt
¾ pound sweet butter, at room temperature
1½ cups sugar
8 eggs
1½ cups finely ground blanched almonds
1 teaspoon almond extract
2 cups finest quality apricot preserves
¾ cup heavy cream, whipped with 2 tablespoons
    confectioner's sugar
½ tablespoon sliced almonds for garnish

Preheat oven to 350 degrees. Butter and flour 2 9-inch cake pans.

Sift the flour, baking powder, and salt together. Set aside. Cream the butter and sugar until very light and fluffy. Beat in the eggs, one at a time. Stir in the ground almonds and almond extract, then lightly stir in the flour mixture until it is just incorporated into the batter. Divide the batter evenly between the 2 pans.

Bake for 40 minutes, until the cakes are golden and a cake tester comes out clean.

Cool the layers in the pans for 20 minutes, then remove from the pans and continue cooling until the layers are room temperature. Carefully split each layer in half horizontally, using a long, sharp knife. Spread the preserves on top of each of the layers and stack them. Spread the top of the cake with the whipped cream, then sprinkle with sliced almonds.

10 to 12 servings

Coffee and Tea

P alatable coffee and tea are requirements. Not every guest will want them but those who do should be served. Although my personal preference is for strong espresso, not decaffeinated, I always see to it that in addition to the espresso maker at the ready, I have brewed regular coffee to serve as well as hot water on hold for a quick pot of tea. Lately I have made only brewed decaffeinated coffee for dinner parties since I have found that at least half the guests request it, especially at night, and those who do not, will not mind drinking it. I never serve instant coffee and instead of tea bags I have a small mesh holder for tea leaves.

Decaffeinated coffee requires some explanation. The decaffeination process, in addition to removing the caffeine, also extracts some of the oils and flavoring agents from the coffee beans. Decaffeinated coffee tends to have a faded, one-dimensional flavor. It is essential that it be fresh and of top quality. Especially when using decaffeinated coffee, buy beans and have them freshly ground (or grind them yourself). Keep coffee in the freezer. With decaffeinated coffee adding about twenty-five percent French roast decaffeinated to decaffeinated Colombian beans will enrich and intensify the flavor dramatically (without making the coffee so strong you would consider it espresso).

Coffee and tea should be freshly made (although a good electric coffee maker can hold it for over an hour). If your tapwater is unsuitable for making tasty coffee, use bottled water.

A Listing of Menus

Dinners: Intimate, Informal, and Grand

INTIMATE DINNERS

Dinner for Two
Beaujolais or Beaujolais Nouveau
Cranberry Borscht
Casserole-Roasted Cornish Hens
Baked Barley
Bibb and Watercress Salad
Cheese
Sabayon with Nectarines

Seafood and Chablis
French Chablis
Zucchini Fritters
Paupiettes of Sole with Shrimp
Brown Rice with Leeks and Chives
Apples Baked in Cider

Breaking the Rules
Red Bordeaux
Old Country Chicken Liver Pâté
with Radish
Swordfish Steaks
in Green Peppercorn Sauce
Garlic-Roasted Potatoes
Broccoli with Lemon Butter
Wilted Romaine and Red Onions
Cheese
Raspberry Cream Tart

A Luxurious Italian Menu
Tuscan White Wine
Warm Artichokes
with Basil Béarnaise
Brunello di Montalcino
Veal Ragout with Peas
and Fresh Pasta
Arugula, Radicchio,
and Endive Salad
Pear-Almond Cake
with Dark Caramel Sauce

Cool Food for a Warm Evening
California Chardonnay
Cold Cucumber and Bulgur Soup
Poached Salmon Steaks
with Lemon-Mustard Sauce
New Potato Salad with Fresh Peas
Sliced Ripe Tomatoes
Double Blueberry Tart
with Gingered Whipped Cream

Northern Italian Specialties
Soave
Mussels and Clams Aglio Olio
Amarone
Fegato alla Veneziana
Herbed Polenta
Bitter Greens with Sweet Vinegar
Pears in Red Wine

A 700-Calorie Dinner
White or Red Wine Spritzers
Asparagus "Guacamole"
with Jicama Chips
Mushroom Timbales
with Red Pepper Sauce
Tilefish en Papillote
Lemon Potatoes
Steamed Broccoli with Oyster Sauce
Minted Melon and Kiwi
Chocolate Meringue Kisses

INFORMAL DINNERS

Dinner in Under An Hour
Red Côtes du Rhône
Parmesan Salad with Fennel,
Mushrooms, and Walnuts
Chicken with Tomatoes
and Balsamic Vinegar
Potatoes with Shallots
Small Steamed Chocolate Puddings

Summer Menu on the Grill
California Fumé Blanc
Individual Pesto Pizzas
Grilled Soy-Glazed Tuna
with Eggplant and Peppers
Walnut Plum Tart

East Coast Informality
White Table Wine or Beer
Corn and Pepper Tart
East Coast Clambake
Buttermilk Coleslaw
Whole Grain Biscuits
Strawberry Ice Cream
Iced Watermelon

West Coast Informality
Dry Chenin Blanc
Simple Sushi
Cold Tomato, Red Wine,
and Basil Soup
Chicken Baked in Walnuts
and Yogurt
Bulgur Salad with Avocado
Chocolate Raisin Cake
Fresh Grapes

Après Outdoors—Before
an Open Fire
American Pinot Noir
Istanbul Bean Soup or Split Pea
and Barley Soup
Sausages Baked in Red Wine
Zucchini and Watercress Stir-Fry
Walnut Wheat Bread
Salad with Goat Cheese
Apple Charlotte with Crème Anglaise

A Bouillabaisse Supper
Châteauneuf-du-Pape Blanc
Assorted Olives
Quick Bouillabaisse
Green Beans
with Goat Cheese Dressing
Apple Bread Pudding

A South-of-the-Border Spread
Chilean Sauvignon Blanc
Seviche
Argentine Cabernet Sauvignon
Stuffed Flank Steak
Baked Sweet Potatoes
Corn on the Cob
Coconut Kheer

An Alsatian Feast
Alsatian Gewürztraminer
Three-Onion Quiche
Choucroute Garnie
Beet and Watercress Salad
Grilled Pineapple with Kirsch

A Hearty Belgian Menu
Belgian Beers
Cream of Endive Soup
Carbonnades à la Flamande
Braised Potatoes, Turnips,
and Carrots
Chicory Salad with Walnut Oil
Frozen Mandarin Mousse

GRAND DINNERS

An Evening in Spring
Pouilly-Fumé or Pouilly-Fuissé
Asparagus Soup
Medallions of Veal Gremolata
Walnut Rice
Cherry Tomatoes
with Sherry Vinegar
Strawberry Cheesecake

A Zesty Summer Dinner
Dry Orvieto Classico
Marinated Mushroom Salad
Grilled Chicken with Pesto
Pan-Seared Zucchini Spears
and Tomato Slices
Sweet Orvieto
Honeyed Sponge Roll with Peaches

Grilling with Style
California Gewürztraminer
Spiced Shrimp
California Cabernet Sauvignon
Butterflied Lamb
with Rainbow Peppers
Cauliflower Dauphinoise
Assorted Cheeses
Strawberry-Rhubarb Tart

A Dinner for a Chilly Evening
California Sauvignon Blanc
or Chardonnay
Scallop-Almond Chowder
with Celery Root Chips
California Merlot
Sautéed Quail with Apples
Cornmeal Timbales
Spinach Salad
with Fresh Chanterelles
Toblerone Mousse

An Autumn Holiday
Celebration
California White Zinfandel
Seafood with Pickled Ginger
California Red Zinfandel
Roast Duck Sauced with Cranberries
Sautéed Sugar Snap Peas
Wild Rice Pilaf with Carrots
and Nutmeg
Honey Cornmeal-Wheat Bread
Maple Pecan Pie

An Eclectic Menu for Six
German, Alsatian,
or American Rieslings
Hot and Sour Scallop Soup
Dilled Chicken in Riesling
Kasha with Onions
Broccoli with Sesame Oil Dressing
Dessert Soufflés:
Rum-Raisin Soufflé
or Irish Coffee Soufflé

A Grand Dinner Party
for a Special Occasion
Champagne
Cucumber and Golden Caviar
Canapés
White Burgundy
Penne with Fennel
and Shiitake Mushrooms
Red Burgundy
Fillet of Beef
with Peppered Onion Confit

Buttered Haricots Vert
Classic Green Salad
Assorted Cheeses
Raspberry Tortoni
Chocolate Thins

Lunches, Brunches, Picnics, and Parties

WARM WEATHER LUNCHES

A Spring Luncheon
Muscadet
Asparagus and Morels
in Mushroom Beurre Blanc
Scallops in White Wine and Cream
Goat Cheeses
Lace Cookies
Fresh Cherries

Cool Italian Classics
Pinot Grigio
Tomatoes and Mozzarella
Vitello Tonnato
Roasted Peppers
Summer Rice Salad
Mango Mousse

A Casual Summer Lunch or Supper
Red Table Wine
Bronson's Baked Clams
Chili-Fried Chicken
Sweet Potato Chips
Tossed Salad with Sprouts
Lemon Tart

Lunch Alfresco
New York State White Wine
Tofu and Vegetable Salad
Mackerel or Bluefish in Soy Marinade
with Buckwheat Pasta
Pink Grapefruit Sorbet

COOL WEATHER LUNCHES

An Autumn Lunch
Chianti Classico
Calamari Salad
Eggplant Lasagne
Green Beans with Garlic
Individual Fig Tartlets

A Pasta Menu for Lunch or Supper
Barbaresco
Smoked Fish Spread
Rigatoni with Hot Sausage
and Broccoli
Fresh Pears and Gorgonzola
Prune Cake

Lunch, Brunch, or Supper for Twelve
Red and White Riojas, or Beer
Grilled Cumin Shrimp
Gazpacho Salad
Picadillo
Sherried Black Beans
Saffron Rice
Oranges in Wine
Spice Squares

Brunch with a Portuguese Touch
Vinho Verde
Caldo Verde
Frittata of Sturgeon and Onions
Carottes Rapées
Two-Crust Pumpkin Pie

A TRIO OF PICNICS

Picnic Quaffs—Rosé Wines, Sangria, Beer

Mexican Picnic
Guacamole
Seviche
Jalapeño Cornbread
Mexican Chicken Salad
Killer Brownies
Watermelon

Greek Picnic
Eggplant Caviar with Garlic
Marinated Artichokes, Peppers,
and Olives
Vine Leaves Stuffed with Brown Rice
Meat, Spinach, and Cheese Pies
Tomatoes and Feta Cheese
Walnut Butter Cookies
Grapes

Indian Picnic
Cold Curry Tomato Soup
Tandoori-Style Chicken
Puri
Cold Spiced Pilaf
Cauliflower and Chilis
Cucumber Raita
Fresh Melon

A Holiday Buffet
Champagne or Sparkling Wine
Cocktail Party Mussels
Fine Liver Pâté
Individual Leek Tartlets
Cold Seafood Mousse
Lemon-Soy Chicken Wings
Pasta Salad with Tomato Concassé
Lentil and Sausage Salad
Cucumber-Dill Salad
Cheese Platter
Christmas Stollen
Lee Haiken's Praline Roulade
Toblerone Mousse
Tropical Citrus Punch

Index

᪥᪥᪥᪥᪥

General Index

almond: apricot torte, 163, 164
  pear cake with dark caramel sauce, 35
  in praline roulade, Lee Haiken, 159
  scallop chowder, 95
anchovy fillets, in vitello tonnato, 119
antipasto, 118
appetizers: artichokes, warm, with basil béarnaise, 33
  asparagus "guacamole," 45, 146
  Bronson's baked clams, 123
  calamari salad, 131
  cocktail party mussels, 156
  cucumber and golden caviar canapés, 108, 161
  eggplant caviar with garlic, 148
  fine liver pâté, 154, 156–57
  grilled cumin shrimp, 137
  guacamole, 146
  individual leek tartlets, 157
  individual pesto pizzas, 53
  marinated mushroom salad, 88
  mussels and clams aglio olio, 41
  old country chicken liver pâté, 28
  olives as, 70
  seafood with pickled ginger, 98
  seviche, 73, 146, 161
  simple sushi, 61
  smoked fish spread, 134
  spiced shrimp, 91, 161; low-calorie version, 90
  tomatoes and mozzarella, 119
  zucchini fritters, 24
apple(s): baked in cider, 26
  bread pudding, 71, 154, 161
  charlotte with crème anglaise, 67
  Golden Delicious, for baking, 67
  with sautéed quail, 95–96

apple cider, see cider
apricot(s), almond torte, 163, 164
Armagnac, 94, 163
artichokes: cooking and trimming, 33
  warm, with basil béarnaise, 33
arugula: in bitter greens with sweet vinegar, 42
  radicchio, and endive salad, 35, 109
  in salad with goat cheese, 66
asparagus: "guacamole," 45, 146
  and morels in mushroom beurre blanc, 116
  selecting, 84
  soup, 84
avocado(s): bulgur salad with, 62
  in guacamole, 146

baked barley, 21–22
baked sweet potatoes, 74
balsamic vinegar: in bitter greens with sweet vinegar, 42
  and chicken with tomatoes, 50–51
  in vinaigrette dressing, 109
barley: baked, 21–22
  and split pea soup, 64
basic pastry, 55
basil: béarnaise, 33; with warm artichokes, 33
  in grilled chicken with pesto, 88–89
  in individual pesto pizzas, 53
  in pesto, 53
  tomato, and red wine soup, cold, 61
basmati rice, see rice
bass (sea or striped), in bouillabaisse, 70
beans, see entries for black beans; green beans; haricots verts; lentils; lima beans; split peas
beef: carbonnades à la Flamande, 79, 80
  fillet of, with peppered onion confit, 108–109, 161

in meat, spinach, and cheese pies, 149
  in picadillo, 136, 137
  stuffed flank steak, 73–74
beer, 136, 145, 155
  ale, 79
  American, 56, 79
  Belgian, 79
  bock, dark, 79
  nonalcoholic, 155
beet(s): in cranberry borscht, 20
  grating and peeling, 20, 78
  and watercress salad, 78
Belgian beef stew (carbonnades à la Flamande), 79–80
beurre blanc, mushroom, asparagus and morels in, 116
Bibb lettuce: in classic green salad, with vinaigrette, 109
  and watercress salad, 22
biscuits, whole grain, 59
bitter greens with sweet vinegar, 42
black beans, sherried, 138
blackfish, in bouillabaisse, 70
blueberry(ies): with blended cottage cheese, 36
  tart with gingered whipped cream, 39
bluefish: in smoked fish spread, 134
  in soy marinade with buckwheat pasta, 127; low-calorie version, 126
borscht, cranberry, 20
Boston lettuce: in classic green salad, with vinaigrette, 109
  in salad with goat cheese, 66
bouillabaisse, quick, 68, 70
braised potatoes, turnips, and carrots, 81
bread(s): honey cornmeal-wheat, 100, 140
  jalapeño cornbread, 146

puri (Indian fried bread), 152–53
walnut wheat, 66, 140
whole grain biscuits, 59
bread pudding, apple, 71, 154, 161
broccoli: effect of vinegar on, 104
and hot sausage with rigatoni, 133, 134
with lemon butter, 30
with sesame oil dressing, 104, 161
steamed, with oyster sauce, 47
Bronson's baked clams, 123
brownies, killer, 147
brown rice, *see* rice
brown rice with leeks and chives, 26
buckwheat groats, *see* kasha
buckwheat pasta with mackerel or
bluefish in soy marinade, 127;
low-calorie version, 126
bulgur: and cucumber soup, cold, 37
salad with avocado, 62
buttered haricots verts, 109
butterflied lamb with rainbow peppers,
91; low-calorie version, 90
buttermilk coleslaw, 58
butter walnut cookies, 150, 161

cabbage: in buttermilk coleslaw, 58
in caldo verde, 141
cake(s): chocolate raisin, 62; advance
preparation of, 60
Christmas stollen, 160–61
honeyed sponge roll with peaches, 89
pear-almond, with dark caramel
sauce, 35, 55, 132
praline roulade, Lee Haiken's,
159–60
prune, 134, 154
spice squares, 139, 154, 161
strawberry cheesecake, 86
calamari, 129
salad, 131
caldo verde (Portuguese vegetable
soup), 140, 141
calves' liver Venetian style (fegato alla
Veneziana), 41
Camembert cheese, 23
canapés, cucumber and golden caviar,
108
cantaloupe, in minted melon and kiwi,
47
caprese (tomatoes and mozzarella),
119
caramel sauce, dark, 35
carbonnades à la Flamande (Belgian
beef stew), 79, 80
carrot(s): carottes rapées, 143
potatoes and turnips, braised, 81
wild rice pilaf with, 99–100
casserole-roasted Cornish hens, 19,
20–21

cauliflower: in broccoli with sesame oil
dressing, 104
and chilis, 153
dauphinoise, 92
caviar: eggplant, with garlic, 148
golden, and cucumber canapés, 108,
161
celery root chips, 95
chanterelles, fresh, with spinach salad,
96
charlotte, apple, with crème anglaise,
67
cheese: as a course, 18, 19, 23, 90,
115, 133, 134, 156, 162
as dessert, 40, 162, 163
as first course, 162
how to serve, 162
ripening of, 162
in salad, 50, 66, 71, 119
with salad, 19, 162
selecting, 12
wine served with, 27, 115, 162, 163
see also entries for Camembert;
chèvre; feta; goat cheese; Gorgonzola; Montrachet; mozzarella;
Parmesan; Roquefort; Vacherin
au Mont d'Or
cheesecake, strawberry, 86, 154
cherries, fresh, 115
cherry tomatoes with sherry vinegar, 86
chèvre cheese: with bread, 19
with salad, 162
see also goat cheese
chicken: baked in walnuts and yogurt,
61
chili-fried, 123
in clambake, 57
dilled, in riesling, 103
fat, rendered, 28
grilled, with pesto, 88–89; low-calorie version, 87
salad, Mexican, 146–47
stock, 22; hints for preparing, 22,
103, 123, 158; simple version of,
103
tandoori-style, 152
with tomatoes and balsamic vinegar,
50–51
wings, lemon-soy, 158
chicken liver(s): in fine liver pâté, 154,
156–57
pâté, old country, 28
chicory salad with walnut oil, 81
chili-fried chicken, 123
chilis and cauliflower, 153
chips: celery root, 95
jicama, 45
sweet potato, 123
chives and leeks, brown rice with, 26
chocolate: brandy served with, 94, 163

in killer brownies, 147
meringue kisses, 47
puddings, small steamed, 35, 51
raisin cake, 62; advance preparation
of, 60
thins, 111
Toblerone mousse, 96
chopped liver, *see* old country chicken
liver pâté
choucroute garnie, 75, 77
chowder, scallop-almond, 95
Christmas stollen, 155, 160–61
cider: apples baked in, 26
hard, 23, 24
sweet, 23, 26, 71
cider sauce, 71
Claiborne, Craig, 22, 79
clambake, 56, 57
clams: Bronson's baked, 123
in clambake, 57
and mussels aglio olio, 41
in seafood with pickled ginger, 98
classic green salad and vinaigrette, 109
clementines, in wine, 139
cocktail party mussels, 154, 155, 156
coconut kheer, 74
coffee, 163, 164
soufflé, Irish, 105
cold cucumber and bulgur soup, 37
cold curry tomato soup, 152
cold seafood mousse, 154, 155,
157–58
cold spiced pilaf, 153
cold tomato, red wine, and basil soup,
61
coleslaw, buttermilk, 58
collard greens, in caldo verde, 141
cookies: chocolate meringue kisses, 47
chocolate thins, 111
lace, 117
walnut butter, 150, 161
corn: on the cob, 74
in cornmeal timbales, 96
and pepper tart, 57
season for, 72
cornbread, jalapeño, 146
Cornish hens, casserole-roasted, 19,
20–21
cornmeal: in herbed polenta, 41–42
timbales, 96
wheat bread, 100, 140
cottage cheese, as low-calorie dessert
topping, 36, 90
crab claws, in seafood with pickled ginger, 98
cranberry(ies): borscht, 20
roast duck sauced with, 98–99
cream of endive soup, 80
crème anglaise, with apple charlotte, 67
croaker, in bouillabaisse, 70

croutons, garlic, 70
cucumber(s): and bulgur soup, cold, 37
   dill salad, 155, 159
   for dipping, 45
   and golden caviar canapés, 108, 161
   raita, 153
   in simple sushi, 61
cumin shrimp, grilled, 137
curry tomato soup, cold, 152
custard sauce, see crème anglaise

daikon radish, as garnish, 28
dandelion greens, in bitter greens with sweet vinegar, 42
dark caramel sauce, 35
desserts, see entries for brownies; cakes; cheesecake; cookies; fruit; fruit desserts; ice cream; mousses; pies; puddings; roulades; sorbet; soufflés; stollen; tartlets; tarts; torte; tortoni
dill-cucumber salad, 155, 159
dilled chicken in riesling, 103
double blueberry tart with gingered whipped cream, 39
dressings, salad, see salad dressings
duck: hints for roasting, 98
   roast, sauced with cranberries, 98–99

East Coast clambake, 57
eel: in bouillabaisse, 70
   in smoked fish spread, 134
egg noodles, 132
   in eggplant lasagne, 131–32
   with veal ragout, 34
eggplant: caviar with garlic, 148
   grilled, with soy-glazed tuna and peppers, 53–54
   lasagne, 131–32
eggs, in frittata of sturgeon and onions, 141
endive: and arugula, radicchio salad, 35
   in classic green salad with vinaigrette, 109
   soup, cream of, 80
entertaining: advance preparation, 19, 36, 40, 51, 60, 72, 73, 87, 90, 106, 114, 118, 119, 126, 136, 140, 154–55
   organization and planning for, 9, 11, 12, 40, 49, 83, 106, 144–45, 154–55
   quick preparation of food and, 40, 49, 83, 115, 133
   serving suggestions for, 56, 154
   simplicity and, 11, 36, 83

see also menu planning
escarole, in bitter greens with sweet vinegar, 42
espresso, 164
   in dark caramel sauce, 35

fegato alla Veneziana (calves' liver Venetian style), 41
fennel: in Parmesan salad with mushrooms and walnuts, 50; low-calorie version, 49
   and shiitake mushrooms with penne, 108
feta cheese: in meat, spinach, and cheese pies, 149
fig tartlets, 132
fillet of beef: cooking method for, 108
   with peppered onion confit, 108–109, 161
fine liver pâté, 154, 156–57
fish: hint for cooking, 37
   poached, 18
   served with red wine, 27
   spread, smoked, 134
   see also entries for bluefish; bouillabaisse; calamari; flounder; mackerel; mako shark; salmon; shellfish; sole; sturgeon; sushi; swordfish; tilefish; trout; tuna
flank steak, stuffed, 73–74
flounder: in bouillabaisse, 70
   in seviche, 73
freezing of food: advance preparation and, 60, 111, 149, 155, 163
   storage and, 13, 20, 22, 53, 98
frittata of sturgeon and onions, 141
fritters, zucchini, 24
frozen mandarin mousse, 81
fruit: as dessert, 36, 40, 49, 56, 62, 78, 83, 87, 90, 115, 148, 151
   see also entries for apples; apricots; blueberries; cantaloupe; figs; grapes; grapefruit; kiwi; lemons; mangoes; melon; nectarines; oranges; pears; pineapple; plums; prunes; raisins; raspberries; rhubarb; strawberries
fruit desserts: apple bread pudding, 71
   apple charlotte with crème anglaise, 67
   apples baked in cider, 26
   double blueberry tart with gingered whipped cream, 39
   frozen mandarin mousse, 81
   grilled pineapple with kirsch, 78
   individual fig tartlets, 132
   lemon tart, 124
   mango mousse, 121
   minted melon and kiwi, 47

oranges in wine, 139
   pear-almond cake, 35
   pears in red wine, 42, 132
   pink grapefruit sorbet, 127
   raspberry cream tart, 30
   raspberry tortoni, 111, 154
   sabayon with nectarines, 22
   strawberry cheesecake, 86
   strawberry ice cream, 59
   strawberry rhubarb tart, 92
   walnut plum tart, 55
garlic: croutons, 70
   with eggplant caviar, 148
   with green beans, 132
   in mussels and clams aglio olio, 41
   roasted potatoes, 29
gastronomy, in America: evolution of, 11
   history of, 8
gazpacho salad, 137
ginger, pickled, seafood with, 98
gingered whipped cream, 39
goat cheese: as a course, 115, 162
   dressing, with green beans, 71
   with salad, 66
   wine served with, 115, 162
   see also chèvre
golden caviar canapés, and cucumber, 108, 161
Gorgonzola cheese: as a course, 133, 134
   as dessert, 40
   selecting, 134
grains, see entries for barley; bulgur; cornmeal; kasha; rice
grapefruit, see pink grapefruit
grapes, as dessert, 62, 148
green beans: with garlic, 132
   with goat cheese dressing, 71
green peppercorn sauce for swordfish steaks, 28–29
green salad, 87; with vinaigrette, 109
greens: bitter, with sweet vinegar, 42
   in caldo verde, 141
   see also salad(s)
gremolata, medallions of veal and, 84
grilled chicken with pesto, 88–89
grilled cumin shrimp, 137
grilled pineapple with kirsch, 78
grilled soy-glazed tuna with eggplant and peppers, 53–54
grilling food: butterflied lamb with rainbow peppers, 91
   suggestions for, 52, 54, 90
   tandoori-style chicken, 152
guacamole: asparagus, 45, 146
   avocado, 146

haddock, in bouillabaisse, 70
Haiken, Lee, 159

halibut, in bouillabaisse, 70
ham: in choucroute garnie, 77
    as garnish, 77
haricots verts, buttered, 109
hazelnut oil: storage of, 13
    in vinaigrette, 109
herbed polenta, 41–42
herbs, freshness and, 13
honey cornmeal-wheat bread, 100
honeyed sponge roll with peaches, 89
hot and sour scallop soup, 103

ice cream, strawberry, 59
iced tea, 145
Indian fried bread (puri), 152–53
individual fig tartlets, 132
individual leek tartlets, 155, 157
individual pesto pizzas, 53
Irish coffee soufflé, 105
Istanbul bean soup, 64
Italian meringue, 111

jalapeño cornbread, 146
jicama, for dipping, 45

kale, in caldo verde, 141
kasha: cooking methods for, 99, 104
    with onions, 104
kheer, coconut, 74
killer brownies, 147
kirsch, grilled pineapple with, 78
kiwi, minted melon and, 47
Kump, Peter, 33

lace cookies, 117
lamb: butterflied, with rainbow pep-
        pers, 91; low-calorie version, 90
    ground, in meat, spinach, and cheese
        pies, 149
lasagne, 129; eggplant, 131–32
leaf lettuce, in salad with goat cheese,
    66
leek(s): and chives, brown rice with,
    26
    tartlets, individual, 155, 157
lemon: butter and broccoli, 30
    mustard sauce, 37, 39
    potatoes, 47
    soy chicken wings, 158
    tart, 124
lemonade, 145
lentil and sausage salad, 155, 159
lettuce: Bibb, 22, 109
    Boston, 66, 109
    leaf, 66
    red leaf, 123
    romaine, 30, 123
lima beans, in Istanbul bean soup, 64
liver: calves', Venetian style, 41

chicken, in fine liver pâté, 154,
    156–57
chicken, in old country pâté, 28
lobster, in clambake, 57
low-calorie menus, recipes, and sugges-
    tions, 36, 44, 49, 83, 87, 90, 126

mackerel: in bouillabaisse, 70
    in smoked fish spread, 134
    in soy marinade with buckwheat
        pasta, 127; low-calorie version,
        126
mako shark, in grilled soy-glazed tuna
    with eggplant and peppers, 53
Mandarine Napoléon, 81
mandarin mousse, frozen, 81
mango mousse, 121
maple pecan pie, 100
marinated mushroom salad, 88, 129
matambre (stuffed flank steak), 72,
    73–74
mayonnaise, quick, 58
meat: spinach, and cheese pies, 149
    see also entries for beef; ham;
        lamb; liver; pork; sausage; veal
medallions of veal gremolata, 84
melon: as dessert, 49, 56, 151
    minted, and kiwi, 47
menu planning, 9, 11, 12–13
    for buffets, 136, 154–55
    for ethnic theme meals, 31, 40, 72,
        75, 79, 118, 129, 133, 136, 140,
        144
    for holiday meals, 75, 94, 97, 154–
        55
    for picnics, 144–45, 152
    with quality ingredients, 9, 12–13,
        18, 36, 48
    with seasonal foods, 9, 12, 72, 83,
        87, 94, 114, 115, 118, 124, 128
    for vegetarian meals, 129
    see also entertaining
menus, a listing of, 165–67
meringue: Italian, 111
    kisses, chocolate, 47
Mexican chicken salad, 146–47
minted melon and kiwi, 47
monkfish, in bouillabaisse, 70
Montrachet cheese, in salad dressing,
    71
morels, and asparagus in mushroom
    beurre blanc, 116
mousse, cold seafood, 154, 155,
    157–58
mousse(s), dessert: frozen mandarin, 81
    mango, 121
    Toblerone, 96; brandy served with,
        94; serving suggestions for, 154,
        155, 161

mozzarella cheese: fresh, 119
    in olive oil, 162
    tomatoes and, 119
mullet, in bouillabaisse, 70
mushroom(s): in casserole-roasted Cor-
        nish hens, 20–21
    cultivated, in penne with fennel, 108
    cultivated, in spinach salad, 96
    in Parmesan salad with fennel and
        walnuts, 50; low-calorie version, 49
    salad, marinated, 88; serving sugges-
        tion for, 129
    shiitake, with fennel and penne, 108
    timbales with red pepper sauce, 45
    in wild rice pilaf with carrots and
        nutmeg, 99–100
    see also chanterelles; morels; shiitake
mussels: in clambake, 57
    and clams aglio olio, 41
    cocktail party, 156
mustard(s): for choucroute garnie, 77
    lemon sauce, 37, 39

nectarines, sabayon with, 22
new potato salad with fresh peas, 39;
    low-calorie version, 36
New York Times Cook Book,
    The (Claiborne), 79
nutmeg, in wild rice pilaf with carrots,
    99–100
nuts, storage of, 13
    see also entries for almonds; pe-
        cans; walnuts

oils, see entries for hazelnut oil; olive
        oil; sesame oil; walnut oil
old country chicken liver pâté, 28
olive oil: selecting, 12
    in vinaigrette, 109
olives, as appetizers, 70
omelet, see frittata
onion(s): confit, peppered, with fillet of
        beef, 108
    with kasha, 104
    quiche, 76
    red, wilted romaine and, 30
    and sturgeon, frittata of, 141
oranges in wine, 139
oysters, in seafood with pickled ginger,
    98

pan-seared zucchini spears and tomato
    slices, 89
papillote, tilefish en, 46
pappardelle (pasta), with veal ragout, 34
Parmesan: salad with fennel, mush-
        rooms, and walnuts, 50; low-calo-
        rie version, 49
    selecting, 12

pasta: buckwheat, with mackerel or
    bluefish in soy marinade, 127;
    low-calorie version, 126
  fresh, 34, 131; how to make,
    132
  fusilli with tomato concassé, 158
  lasagne, eggplant, 131–32
  method for cooking, 131, 132
  penne with fennel and shiitake
    mushrooms, 108
  rigatoni with hot sausage and broc-
    coli, 134
  rotelle with tomato concassé, 158
  and veal ragout with peas, 34
pastry: basic, 55
  sweet tart, 30
  see also entries for pies; quiche;
    tartlets; tarts
pâté(s): chicken liver, old country, 28
  fine liver, 154, 156–57
paupiettes of sole with shrimp, 23, 24
peaches, with honeyed sponge roll, 89
pear(s): about, 134
  almond cake with dark caramel
    sauce, 35, 55, 132
  with cheese course, 40, 133, 134
  as dessert, 40
  in red wine, 42, 132
peas: fresh, in new potato salad, 39
  Sugar Snap, sautéed, 99
  veal ragout with, 34
  see also snow peas; split peas
pecan maple pie, 100
penne with fennel and shiitake mush-
    rooms, 108
pepper(s): availability of, 90, 91
  chilis and cauliflower, 153
  and corn tart, 57
  grilled, with soy-glazed tuna and
    eggplant, 53–54
  jalapeño, in cornbread, 146
  rainbow, with butterflied lamb, 91
  red, sauce with mushroom timbales,
    45
  roasted, 119
  rouille, 70
peppercorn sauce, green, with swordfish
    steaks, 28–29
peppered onion confit, 108–109
pesto, 53
  with grilled chicken, 88–89
  pizzas, 53
  uses for, 53, 88
phyllo leaves, for meat, spinach, and
    cheese pies, 149
picadillo, 136, 137
pickled ginger, with seafood, 98
pie(s): maple pecan, 100
  two-crust pumpkin, 143; serving

suggestion for, 94
  see also tarts
pilaf(s): cold spiced, 153
  wild rice, with carrots and nutmeg,
    99–100
pineapple(s), grilled, with kirsch, 78
  selecting, 78
pink grapefruit sorbet, 127
pizza(s): dough for, 53
  individual pesto, 53
plum(s), walnut tart, 55
poached salmon steaks with lemon-
    mustard sauce, 37; low-calorie
    version, 36
polenta, herbed, 41–42
porgy, in bouillabaisse, 70
pork tenderloin, smoked, in choucroute
    garnie, 77
Portuguese vegetable soup (caldo
    verde), 140, 141
potato(es): garlic-roasted, 29
  lemon, 47
  new, 39, 47, 51
  salad with fresh peas, 39
  with shallots, 51; low-calorie version,
    49
  turnips and carrots, braised, 81
  see also sweet potatoes
poultry, see entries for chicken;
    Cornish hens; duck; quail
praline roulade, Lee Haiken's, 159–60
prune cake, 134, 154
pudding(s): apple bread, 71, 154, 161
  chocolate, steamed, 35, 51
  coconut kheer, 74
pumpkin pie, two-crust, 94, 143
punch(es): sparkling wine, cranberry
    juice, 155
  tropical citrus, 155, 161
puri (Indian fried bread), 152–53

quail, sautéed, with apples, 95–96
quiche, three-onion, 76
quick bouillabaisse, 68, 70
quick mayonnaise, 58

radicchio: and arugula, endive salad,
    35, 109
  in salad with goat cheese, 66
radish, white (daikon), as garnish, 28
raisin(s): chocolate cake, 62; advance
    preparation of, 60
  in Christmas stollen, 160
  rum soufflé, 104–105
raita, cucumber, 153
raspberry: cream tart, 30
  tortoni, 111, 154
red leaf lettuce, in tossed salad, 123
red onions, wilted romaine and, 30

red pepper sauce, 45
red wine: cold tomato and basil soup,
    61
  pears in, 42
  sausages baked in, 64
rendered chicken fat, 28
rhubarb, strawberry tart, 92
rice, cooking method for, 99
rice, basmati, in cold spiced pilaf, 153
rice, brown: with leeks and chives, 26
  vine leaves stuffed with, 148–49
  walnut, 84
rice, long-grain: in coconut kheer, 74
  in cold spiced pilaf, 153
  saffron, 138
  salad, summer, 121
  in simple sushi, 60–61
rice, wild, in pilaf with carrots and nut-
    meg, 99–100
riesling, dilled chicken in, 103
rigatoni with hot sausage and broccoli,
    133, 134
roast duck sauced with cranberries,
    98–99
roasted peppers, 119
romaine lettuce: in tossed salad, 123
  wilted, and red onions, 30
Roquefort cheese, with sweet wine, 163
rouille, 70
roulade: honeyed sponge roll, 89
  Lee Haiken's praline, 159–60
rum, raisin soufflé, 104–105

sabayon with nectarines, 22; advance
    preparation of, 19
saffron rice, 138
salad(s): arugula, radicchio, and en-
    dive, 35, 109
  beet and watercress, 78
  Bibb and watercress, 22, 109
  bitter greens with sweet vinegar, 42
  broccoli with sesame oil dressing,
    104, 161
  bulgur, with avocado, 62
  buttermilk coleslaw, 58
  calamari, 131
  carottes rapées, 143
  chicory, with walnut oil, 81
  cucumber-dill, 155, 159
  gazpacho, 137
  with goat cheese, 66
  green, 87; with vinaigrette, 109
  green beans with garlic, 132
  green beans with goat cheese dress-
    ing, 71
  lentil and sausage, 155, 159
  marinated mushroom, 88, 129
  Mexican chicken, 146–47
  new potato, with fresh peas, 39

Parmesan, with fennel, mushrooms, and walnuts, 50; low-calorie version, 49
pasta, with tomato concassé, 158
spinach, with fresh chanterelles, 96
summer rice, 121
tofu and vegetable, 127
  tossed, with sprouts, 123
  wilted romaine and red onions, 30
salad dressing(s): goat cheese, 71
  mayonnaise, quick, 58
  sesame oil, 104
  vinaigrette, 109; variations of, 22, 35, 42, 66, 78, 127
  walnut oil, 81
  yogurt, 123
salmon: quality and freshness of, 37
  smoked, for sushi, 61
  steaks, poached, with lemon-mustard sauce, 37; low-calorie version, 36
sauce(s): basil béarnaise, 33
  green peppercorn, 28–29
  lemon-mustard, 37, 39
  mushroom beurre blanc, 116
  red pepper, 45
  thickening of, 21, 95
sauce(s), dessert: cider, 71
  crème anglaise, 67
  dark caramel, 35
  sabayon, 22
sauerkraut, in choucroute garnie, 77
sausage(s): baked in red wine, 64
  in choucroute garnie, 77
  garlic, in caldo verde, 141
  hot, and broccoli with rigatoni, 133, 134
  and lentil salad, 155, 159
  types of, 64, 77, 141, 159
sautéed quail with apples, 95–96
sautéed Sugar Snap peas, 99
Savoy cabbage, in caldo verde, 141
scallop(s): almond chowder, 95
  in cold seafood mousse, 157
  in seviche, 73
  soup, hot and sour, 103
  in white wine and cream, 116–17
sea bass, in bouillabaisse, 70
seafood mousse, cold, 154, 155, 157–58
seafood with pickled ginger, 98
seaweed, for clambake, 57
sesame oil: cooking with, 12
  dressing, with broccoli, 104
seviche, 73, 146, 161
shallots, potatoes with, 51; low-calorie version, 49
shark, see mako shark
shellfish, see entries for clams; lobster; mussels; scallops; shrimp

sherried black beans, 138
shiitake mushrooms and fennel with penne, 108
shrimp: in cold seafood mousse, 157
  grilled cumin, 137
  with paupiettes of sole, 23, 24
  salting, to improve texture, 91
  in seafood with pickled ginger, 98
  spiced, 91, 161; low-calorie version, 90
simple sushi, 60, 61
small steamed chocolate puddings, 35, 51
smoked fish spread, 134
snow peas, as substitute ingredient, 39, 99
sole, paupiettes of, with shrimp, 23, 24
sorbet, pink grapefruit, 127
soufflé(s): Irish coffee, 105
  rum-raisin, 104–105
soup(s): asparagus, 84
  caldo verde (Portuguese vegetable), 140, 141
  chicken stock, 22
  cranberry borscht, 20
  cream of endive, 80
  cucumber and bulgur, cold, 37
  curry tomato, cold, 152
  hot and sour scallop, 103
  Istanbul bean, 64
  scallop-almond chowder, 94, 95
  split pea and barley, 64
  tomato, red wine, and basil, cold, 61
soy sauce, selecting, 12
sparkling wine, cranberry juice punch, 155
spiced shrimp, 91, 161; low-calorie version, 90
spices, freshness and, 13
spice squares, 139, 154, 161
spinach: in caldo verde, 141
  meat and cheese pies, 149
  salad with fresh chanterelles, 96
split pea and barley soup, 64
sprouts, in tossed salad, 123
squid, see calamari
steamed broccoli with oyster sauce, 47
stews, 136
  bouillabaisse, 68, 70
  carbonnades à la Flamande, 79, 80
  veal ragout with fresh peas and pasta, 34
stock, chicken, 22; hints for preparing, 22, 103, 123, 158; simple version of, 103
stollen, Christmas, 155, 160–61
strawberry(ies): cheesecake, 86, 154
  as dessert, 83, 90
  ice cream, 59

with pink grapefruit sorbet, 127
  rhubarb tart, 92
striped bass, in bouillabaisse, 70
stuffed flank steak, 72, 73–74
sturgeon and onions, frittata of, 141
Sugar Snap peas, sautéed, 99
summer rice salad, 121
sushi, simple, 60, 61
sweet potato(es): baked, 74
  chips, 123
sweet tart pastry, 30
Swiss chard, in caldo verde, 141
swordfish steaks: in green peppercorn sauce, 27, 28–29
  in grilled soy-glazed tuna with eggplant and peppers, 53

tandoori-style chicken, 152
tart(s): blueberry with gingered whipped cream, 39
  corn and pepper, 57
  lemon, 124
  raspberry cream, 30
  strawberry-rhubarb, 92
  walnut plum, 55
tartlets: individual fig, 132
  individual leek, 155, 157
  see also pies
tea, 164; iced, 145
three-onion quiche, 76
tilefish: in bouillabaisse, 70
  en papillote, 46
timbales: cornmeal, 96
  mushroom, with red pepper sauce, 45
Toblerone mousse, 96, 154, 155, 161
tofu and vegetable salad, 127
tomato(es): cherry, with sherry vinegar, 86
  chicken with, and balsamic vinegar, 50–51
  concassé, with pasta salad, 158
  curry soup, cold, 152
  hothouse, 9, 12
  and mozzarella, 119
  selecting, 119
  slices and zucchini spears, pan-seared, 89
  soup, cold, with red wine and basil, 61
  in tilefish en papillote, 46
  vine-ripened, 9, 12
torte, almond-apricot, 163, 164
tortoni, raspberry, 111, 154
tossed salad with sprouts, 123
tropical citrus punch, 155, 161
trout, in smoked fish spread, 134
tuna: raw, for sushi, 61
  soy-glazed, grilled, with eggplant and

peppers, 53
in vitello tonnato, 119
turkey: hints for roasting, 98
as substitute ingredient, 97, 98
turnip(s): potatoes and carrots, braised, 81
white, for dipping, 45
turnip greens, in caldo verde, 141
two-crust pumpkin pie, 94, 143

Vacherin au Mont d'Or cheese, with sweet wine, 163
veal: medallions of, gremolata, 84
ragout with peas and fresh pasta, 34
in vitello tonnato, 119
vegetables: asparagus and morels in mushroom beurre blanc, 116
broccoli with lemon butter, 30
broccoli, steamed, with oyster sauce, 47
cauliflower and chilis, 153
cauliflower dauphinoise, 92
celery root chips, 95
cherry tomatoes with sherry vinegar, 86
corn on the cob, 74
eggplant lasagne, 131–32
eggplant and peppers, grilled, 53–54
garlic-roasted potatoes, 29
green beans with garlic, 132
haricot verts, buttered, 109
lemon potatoes, 47
potatoes with shallots, 51
potatoes, turnips, and carrots, braised, 81
rainbow peppers, with butterflied lamb, 91
Sugar Snap peas, sautéed, 99
sweet potato chips, 123
sweet potatoes, baked, 74
zucchini and watercress stir-fry, 64, 66
zucchini fritters, 24
zucchini spears and tomato slices, pan-seared, 89
see also salads
vegetarian menu suggestion, 130
vermouth, used in cooking, 33
vinaigrette dressing, with green salad, 109
vine leaves stuffed with brown rice, 148–49
vitello tonnato, 118, 119

walnut(s): butter cookies, 150, 161
with cheese and pears as dessert, 40
chicken baked in, and yogurt, 61
hints for grinding, 150
in Parmesan salad with fennel and

mushrooms, 50; low-calorie version, 49
plum tart, 55
rice, 84
wheat bread, 66, 140
walnut oil, salad dressing from, 81
warm artichokes with basil béarnaise, 33
wasabi paste, in simple sushi, 61
watercress: and beet salad, 78
and Bibb salad, 22, 109
in bitter greens with sweet vinegar, 42
in tossed salad, 123
and zucchini stir-fry, 64, 66
watermelon, as dessert, 56
whipped cream, gingered, 39
white wine and scallops, cream in, 116
whiting, in bouillabaisse, 70
whole grain biscuits, 59
wild rice: pilaf with carrots and nutmeg, 99–100
selecting, 99
wilted romaine and red onions, 30
wine, see wine index

yams, compared to sweet potatoes, 74
yogurt: chicken baked in, and walnuts, 61
in cucumber raita, 153
salad dressing, 123

zucchini: fritters, 24
spears and tomato slices, pan-seared, 89
and watercress stir-fry, 64, 66

Wine Index

aging capability of, 27, 31, 40, 83, 90, 94, 106, 163
amarone, 40
amount served per person, 14, 155
aperitifs, 31, 87, 97, 133, 136
Argentina, 72
Asti spumante, 87, 163; used in cooking, 89

Bandol, 145
Barbaresco, 133
barbera, 44
Bardolino, 40
Barolo, 133
Barsac, 163
Beaujolais, 14, 19
Beaujolais nouveau, 19
Beaujolais-Villages, 19, 122

bianco Toscano, 31
Biondi-Santi, Franco, 31
Biondi-Santi brunello di Montalcino, 31
blanc de noirs, 145
Bordeaux, 18, 27, 31, 122
Brouilly, 19
brunello, 18
brunello di Montalcino, 31
Burgundy, 18, 56, 63, 79, 83, 106, 122

cabernet franc, 27
cabernet sauvignon, 27, 40, 60, 63, 72, 90, 94, 126, 129
California, 18, 23, 36, 56, 60, 83, 90, 94, 97, 101, 122, 126, 145, 163
Napa County, 36
Napa Valley, 52, 63
Sonoma County, 36
canaiolo, 129
Chablis, 23, 36, 56, 94
chablis, 23, 56
Champagne, 36, 75, 108, 155, 163; see also sparkling wine
chardonnay, 18, 23, 36, 56, 60, 72, 83, 94, 106, 126, 155
Chassagne-Montrachet, 106
Château d'Yquem, 163
Châteauneuf-du-Pape, 49, 68
Chénas, 19
chenin blanc, 60, 90; used in cooking, 24, 103
Chianti, 11, 44, 122, 129
Chianti Classico, 129
Chile, 72
Chiroubles, 19
cinsault, 49
compatibility of, with food, 8, 11, 13, 19, 23, 27, 36, 40, 49, 52, 60, 63, 68, 72, 75, 83, 87, 90, 94, 97, 101, 106, 114, 115, 118, 122, 126, 129, 133, 136, 140, 162, 163
cooking with, 13, 101, 157
red, 28, 34, 42, 61, 64, 73, 98
white, 20, 24, 37, 57, 70, 77, 84, 89, 101, 103, 116, 119, 139, 156
Cornas, 49
Côte-Rôtie, 49
Côtes de Brouilly, 19
Côtes du Rhône, 49, 122
Côtes du Rhône Villages, 49
Crozes-Hermitage, 49

decanting, 14, 15
dessert wines, 75, 87, 94, 97, 101, 140, 155, 163
see also late harvest
dolcetto, 87

Eszencia, 163
European hybrid grapes, 126

Fleurie, 19
France, 18, 52, 68, 94, 122, 163
    Alsace, 75, 101, 145
    Beaujolais, 19
    Bordeaux, 27, 94
    Brittany, 115
    Burgundy, 19, 36, 49, 83, 106
    Chablis, 23, 106
    Chalon, 106
    Champagne, 155
    Côte de Beaune, 36, 106
    Côte de Nuits, 106
    Côte d'Or, 106
    Loire Valley, 83, 145
    Mâcon, 36, 83, 106
    Provence, 68, 145
    Rhône, 49
Frascati, 13
fumé blanc, 52, 83
    see also sauvignon blanc

Galestro, 31
gamay, 19
Gattinara, 133
Gavi, 87, 133
Germany, wines from, 163
    Mosel-Saar-Ruwer, 101
    Rhine, 101
gewürztraminer, 75, 90
Gigondas, 49
grenache, 49
grignolino, 87

Hazan, Victor, 31
Hermitage, 49
Hungary, 163

Italian Wine (Hazan), 31
Italy, 18, 163
    Chianti, 129
    Friuli-Venezia Giulia, 118
    Orvieto, 87
    Piedmont, 87, 133
    Trentino-Alto Adige, 118
    Tuscany, 11, 31, 129

Valtellina, 133
Veneto, 40, 87, 118

Johannisberg riesling, 90, 101, 163
jug wine, 14, 23, 56, 60
Juliénas, 19

late-harvest, 75, 97, 101, 163
light (low-calorie), 44

Mâcon blanc, 94
Madeira, 140
malbec, 72
Mercurey, 106
merlot, 27, 40, 94, 126
methods of producing, 19, 40, 87,
    115, 145, 155, 163
Meursault, 36
Mondavi, Robert, 52, 83
Montrachet, 36
Morgon, 19
Moulin-à-Vent, 19
Muscadet, 115
muscat, 145
Muscat de Beaumes-de-Venise, 163

nebbiolo, 133
New York State, wines from, 101, 126

Oregon, 63
Orvieto, 87; used in cooking, 89

Peru, 72
picolit, 163
pinot bianco, 40
pinot grigio, 40, 87, 118, 133
pinot meunier, 155
pinot noir, 63, 106, 126, 145, 155
port, 140
Portugal, 140
Pouilly-Fuissé, 83
Pouilly-Fumé, 52, 83
primitivo, 97

riesling, 101, 126; used in cooking,
    101, 103
Rioja, 13, 122, 136
role of, in America, 8, 13

rosé d'Anjou, 145
rosso di Montalcino, 31

Saint-Amour, 19
St. Émilion, 14
St. Joseph, 49
Sancerre, 13
sangiovese, 31, 129
sangiovese grosso, 31
sangria, 145
Santenay, 106
Sauternes, 163
sauvignon blanc, 44, 52, 56, 72, 83,
    94, 126
    see also fumé blanc
Schloss Johannisberg, near Frankfurt,
    Germany, 101
selecting, 11, 13–14, 97; see also
    compatibility of, with food
serving, 14–15, 163
seyval blanc, 126
Soave, 40
South America, 72
Spain, 122
    Rioja, 136
spanna, 133
sparkling wine, 40, 60, 133, 155, 163;
    see also Champagne
spritzers, 44
storage of, 14
syrah, 49

table wine, 56, 122
Tavel, 145
temperature served at, 14, 19, 163
tocai, 87
Tokay aszú, 163

Valpolicella, 40
vinho verde, 140
vinifera grapes, 63, 126
vin santo, 163
Volnay, 106
Vouvray, 60, 163

Washington State, 101, 126

zinfandel, 14, 44, 97, 122, 145; used
    in cooking, 98

Credits

All photographs by Matthew Klein, with the exception of the following: Champagne News and Information Bureau, New York, 14 middle & bottom; Fetzer Vineyards, Redwood Valley, California, 14 top; Robert Mondavi Winery, Oakville, California, 54 bottom; Arnold Rosenberg, 38, 117, 120; Bruce Wolf, 58; Dan Wynn, 99.

Food Stylists

Vicky Cheung, jacket, 10 bottom, 11, 46, 69, 80, 85 bottom, 135 bottom; Laurie Goldrich, 58, 147, 150, 151; Darilyn Lowe, 6 all, 7 both, 10 top, 15, 20, 24, 39, 42 top, 46 top, 46 middle, 47, 51 both, 55, 59 top, 92, 107 top, 116, 121, 125 top, 131, 135 both, 139 bottom, 143; Zabel Meshejian, 124; Deborah Mintcheff, 34, 62 top, 65 bottom, 73, 110 bottom right, 158; Arturo Pesavento, 29 top; Andrea Swenson, 2, 17, 21, 25, 29 bottom, 42 bottom, 50, 59 bottom, 65 top, 76, 85 top, 93, 102, 107 bottom, 110 top, 113, 125 bottom, 138 top, 142, 159.

Props

Linda Cheverton, jacket, 2, 10 bottom, 17, 21, 25, 42 bottom, 50, 65 top, 76, 85 top, 93, 102, 107 bottom, 110 top, 113, 125 bottom, 135 bottom, 138 top, 142, 159; Pamela Zacha Levitt, 69, 124. The author and publisher would like to thank the following New York shops: Ad Hoc Housewares, 124; Baccarat, 2, 21, 50, 85 top, 93, 110 top, 110 bottom right, 125; Bazaar de la Cuisine, 38; Cardel, Ltd., 34; Ginori, 62, 130; Gordon Foster, Ltd., 125, 138 top, 142, 159; Hellenic Organization of Industries and Handicrafts, 150; James Robinson, Ltd., jacket, 20, 65 top, 110 top, 125; James II Galleries, 43; La Cuisinière, 117; Lee Bailey/Henri Bendel, 34, 124; Lucidity, 124; Pan American Phoenix, 147; Pierre Deux, jacket, 43, 110 top, 138 top; D. Porthault, 130; Tiffany & Co., 158; Tognana, 73; Very Special Flowers, jacket, 2, 42, 93, 102.